THE MAGIC OF
YOUR RADIAL ARM SAW

OTHER BOOKS BY R. J. DE CRISTOFORO

Woodworking techniques: Joints and Their Applications

De Cristoforo's Housebuilding Illustrated

How to Build Your Own Furniture

Handtool Handbook For Woodworking

The Practical Handbook Of Carpentry

Plywood Projects You Can Build

Concrete And Masonry Techniques And Design

THE MAGIC OF
YOUR RADIAL ARM SAW

R. J. De Cristoforo

Reston Publishing Company, Inc.
A Prentice-Hall Company
Reston, Virginia

CAT. NO. 35601-15

WARNING—MANY PHOTOGRAPHS IN THIS BOOK WERE TAKEN WITHOUT GUARDS IN PLACE. OCCASIONALLY A GUARD IS ADJUSTED A BIT SO IT WON'T HIDE AN OPERATION. IN ALL CASES THIS IS ONLY DONE FOR PHOTOGRAPHIC CLARITY. NEVER WORK WITHOUT CORRECTLY ADJUSTED GUARDS AND OTHER SAFETY DEVICES.

This handbook provides basic information relating to radial arm saws. It is not intended to replace instructions or precautions given by the maker or vendor of any radial arm saw that you may consider using. Additionally, while this handbook contains many safety tips, it is not possible to provide precautions for all possible hazards that might result. Standard and accepted safety procedures should be applied at all times.

Table of Contents

Description of a dadoing tool—types of dadoing tools—the dado assembly—the "Quick-set" dado—general practice—importance of feed speed—the simple dado—feed direction—cutting duplicate dadoes—extra-wide dadoes—using stop blocks to gauge work position—repeat passes—dadoes at an angle—setting up to cut grooves—forming extra-wide grooves—how to cut end and edge rabbets—extra-wide rabbets—what "stopped" and "blind" dadoes and grooves are and how to cut them—variable depth dadoes and rabbets—corner dadoes—how to make a V-block—V-shaped cuts —fluted panels—decorative cuts—piercing—using the dadoing tool in horizontal position—a special fence and a special guard—cutting edge rabbets—beveled rabbets—decorative scallops—a special table—typical uses for the special table—rabbeting—stopped edge-grooves—circular rabbets—making and using V-blocks—horizontal work by feeding the cutter—a second special table—typical uses for the second table.

Various ways of doing shaping—the shaper head and how it is mounted—types of shaper knives and how they are installed—general practice—working **with** the grain of the wood—pass sequence for four edges—importance of guards—how to make a special shaper fence—straight shaping—difference between partial and total cuts—end cuts—a sophisticated ready-made shaper fence and its advantages—how to produce strip moldings—shaping circular work—fancy scallops—how to do surface shaping—cross-grain cuts—how to set up for shaping curved edges—jigs and guides to make—freehand-shaping procedures—pattern shaping—how to do fluting or reeding on round or square stock—coving with shaping knives—a two-knife shaper head and how it is mounted and used—jointing—panel raising —forming louvers.

Why a portable router is used—the attachment for mounting a portable router—typical work—router bits and cutters—integral pilots—ball bearing pilots—general practice—feed direction and feed speed—making straight cuts—stopped cuts—grooving—shaping with a fence—a special setup for the router—routing circular work—how to work on irregular edges—doing internal routing—pattern routing—forming curved grooves—freehand routing—moldings—controlling cut-spacing—how to make special tables for the router—typical applications on the special tables.

Preface

Woodworking covers hundreds of basic sawing operations and special techniques, as well as thousands of uses for wood and wood products, factors that account for the popularity of versatile power tools. The tool itself is an expert. It is consistently accurate and so lessens the possibility of human error, substitutes for muscle, and shortens production time.

The advantage of a power saw is obvious the first time it is used to do sizing operations like crosscutting and ripping, especially if such chores were previously done with a hand saw. Hand tool woodworking is intriguing, but expertise comes after a longer period of apprenticeship than is required with power tools. With a hand saw, guidance and squareness of the cut depend on the operator's skill. With a radial arm saw, the work is placed on the tool's table against a guide fence and the saw blade is pulled through for the cut. The result, with a minimum amount of time and effort, is a straight, square cut.

Actually, there are many areas of woodworking where only simple sawing is enough to get a job done correctly. For example, this is true in house framing, utilitarian shelves in a garage, open shelves in a closet, a bookcase of boards supported by bricks or concrete blocks—all projects that only require straight sawing of lumber or plywood to a specific length and width.

But most craftspeople soon graduate from elementary work to more advanced constructions. Building a piece of furniture or a built-in, or making a Grandfather's clock, call for more than basic saw cuts. The inducement can be many things—the creative instinct, dissatisfaction with commercial products, the economics of do-it-yourself work, the therapeutic value of a workshop, the possibility of a career in wood construction industries, and, so important today, the advantages of an on-hand means of doing house repairs or remodeling work.

When craftspeople get deeper into woodworking, they become aware of the need for more than basic sawing. There are holes to be drilled, wood connections more intriguing and longer-lived than the butt, edges and sometimes surfaces to be shaped or molded, curved forms, pierced and raised panels, components that require bending, multiple duplicates to be made, sanding jobs, taper cuts, special connections that need a compound angle—the list goes on.

When work scope ranges from the simple shelf to the heirloom desk, there is need for a power tool that does more than saw; this is justification enough for an in-depth treatment of the radial arm saw, since the modern concept is truly multipurpose. It originated as a sawing tool. It has evolved as a one-tool shop.

The aim of this book is to demonstrate how a radial arm saw should be used and to show the myriad operations it can perform—for anyone.

It's a book for users—tyro or advanced—written in the shop where everything spoken of or pictured was tested and proven. The beginner should start at page one. Others can check chapter headings or the index to find information on a particular procedure. Often, even knowledgeable woodworkers, going through a treatise page by page, discover a woodworking method that is more practical or quicker than the system in force.

The appeal of the power tool lies in its disinterest. Its potential is available to anyone who pushes the "on" button—tyro/homeowner or professional, male or female, student or teacher, furniture maker or boat builder. If the procedure is correct, the results will be the same for all.

The power tool's disinterest should also be considered another way. It's a powerful machine designed for wood fabrication and it can't sense what's in the cut-line. It won't shy from non-wood materials like fingers.

Statistics tell us that as many, if not more, professionals are hurt on power tools as amateurs. So safe use is not a matter of experience. If it were, then all beginners would be scarred during the learning period. The worker who follows correct procedures and who will keep his hands and body away from cut-areas no matter what, will always be safe. The person with some experience who allows himself to become casual and careless is the one who might be hurt.

Safety has to do with correctly using the tool, which means, among other things, keeping guards in place, following safety instructions which apply to shop housekeeping and dress as much as to tool use, and, most important, never allowing confidence to lead to carelessness. Respect for the tool, even a good degree of fear, are the greatest safety factors of all.

There are hundreds of tool-use illustrations in this book, but not all of them were posed with guards in place or with guards situated as they should be. **This is done only because the correct guard setup would conceal what is being done.**

You are the master of the tool, but don't let your ego make you vulnerable. When facing a strange procedure, don't hesitate to try a dry run (no power) before you actually cut.

> There are two classic phrases—
> "Measure twice, cut once."
> "Think twice before cutting."

Thanks to Ivan J. Hahn of the DeWalt organization for providing tools and accessories needed to do the book, and to William F. Rooney of Louisiana-Pacific Corporation who provided the wood and wood products needed for photo props and to build the radial arm saw shop.

Chapter 1
The Good Craftsperson
Works Safely

Knowing the potential hazards in all things we do or use is the prime factor toward leading an accident-free life—it doesn't matter whether one is walking, driving, mowing the lawn, pruning a tree, or using a power tool. Safety as a state of mind is as important as knowing a set of rules. It's not unusual for the worker who never gets scratched when power tooling to do some damage when switching to a chisel, screwdriver, or hammer. In this case the difference is in the regard the worker has for the tool he is using.

Safety rules are a bore to write and read but they can't be ignored. Those that apply to power tools and general shopwork are as critical as the warnings posted on signs around swimming pools or at the beach or a cliff's edge.

TO DO AND NOT TO DO. Power tools are equipped with guards that should be kept in place and in working order. The main guard of a radial arm saw is shown in Figure 1-1. The upper part of the guard covers more than 50% of the blade and is adjustable for various sawing operations. The lower part of the guard covers the remainder of the blade but is designed to automatically ride the surface of the workpiece and return to its original position when the cut is complete.

The upper guard has a sawdust ejection chute with a turnable rubber nozzle so waste can be directed away from the operator when ripping. The guard also grips an antikickback device which must be correctly adjusted for all ripping operations. Since the device does shield the front of the blade, often it is left in place even for crosscutting. If used in this manner, it must be adjusted so it won't interfere with the cut.

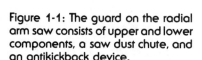
Figure 1-1: The guard on the radial arm saw consists of upper and lower components, a saw dust chute, and an antikickback device.

An accessory antikickback unit (Figure 1-2) includes a fixed tine which serves as a "splitter." Its purpose is to ride in the groove formed by a saw cut to keep the wood from binding the blade.

Other types of guards that are available include the one shown in Figure 1-3. This one was specifically designed for shaping and molding work but it can be used in other ways, as we will show.

Figure 1-2: A special antikickback unit is available as an accessory. Its fixed center tine serves as a splitter to keep work from binding the blade when doing rip cuts.

Figure 1-3: Another guard available is this one designed for shaping operations. It may also be used with other accessories, as we will show.

In addition to commercial guards that come with the tool or are available as accessories, there are many safety devices the operator can, and should, make for himself, among them the adjustable shield shown in Figure 1-4. This consists of a piece of rigid plastic attached to the end of a piece of 1/2" bar stock which is gripped in the guard in place of the antikickback device. It provides a cover at the front of the blade without interfering with vision.

Figure 1-4: A typical safety device the worker can make for himself. It shields the front of the blade without interfering with visibility. It is not a substitute for the antikickback unit.

When the shield can't be used because of stock thickness, for example, it can be removed and the bar alone used as shown in Figure 1-5. The homemade guard is **not** a substitute for the antikickback unit. Construction details are shown in Figure 1-6.

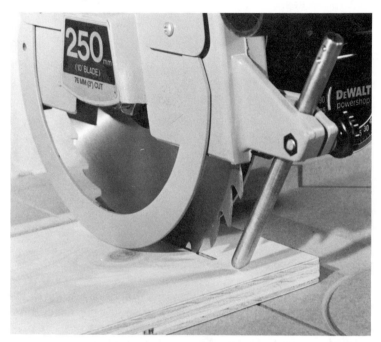

Figure 1-5: The homemade guard, with the plastic shield removed, can be used like this.

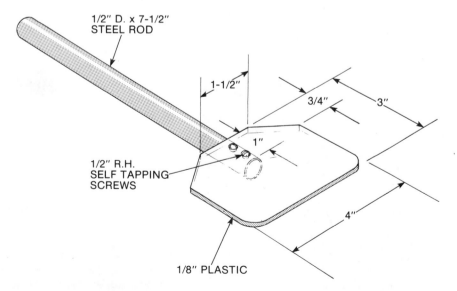

1/2" D. x 7-1/2" STEEL ROD

1-1/2"

3/4"

3"

1"

1/2" R.H. SELF TAPPING SCREWS

4"

1/8" PLASTIC

Figure 1-6: Construction details of the guard.

OTHER SAFETY ITEMS. Most important are safety goggles and a dust mask or respirator (Figure 1-7). It is wise practice to wear safety goggles for all operations, even the simple sawing chores. Don't depend on prescription glasses to provide eye protection; that is not their purpose. You can buy safety goggles designed to fit over vision lenses.

Figure 1-7: Safety goggles and a respirator. These should never be stored in a drawer or cabinet. Keep them visible so you won't forget to use them.

A dust mask usually is recommended for operations that create much dust. Many people think this refers only to sanding. It's not so; even crosscutting and ripping chores produce dust, and the dust from the adhesive in some plywoods can be irritating to throat and lungs. A respirator is a good safety factor, so why not reach for it every time you reach for safety goggles?

The key lock in the tool's power control center (Figure 1-8) will prevent unauthorized use but only if you remove it when you are through working. Leaving it in place negates its purpose.

Figure 1-8: You can't start the machine unless the key lock is inserted and turned. Don't leave the key in place when you are out of the shop.

SHOPKEEPING AND DRESS. Keep the tool, its table, benches, and floor area clean —free of sawdust, chips, and scraps. Litter can cause slipping or tripping, and this invites accidents.

There is such a thing as a dangerous environment for a power tool. It's not wise to use it in a damp or wet location or to expose it to rain.

Good lighting is important. The shop should be generally well lighted and the tool should have its own light, preferably adjustable, so shadow-free illumination can be provided for any operation.

Protect the tool's table from variable humidity conditions. Occasionally brush on a generous application of penetrating sealer. After ten or fifteen minutes wipe off excess sealer with a lint-free cloth and, when the coating is dry, sand lightly with fine sandpaper.

A shop uniform makes sense. Don't wear gloves, a necktie, or any loose clothing that might snag on stationary or moving tool parts. All jewelry should be removed. Wear a hair covering, especially if the hair is long, for safety reasons and to protect from dust. Wear nonslip shoes, preferably with steel toes.

GOOD SHOP PRACTICE. Socializing and shopwork don't mix well. Don't allow visitors, young or old, in the shop while you are working.

Make the workshop childproof by correctly using the key lock, of course, but also by padlocking to prevent entry and, perhaps, by installing a lockable master switch that controls all electrical equipment in the area.

Don't overreach when making any kind of cut. Stable footing and balance are critical. Don't struggle with large pieces of work. Seek help if you need it but be sure the assistant knows what you plan to do.

Disconnect the tool before making accessory changes. Do this even though you have turned off and removed the key lock. Always check the position of the "off" switch or button before plugging in.

Keep all cutting tools clean and sharp for quality work and safest performance. A dull tool requires more feed pressure and this creates a situation where your hands might slip.

When practical, it is good practice to hold work with a clamp. Don't ever hand-hold work so small that it puts you in a danger zone.

Don't use the tool like a step ladder. Serious injuries can occur if the tool tips or you unintentionally contact a cutting tool.

Never force a cutting action on any tool. This usually indicates that the cutting tool is dull or that you are cutting too deeply. Many very deep or oversize cuts must be made by repeat passes.

Always complete the "pass." For example, when crosscutting, a board will be severed when the blade has passed through it, but the pass will not be complete until you have returned the blade to its neutral position behind the guide fence. Then you turn off the motor and wait for the blade to stop turning before removing the work.

Always move work so you are feeding against the direction of rotation of the blade or cutter.

Don't leave a power tool running when it is necessary to move to another chore regardless of how little time is involved. In fact, it is wise to wait for the cutting tool to stop turning before moving away from the tool.

GOOD TOOL PRACTICE. Various saw cuts and other operations require the tool to be secured in particular attitudes. These positions are firmed through the use of knobs or levers. Other adjustments may be made with keys or wrenches. Make it a habit to see that locking components are secure and that adjustment components have been removed before you turn on the machine.

Use only recommended accessories. Don't ask an attachment to do a job for which it was not designed.

Be sure to mount saw blades and other cutters so they rotate in the correct direction. For example, when facing the motor arbor, the saw blade must rotate toward the back of the machine (clockwise).

Mount any accessory by carefully following the instructions that come with the tool.

Don't use saw blades of larger diameter than are recommended for the tool.

When mounting a saw blade be sure the arbor and the arbor collars are clean and that the recessed surface of the collars face the blade. Use the provided wrenches to lock the blade in place.

Check the tool before you use it and occasionally thereafter to be sure the components are in correct alignment.

Don't leave any cutting tool on the main arbor when you are using the rear auxiliary shaft, but do keep the saw guard mounted. It will serve to cover the unused arbor.

It is usually not advisable to oil or grease the tool's arm tracks or motor but check the owner's manual for specific instructions.

Never do ripping operations without the guard correctly adjusted and the antikickback device in place. Never rip from the wrong direction. Check the warnings and arrows on the tool's guard.

Keep the antikickback unit in place even when crosscutting, but adjust it to clear the workpiece.

Don't work without the lower part of the saw guard in position.

Always be alert. Don't work if you are tired, upset, or have had an alcoholic drink or two.

Don't work with a damaged tool. Check for parts alignment, excessive friction between moving parts, mounting arrangements of cutting tools and guards—or any condition that might affect the tool's performance. Replace damaged parts or have them properly repaired.

Above all, know the power tool. Carefully read and reread the owner's manual. Learn its applications and its limitations—use it wisely and safely.

ELECTRICAL CONSIDERATIONS. The tool should be grounded when in use to protect the operator from electrical shock. Should there be a malfunction or a breakdown, the grounding system provides a path of least resistance for electric current and reduces the risk of shock. The tool's electric cord has an equipment-grounding conductor and a grounding plug. In order for the system to work, the plug must be used in a matching outlet that is correctly installed and grounded in accordance with local codes and ordinances.

When the tool is organized for use on less than 150 v, its plug will resemble the one shown in Figure 1-9A. The grounding pin, which must never be removed, fits the specially shaped third hole in the outlet.

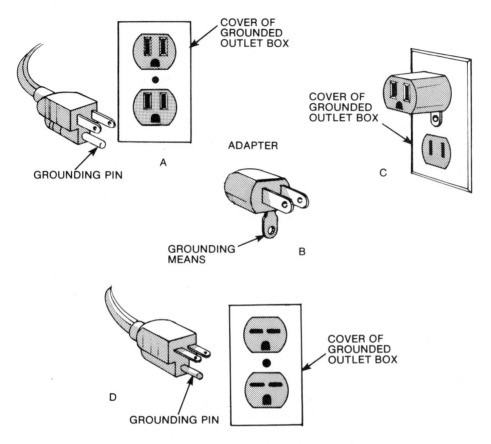

Figure 1-9: Methods of grounding. Never remove the grounding pin from a three-prong grounding plug. Be sure the outlet box is correctly grounded.

If the outlet is designed for a two-prong plug, an adapter like the one shown in Figure 1-9B, mounted as in Figure 1-9C, may be used to accommodate the grounding plug. The extending lug on the adapter (usually green colored) must be firmly attached to an outlet box **you know is correctly grounded.** It's recommended that such adapters be only temporarily used until a correctly grounded outlet box can be installed, preferably by a qualified electrician.

If the tool is organized for use on 150-250 v, it will have a plug like the one shown in Figure 1-9D and must be used with a matching, correctly grounded receptacle that is wired to deliver the correct voltage. Adapters are not available—should not be used—with this type of plug.

Incidentally, the adapter shown in Figures 1-9B and C is not used in Canada.

It is not advisable for the amateur to disassemble the tool or try to do any rewiring in the electrical system. This should be done in the manufacturer's service center or, if more convenient, by a local, professional service person. Anyone who decides to do an electrical repair should remember that the green-colored wire—sometimes green and yellow—is the "grounding" wire. It must never be connected to a **live** terminal.

Check with a qualified electrician or service person if the grounding instructions are not understood or if there is any doubt about whether the tool is properly grounded.

Repair or replace a worn or damaged cord immediately.

The shop's electrical system should include a circuit to be used exclusively by the tool. In the radial arm saw shop that will be shown later, the circuit was installed in the wall before benches and cabinets were constructed. Note that the outlet box (Figure 1-10) is recessed enough so it can be concealed by a small, hinged door (Figure 1-11). Adding a small lock to the door would provide another safety factor.

In summary, working safely has to do with knowing the tool, using it correctly, working sensibly, and accepting operator responsibility. The machine can't think; that's your job. Don't become overconfident or casual. Always be alert, aware that accidents can happen. No tool—powered or for hand use—is automatically "safe."

Remember our previous warning—MANY PHOTOGRAPHS IN THIS BOOK WERE TAKEN WITHOUT GUARDS IN PLACE. OCCASIONALLY A GUARD IS ADJUSTED A BIT SO IT WON'T HIDE AN OPERATION. IN ALL CASES THIS IS ONLY DONE FOR PHOTOGRAPHIC CLARITY.

NEVER WORK WITHOUT CORRECTLY ADJUSTED GUARDS AND OTHER SAFETY DEVICES.

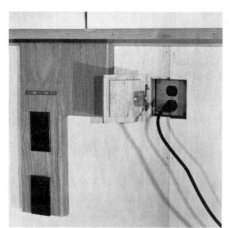

Figure 1-10: The radial arm saw shop that will be shown later has a circuit that is exclusively for the tool. The outlet box was recessed in the wall so it could be concealed with a small hinged door.

Figure 1-11: The door is mounted with a spring hinge so it will stay shut. Adding a small lock would provide another safety factor.

Chapter 2
The Words
We Use

Abrasive. Cutting particles of materials like flint, aluminum oxide, garnet, emery. Applied to various backings and supplied in different shapes—discs, squares, and strips being most common.

Abrasive paper. A backing coated with an abrasive. The common term is "sandpaper." The word "paper" doesn't always apply. Some abrasives are backed with cloth.

Abrasive wheel. A wheel composed of bonded abrasive material. A more common term is "grinding wheel." Used, for example, to sharpen tools and grind metals.

Across the grain. Indicating an action that is at right angles to wood grain direction. "Crossgrain" means the same.

Adhesive. A medium used to bond separate pieces. Glues and cements are adhesives.

Bead. A semicircular shape that is higher than adjacent surfaces. Usually a decorative detail.

Bevel. An edge-cut that does not form a right angle with adjacent surfaces. For example, a rip cut made at 30° produces a beveled edge.

Brad. Small, thin nail. Used for light assembly work. Sold by length and gauge rather than the **penny** (d) designation used for larger nails.

Butt. Literally, to thrust one part against another.

Butt joint. A wood connection that only involves square cuts. Example: a board that is surface-nailed into the edge of a second board.

C-clamp. A gripping device shaped like the letter C and available in many sizes. Pressure is applied with a thumbscrew, sliding pin, or knurled knob.

Chamfer. An angular cut that does not remove the entire edge of the stock.

Cleat. A support or reinforcement piece. A shelf may rest on a cleat. Boards can be joined with surface-mounted cleats.

Clinch. A reinforcement procedure with nails. A projecting nail-end is bent back against the surface from which it protrudes. The effect is to "clinch" the parts together.

Compound Miter. A cut made by combining a blade tilt with an arm swing. Usually done to form a structure with sloping sides. Example: a shadow box picture frame.

Countersink. An inverted cone shape usually done so flathead screws can be driven flush with surfaces. Often used to describe nails set below wood surfaces so they can be hidden with wood dough.

Cove.   An arch-like cut made along an edge or into a surface. Cove shapes are found on many molding designs.

Crosscut.   A saw cut made across the wood grain. Cutting a board into specific lengths is a crosscutting operation.

Cross miter.   Called a bevel or simply a miter but specifically, a bevel cut made across the grain.

Dado.   A U-shaped cut made across the grain. Often called a "gain."

Depth of cut.   Applies in various ways. A saw's capacity is often referred to as "maximum depth of cut." Depth of cut may also mean how far into the work the saw or other tool should penetrate.

Direction of rotation.   How a tool turns. When the blade of a radial arm saw is viewed from the left it is turning in a clockwise direction.

Dovetail.   A fan-shaped tenon. A dovetail joint is an interlocking wood connection—a fan-shaped tenon fits a similarly shaped slot.

Dowel.   A wooded pin available in various diameters and lengths. Common use: to reinforce various types of wood joints.

Dressing.   To bring a piece of lumber to required squareness or smoothness.

Feed direction.   The direction in which wood is moved past a saw blade or other cutting tool, or the direction in which the cutting tool is moved.

Feed speed.   Refers to how fast the work or the cutting tool is moved.

Finishing nail.   A nail with a special head that allows it to be easily set below the surface of the wood. Usually used when hiding the nail is good practice.

Flute.   The opposite of "bead." A semicircular shape that is below adjacent surfaces.

Gang cutting.   Holding several pieces so all can be cut at the same time.

Grain.   The pattern created by the fibers in wood. Different wood species have peculiar grain patterns. The pattern is also affected by how the wood is sawed at the mill.

Grit.   The size of the particles on abrasive paper. The smaller the grit, the smoother the surface.

Groove.   A U-shaped cut, like a dado, but made in line with the wood grain. The operation known as "grooving" is also often called "ploughing."

Hardboard.   A man-made material used in building and furniture construction. Specially treated wood fibers are subjected to heat and pressure to form dense, grainless panels.

Hardwood.   Wood obtained from deciduous trees—oak, maple, birch, ash, and so on. The term is botanical and does not indicate the actual hardness of any species.

Heeling.   A sawing action that indicates a misalignment. In effect, the "back" teeth of the blade are not following the cut-path of the "front" teeth.

Infeed.   The side of a cutting tool from which a cut is started. Example: when feeding from right to left, the right side is the infeed side.

Inlay.   A recess in one surface made to take a similarly shaped piece of contrasting material. Usually done for ornamentation.

In-rip.   Common saw blade position when work is cut lengthwise (ripped). The saw blade is between the motor and the tool's column. Work-feed is from right to left.

Jig.   A special device designed to increase a tool's versatility, to simplify an operation, or to minimize the possibility of human error. Most jigs are home-made. Many are shown in this book.

Kerf (see Figure 2-1).   The normal cut made with a saw blade. It can be through the wood to separate pieces or its depth can be less than the thickness of the stock.

Figure 2-1: The "kerf" is the cut made with a saw blade. It may pass through the stock to separate pieces or merely penetrate the stock to a particular depth.

Miter.   An angular cut, a common one being across the grain at a 45° angle. A MITER JOINT is formed when two such pieces are butted at the cut-line.

Moldings.   Decorative pieces applied to surfaces and in corners. Moldings are often used to construct picture frames.

Mortise.   A rectangular or square cavity that can be formed by drilling or by working with a router bit. One part of MORTISE-TENON joint.

Notch.   A U-shaped cut made in the edge of wood.

Outfeed.   The side of a cutting tool where the cut ends. Example: when feeding from right to left, the left side is the outfeed side.

Out-rip.   Saw blade position when very wide work is cut lengthwise (ripped). The saw blade faces the front of the table. Work-feed is from left to right.

Pass.   The action of moving work past a saw blade or other cutting tool or of moving a cutting tool to do a particular job.

Pivot.   A central point established so a piece of work can be rotated against a cutting tool. Applies, for example, to sanding, saber sawing, and shaping.

Plywood.   A man-made panel composed of various layers of thin sheets of wood usually placed so the grain in alternate sheets runs in opposite directions. Plywoods are also available with cores of solid wood or particleboard. Many types available. Surface veneers can be exotic hardwoods, more economical species, or even hardboard.

Pusher.   A special device used to move material past a cutting tool. The idea is to keep the hands away from danger areas. Especially important for ripping operations.

Rabbet.   An L-shaped cut that can be made along ends or edges of material. Usually, the L-shape is sized to suit the insert piece which is merely cut square. The two pieces, when assembled, form the RABBET JOINT.

Raised panel.   A panel of wood with slanted edges so its center area is higher than perimeter points. Often seen on doors and drawer fronts.

Rip miter.   Actually a bevel but often identified as a miter, especially when two such cuts are joined to form a 90° corner.

Ripping.   Saw cuts made in line with the grain of the wood.

Rout.   A woodworking procedure that involves high-speed cutters. The cutters may have profiles or straight shanks. Routing has practical applications as well as decorative ones.

Rpms.   The number of revolutions a tool makes in a minute.

Shim.   Usually, an adjustment piece. Shim applies since such pieces are generally slight in thickness.

Slot.   A slot is like a dado—a U-shaped cut.

Softwood.   Wood obtained from evergreen trees—pine, fir, redwood, cedar, larch, and so on. Like HARDWOOD the term is botanical and does not indicate wood density.

Spline.   A joint reinforcement used on miter joints, edge-to-edge joints, and similar connections. Thin plywoods and hardboards are good spline materials.

Stop (stop block).   A device used to control the length of a cut or to position work so the same cut can be made on many pieces.

Strip cut.   To cut slim strips from the edge of a board.

Tee nut.   A commercial product that makes it possible to easily install metal threads in wood.

Template (pattern).   A device that helps duplicate designs or that can serve as a guide to assure accuracy when making duplicate cuts or forming many similar pieces.

Tenon.   A projection with two or more shoulders. Usually rectangular or square and sized to fit a MORTISE.

Tongue.   Also a projection but always with two shoulders. Often sized to fit a groove on a mating board to form the TONGUE AND GROOVE joint.

Chapter 3
Getting Acquainted

The radial arm can be considered a power tool that combines the solid precision of a stationary tool with the flexibility of a portable electric saw. If you note that the portable saw is largely controlled by wrist action and that the radial arm saw adds shoulder, elbow, and arm movement, you can see that the combination offers practical results and bonus applications that increase the scope of work and operational convenience and accuracy.

It is not unusual to see a radial arm saw used as a primary tool at a house construction site. This is so, especially when the machine is equipped with side extensions, because the saw makes it easy to trim and shape house components like studs, rafters, and joists, or lumber pieces that are otherwise difficult to handle. The work sits solidly on the tool's table, the saw blade is pulled through for the cut. The workpiece may be 5' or 20' long. Trimming it and squaring it are no problem.

This particular application—part of the tool's history—tended to cast it as a "contractor's tool," widely acclaimed as a super crosscut or cutoff machine. It still is, but added refinements and features, together with specially designed accessories, have justified its place in the one-tool shop or multipurpose category.

The modern concept does more than saw. It can dado and rabbet, shape and mold, do routing and saber sawing, sand and grind, drill, polish, surface, joint —do more than 90% of the operations involved in general woodworking.

The often-asked question about basic operational differences between a table saw and a radial arm saw can be answered by describing crosscut actions. On a table saw, the saw blade projects from beneath the table. Work is placed on the table and held against a miter gauge. Both the work and the miter gauge are moved past the saw blade to make the cut. On the radial arm saw, the blade is above the table. Work is placed on the table against a guide fence. The work remains stationary while the blade is pulled through for the cut.

Accessories for a table saw are usually limited to dadoing tools and molding heads (shaping units). The radial arm saw can handle other accessories and so has a broader work scope.

TYPES AND SIZES. A modern radial arm saw, popular with professional people and homeworkers, is shown in Figure 3-1. This is the unit that will be seen throughout this book. Its 2-1/4 hp, totally enclosed motor drives a 10" saw blade at 3450 rpm. Its work capacities, which include a 3" depth of cut, 14-1/2" crosscut, and a better than 24" rip cut, make it a good tool for general shop work. Features include a brake built into the motor which automatically stops

Figure 3-1: The modern radial arm saw has power, good capacities, and many convenience features. This is the unit that will be seen throughout this book.

the blade after the switch is turned off, an accessory arbor designed to take a three-jaw chuck, scales for bevel, miter and rip cut settings, and automatic stops so a cutting tool can be easily positioned for frequently done operations. It has a dual voltage motor which means that although it may be factory connected for 120-v use, it can be reconnected to work on a 240-v circuit.

The intermediate unit shown in Figure 3-2 has open motor construction developing 2 hp to turn a 10″ saw blade at 3450 rpm. It operates on 120 v and has a manual brake; a button, located at the rear of the motor, is pushed by the operator when he wishes to shorten blade stop time. Capacities are—3″ depth of cut, 13″ crosscut, and 24″ or more rip cut. The unit is equipped with necessary scales and provides the convenience of automatic stops.

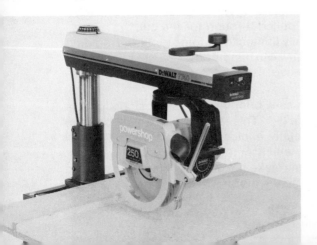

Figure 3-2: An intermediate unit, capable of all the major woodworking chores but lacking a few features. For example, it has a manual brake and a single voltage motor.

The major difference between the model shown in Figure 3-3 and the one in Figure 3-2 is in the location of the control handle used to raise or lower the radial arm. On this unit it is at the back of the machine, on top of the column.

Although the unit in Figure 3-4 might be considered a contractor's tool, it is often selected by serious amateurs because of its capacity for heavy work. The dual voltage motor develops 3-1/2 hp and has a built-in brake to automatically stop the blade quickly after the switch is turned off. The blade diameter is 12"; rpm equals 3450, and it is capable of a 4" depth of cut, 16" crosscut, and 27" rip cut. Despite its ruggedness, this tool has all the features that contribute to efficient woodworking—scales, automatic stops, and so on. The tool's net weight is about 60% greater than the other saws shown here.

Figure 3-3: Note here that the arm controls have been set at the rear of the machine. Otherwise it is similar to the model shown in Figure 3-2.

Figure 3-4: A typical contractor's radial arm saw, one that is often selected by the serious amateur who seeks extra heavy construction. This tool develops 3-1/2 hp and turns a 12" saw blade.

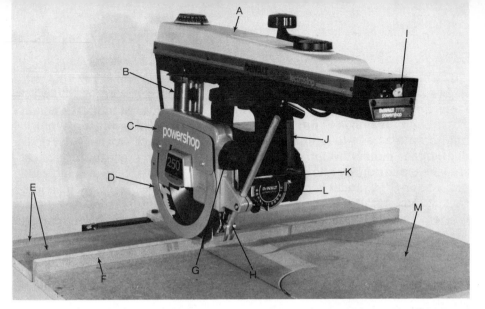

Figure 3-5: Nomenclature: (A) Radial arm—adjustable vertically, swings 180° radially; (B) column—rigid support for the radial arm and all top-side mechanisms; (C) main guard—covers 50% of blade, adjusts to suit various operations, used with tools other than saw blades; (D) lower guard—on each side of blade, lifts/lowers to accommodate stock thickness; (E) movable table boards—two pieces, allow for various guide fence positions; (F) guide fence —basic uses include positioning work for crosscutting or ripping, considered replaceable; (G) dust spout—adjustable, directs waste away from operator; (H) antikickback bar and fingers—main function to prevent saw blade from pulling work toward operator on rip cuts, adjusts to stock thickness; (I) power control center—includes "on" and "off" buttons and a key lock to prevent unauthorized use; (J) control handle—main function to move tool mechanism along radial arm; (K) bevel lock—secures tilt settings; (L) bevel scale—read out for motor tilt settings, includes auto-stops at frequently used positions; (M) fixed table—main support area for various operations, adjustable for parallelism to the radial arm.

NOMENCLATURE—TOOL CONTROLS. The controls of the radial arm saw are the key to its successful operation. These and other components are identified in Figures 3-5 and 3-6. Become familiar with all the parts and their names because we will frequently refer to them. At this point, especially if you have never done radial arm saw woodworking, you should try some "dry runs." That is, use the various controls without plugging in the tool. Adjusting the machine for various operations and testing the locking knobs and levers before actually operating it is good practice.

A BASIC SAWING ACTION. This action is demonstrated by the crosscut procedure shown in Figure 3-7. The feed direction indicates how the cutting tool is moved. From its neutral position behind the guide fence, the saw blade is pulled forward and severs the stock. The blade rotates down and toward the rear of the machine. This action tends to keep the work down on the table and against the guide fence. The feed-speed of the blade (that is, how fast the blade is pulled through the work) should always be conservative. Rushing the cut will produce rough edges, can cause the blade to stall since its teeth won't have time to work as they should, and might prompt the blade to climb like a wheel.

The cut is complete when the blade has severed the stock, but the crosscut action is not finished until the blade has been moved back to its neutral position behind the guide fence and is allowed to come to a complete stop.

30

Figure 3-6: Nomenclature: (A) Miter scale—read out for arm swing settings (miter cuts); (B) elevation control—turns to raise or lower the radial arm, 360° turn equals 1/8" adjustment; (C) miter lock—secures radial arm for miter-cut operations, includes auto-stops at frequently used positions; (D) rip scale—read out for blade-to-fence settings, provides for "in" or "out" ripping; (E) rip pointers—adjustable, two provided, one for "in" ripping, one for "out" ripping; (F) rip lock—locks mechanism at any position on radial arm, main function, securing blade for rip cuts; (G) yoke lock—secures mechanism for ripping operations but locking function available to any position, auto-stops included; (H) base—secured to tool's support frame, supports the column, designed to allow base-to-column adjustments; (I) accessory arbor—designed specifically for mounting a three-jaw chuck; (J) table clamps—one at each end of table, secures table boards and fence, also used to secure some accessories and special tables you can make.

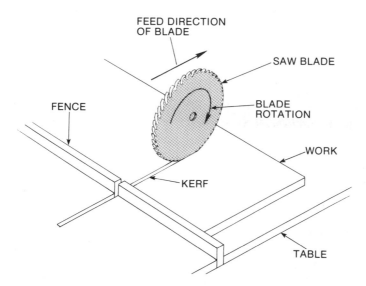

Figure 3-7: A basic cut action of the radial arm saw. Notice that while the feed direction of the blade is forward, the blade turns clockwise so cutting action is down and toward the rear of the machine.

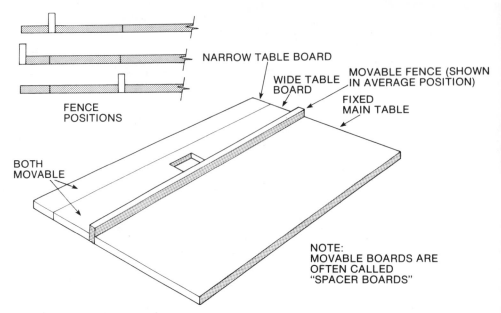

NARROW TABLE BOARD

WIDE TABLE BOARD

MOVABLE FENCE (SHOWN IN AVERAGE POSITION)

FIXED MAIN TABLE

FENCE POSITIONS

BOTH MOVABLE

NOTE:
MOVABLE BOARDS ARE OFTEN CALLED "SPACER BOARDS"

Figure 3-8: Parts of the saw's table. Possible guide-fence positions are shown in the upper left-hand corner.

THE TABLE. The table (Figure 3-8) consists of one main piece that is fixed and two movable boards which, for average work, are situated behind the guide fence, as the drawing shows. The illustration also suggests various guide-fence positions that are useful for many accessory operations and that help to increase capacity, for example, during ripping operations.

It is standard on a radial arm saw for the saw blade to cut into the table; it must do this in order to sever the stock. Each time you change the saw blade's position—this is done most often during miter sawing—a new cut is made in the table. Because of this unavoidable kerfing, the table can become unsightly and develop a rough work surface.

Most workers will kerf the table for frequently used sawing positions such as crosscutting, right hand 45° miter, and ripping; ripping operations require a shallow trough since they must accommodate various widths of stock.

Additional table kerfs can be avoided by using a thin, protective cover. The cover can be a sheet of 1/4" plywood tack-nailed to the regular table or a removable slide-on unit like the one shown in Figure 3-9. The slide-on auxiliary table is made as shown in Figure 3-10. Its advantages are that it is easy to mount whenever it is needed, and it doesn't add nail holes in the regular table.

THE GUIDE FENCE. Consider the guide fence a replaceable item. If you used the radial arm saw for only crosscutting, then a single fence might last a lifetime, but since the saw is used for many types of cuts, the fence would soon be kerfed to the point of weakness. Also, extra fences as well as special fences contribute convenience and accuracy to many sawing and nonsawing operations.

Since the basic fence is nothing but a straight piece of material, you can quickly make a number of them to have on hand for particular applications (Figure 3-11). This doesn't mean that a used fence should be discarded. Keep it on hand as you would any accessory for reuse when work requires it.

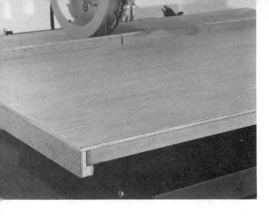

Figure 3-9: An auxiliary cover can be a sheet of 1/4" plywood tack-nailed to the regular table, but a slide-on unit like this one is more convenient to remove.

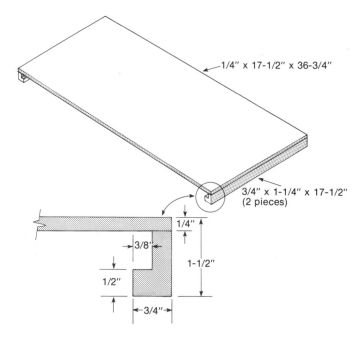

1/4" x 17-1/2" x 36-3/4"

3/4" x 1-1/4" x 17-1/2"
(2 pieces)

1/4"

3/8"

1-1/2"

1/2"

3/4"

Figure 3-10: Construction details of the slide-on auxiliary table.

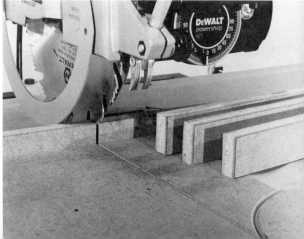

Figure 3-11: It is advisable to make extra guide fences right at the start. "Used" ones are not discarded but are stored like any accessory.

Figure 3-12: The motor's 5/8" x 1-1/2" main arbor is longer than needed to secure a saw blade so that it can be used to grip other types of woodworking tools.

MOUNTING A SAW BLADE. The tool's main arbor (Figure 3-12) is at the left end of the motor. It has a 5/8" diameter and is 1-1/2" long; this is more length than is needed to grip a saw blade but allows the arbor to hold other cutting tools. The end of the arbor has hexagonal recess to accommodate an Allen wrench, which is used to hold the arbor when cutting tools are secured. Two collars with recessed sides and a nut with left-hand threads are also provided.

To mount a saw blade, place a collar on the arbor so that its recessed side faces the end of the arbor. Place the saw blade so that it will rotate in a clockwise direction, and then add the second collar so that its recessed side is against the blade. Place the nut and tighten it by using the two wrenches that come with the tool, as shown in Figure 3-13. The nut has left-hand threads so it can't be loosened by normal tool rotation. This means it is tightened by turning it counterclockwise.

Figure 3-13: A saw blade is mounted between collars with the recessed surface of the collars placed against the blade. The arbor is held with an Allen wrench; the nut is tightened by turning it counterclockwise.

To remove a saw blade or other cutting tool, use both wrenches but turn the nut clockwise. Once the nut is loose you can spin it off the arbor, but keep the Allen wrench in place so the nut will slide down and come to rest on the table (Figure 3-14).

Figure 3-14: To remove a saw blade or other cutting tool, turn the nut clockwise. Leave the Allen wrench in place so that when you spin the nut off the arbor it will slide down the shaft and come to rest on the table.

Be sure to mount saw blades and other cutting tools so they will turn in the direction indicated by the arrow that is stamped or printed on the blade.

NEUTRAL CROSSCUT POSITION. This position is shown in Figure 3-15. The blade is as far back as it can go, behind the guide fence, where it can't interfere with or touch work that will be placed against the fence for sawing. The tool is turned on after the work is positioned and then the blade is pulled through. Return the saw blade to the neutral crosscut position after the work is severed. Wait for the blade to stop turning before you remove the work.

Figure 3-15: This is the neutral crosscut position. The blade is at the back of the radial arm and behind the guide fence.

IN-RIP POSITION. This position, shown in Figure 3-16, will accommodate most ripping operations. The following procedure is used to change from crosscutting to in-ripping. Pull the blade to the front of the arm and then elevate it to clear the table. Loosen the yoke lock and swivel the yoke 90° toward the column so the blade will be parallel with the guide fence. Secure the yoke lock and lower the blade so its teeth will be in the rip trough. Set the blade for the width of cut required and then tighten the rip lock. Cut-width is determined by measuring from the fence to the side of the blade that faces it. If the blade has set teeth, measure from the point of a tooth that is set toward the fence.

When in-ripping, the feed direction (the direction in which the work is moved) is from right to left—against the blade's direction of rotation.

Figure 3-16: The in-rip position. The saw blade is square to the table and parallel to the guide fence. Work is fed, as indicated by the arrow, from right to left.

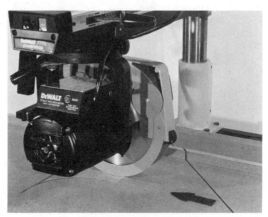

OUT-RIP POSITION. When cut-width is greater than can be accomplished in the in-rip position, the saw blade is positioned as shown in Figure 3-17 by following the procedure outlined for in-ripping, except that the yoke is swiveled 90° toward the front of the arm. Maximum rip cut is possible when the blade is set completely forward and the guide fence is moved to the back of the machine, where it is separated from the main table by the two movable table boards.

When using the out-rip position, feed the work from left to right.

Figure 3-17: The out-rip position is similar to the in-rip position, except that the saw blade faces away from the column instead of toward it. Here, work-feed direction (arrow) is from left to right.

THE RIP SCALE. The rip scale located on the right side of the radial arm (Figure 3-18) makes it possible to quickly set the blade to the cut-width required for either in-ripping or out-ripping. The top part of the scale is read for in-ripping positions, the bottom part for out-ripping. Each scale has its own adjustable pointer. The pointers should be adjusted at the outset by following instructions in the owner's manual; they will have to be readjusted should you change to a saw blade of heavier gauge than the original one.

Figure 3-18: Read-out scales for both in- and out-ripping are on the right side of the radial arm. Note that both metric and inch scales are marked.

ANTIKICKBACK DEVICES. The design supplied with the machine is shown in Figure 3-19, set up as it should be when the tool is used for in-ripping. The bar is locked in the saw guard so that the curved tines will ride the surface of the work. The tines dig into the work and hold it in case the saw blade's rotation should move the work back toward the operator. The tines must ride the surface of the work. If they don't, they can't function.

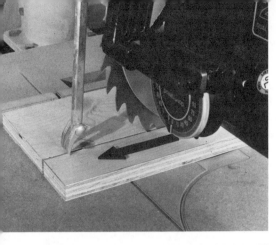

Figure 3-19: The antikickback device is organized as shown here. The curved tines ride the surface of the work and will dig in should the saw blade tend to move the work back toward the operator. This is the in-rip position. Arrow shows direction of work-feed.

An accessory antikickback device (Figure 3-20) includes a fixed "splitter," which rides in the kerf made by the saw blade to keep the kerf from closing and thus from binding the saw blade. There is more tendency for kickback when the work binds the blade. In the photograph, the curved tines have been elevated only to illustrate the splitter.

Figure 3-20: The accessory antikickback device includes a "splitter" that rides in the saw kerf. Its purpose is to keep the wood from binding the blade.

SIMPLE MITER-CUT POSITION. The most common miter cut—frequently used, for example, on picture frames—calls for a 45° cut across the surface of the stock. The saw is set up for this operation as shown in Figure 3-21. To make the miter cut, follow this procedure. Raise the blade to clear the table and then loosen the miter lock. Swing the radial arm to the right until it clicks into the 45° auto-stop. Tighten the miter lock and lower the blade to its cut position. Miter cuts that are not 45° can be set by reading the radial arm's position on the miter scale located at the rear of the arm above the column.

Figure 3-21: Simple miter-cut position with the radial arm swung 45° to the right. Miter cuts of this type are made as easily as simple crosscuts.

CROSS-MITER (OR BEVEL) POSITION. Miter or bevel cuts across the stock are made with the tool set as shown in Figure 3-22. To reach this position, first raise the blade well above the table (about 15 turns), then loosen the bevel lock and tilt the motor until the unit clicks into the 45° auto-stop. Secure the bevel lock and lower the blade to its cutting position.

Cuts that are not 45° can be determined by reading the tilt angle on the bevel scale.

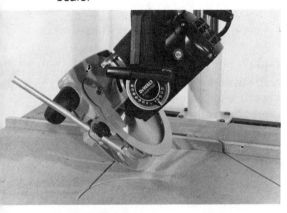

Figure 3-22: The blade set up for cross-mitering (or beveling). This is basically a crosscut position but with the blade tilted to the required angle.

RIP-MITER (OR BEVEL) POSITION. If you position the tool as described for cross-miter cuts and then swivel it 90° toward the column as if for in-ripping, you would reach the position shown in Figure 3-23, which is right for miter and bevel cuts (also chamfers) that are made parallel to the grain of the wood. This setup is like a ripping operation but with the blade tilted. When the tool is positioned as shown in the illustration, work-feed direction is from right to left.

Figure 3-23: Here, the saw is set up for in-ripping but with the blade tilted so the result will be a rip miter (or bevel). Work-feed direction is from right to left.

THE HORIZONTAL CUTTING POSITION. Here (Figure 3-24) the motor is tilted a full 90° so the cutting tool is parallel to the table. This attitude is a unique feature of the radial arm saw and has many applications. Tools that can be driven in this position include saw blades, dadoes, shaping heads, and rotary planers. Later in the book we'll see how all these things work.

Figure 3-24: The horizontal cutting position, shown here with a saw blade on the arbor, is used for many operations. Later chapters will describe particular applications.

Work-feed direction is from right to left when the tool is in the position shown in the photo. Many woodworking techniques are accomplished by placing a cutting tool in horizontal position and moving it while the work remains stationary. These techniques generally require a special table (that has to be constructed) and particular organizing. Such advanced procedures will be described in later chapters.

THE TABLE KERFS. To form the most commonly used kerfs—those shown in Figure 3-25—either in the tool's table or an auxiliary cover, follow this procedure.

Elevate the blade to clear the table and set it in its neutral crosscut position (behind the guide fence). Turn the saw on and use the elevation control to slowly lower the blade until it is cutting 1/32" to 1/16" into the table. Grip the control handle firmly while you are doing this. Then, slowly pull the blade forward to its maximum crosscut position and secure the rip lock. At this point you will have the crosscut kerf and a guide kerf in the fence.

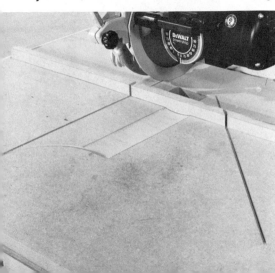

Figure 3-25: The basic table kerfs. Many operators will cut these in the regular table but will switch to an auxiliary table when the operation calls for other table kerfs.

Loosen the yoke lock and slowly turn it in a clockwise direction until the auto-stop clicks into position. Now, the blade will be in the in-rip position and you will have formed a 90° curved kerf which is called the "swing line."

After the swing line is formed, secure the yoke lock, loosen the rip lock, and very slowly move the blade back until it barely touches the guide fence. This is actually a coving operation—a technique we'll discuss later—that forms the rip trough. In effect, the rip trough is a continuous kerf that allows the blade to be set for various in-ripping chores.

The swing line and the rip trough can be extended to accommodate out-ripping operations. To do this, return the blade to the maximum crosscut position and secure the rip lock. Then, with the motor on, loosen the yoke clamp and rotate the yoke counterclockwise until it clicks into the out-rip position. Secure the yoke lock, loosen the rip lock, and slowly move the blade back to form a new trough that will mate with the original one. Now you have a 180° swing line and a full-length rip trough.

Elevate the blade to clear the table and return it to the neutral crosscut position. Loosen the miter lock and swing the radial arm to the right until it clicks into the 45° position. Slowly lower the blade until it kerfs the table and then pull it forward until it reaches maximum 45° miter position. Turn off the motor, elevate the blade to clear the table, and then return it to the neutral crosscut position.

When the kerfing is complete, touch up all the cut-lines with a piece of very fine sandpaper so there will be no rough edges. Brush on a generous coat of penetrating sealer, making sure that the sealer penetrates all kerfs. Wipe off excess sealer with a lint-free cloth after 15 or 20 minutes. Lightly sand the entire table with fine sandpaper after the sealer is dry. Many operators occasionally apply a coating of paste wax to keep the table clean and smooth.

Chapter 4
The Shop

Working arrangements for the radial arm saw range from a simple stand you can make or buy, to a complete shop designed around the tool and planned for compactness, efficiency, and pleasant use.

A first problem to resolve when the tool is acquired is how to set up so that it can be quickly used. A solution is to add a steel leg stand to the initial purchase (Figure 4-1). The units come with all necessary hardware, require minimum assembly time, and are predrilled to accept the tool as well as casters you may wish to add. The leg braces are for reinforcement but can also be used to support a shelf.

Figure 4-1: A steel leg stand is a quick and easy way to provide a mounting arrangement for the radial arm saw. The leg braces can be used to support a shelf.

A step up in the stand area is the steel cabinet shown in Figure 4-2. This is an excellent base for the machine and provides considerable storage space for accessories, instructional materials, and so on. Like the leg stand, the unit has all necessary nuts and bolts and is predrilled for the tool and for casters. Leveler feet are standard equipment. They provide some adjustment for tool-table height but are especially useful when the cabinet is on an uneven floor.

Many craftspeople custom design the interior of their cabinet, installing wooden shelves or drawers to suit their particular needs.

A 2 x 4 STAND. The stand shown in Figure 4-3 is designed for easy cutting and assembly and can be made by anyone not wishing to invest in a ready-made steel unit. All parts, except for the top, are standard 2 x 4s (which actually measure 1-1/2" x 3-1/2") and only require simple crosscuts to the lengths called out on the drawing.

Figure 4-2: A cabinet stand supports the saw and provides storage space for accessories. It can be fitted with drawers you buy or make. The back of the door has special trays for small items.

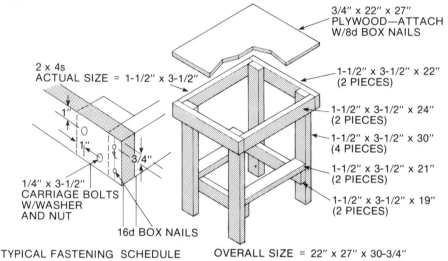

3/4" x 22" x 27" PLYWOOD—ATTACH W/8d BOX NAILS

2 x 4s
ACTUAL SIZE = 1-1/2" x 3-1/2"

1-1/2" x 3-1/2" x 22" (2 PIECES)

1-1/2" x 3-1/2" x 24" (2 PIECES)

1-1/2" x 3-1/2" x 30" (4 PIECES)

1-1/2" x 3-1/2" x 21" (2 PIECES)

1-1/2" x 3-1/2" x 19" (2 PIECES)

1"

1"

3/4"

1/4" x 3-1/2" CARRIAGE BOLTS W/WASHER AND NUT

16d BOX NAILS

TYPICAL FASTENING SCHEDULE

OVERALL SIZE = 22" x 27" x 30-3/4"

Figure 4-3: A basic stand that can be quickly made. All parts, except for the top, are of standard 2 x 4 lumber. The fastening detail that is shown will produce the strongest assembly.

Of course, the machine must be used to saw the parts and this calls for a temporary but sturdy platform on which to rest it. It can be an existing workbench or a "stand" made by spanning across two, closely spaced, sturdy sawhorses with a sheet of heavy plywood. Be sure the tool is solidly placed whichever you choose. Also, if you are a novice or have never used a radial arm saw, go ahead to Chapter 7, "The Basic Cuts," to see how crosscutting is accomplished.

The pieces are assembled as shown in the drawing. This calls for some drilling, which can be done with a hand drill, a bit and brace, or with a portable electric drill. Nails can be substituted for the carriage bolts, but the assembly will not be as strong. Use glue in all joints.

Plate-type swivel casters can be attached to the bottom of the legs but use those that have a locking device so the tool can't move about when you are using it.

PLYWOOD STAND. A more elaborate stand that can be made is shown in Figure 4-4. This stand is incorporated in the complete radial arm saw shop that will be described later (Figure 4-5). Construction details appear in Figure 4-6. This project requires ripping as well as crosscutting operations, so the novice is again urged to consult Chapter 7 to see how these jobs are done. If you start the project with a full sheet of plywood—or any piece that is unwieldy—have someone help you support the work while you are making initial sizing cuts. Be sure that the helper knows the procedure involved.

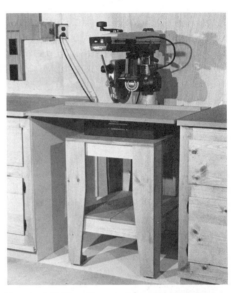

Figure 4-4: A more elaborate stand—one that is all-plywood construction.

Figure 4-5: The plywood stand is the unit that is used in the super shop. When the stand is equipped with casters, the tool may be used at any building site.

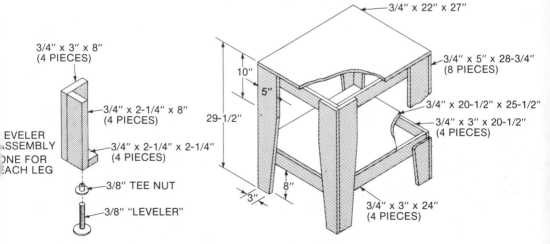

3/4" x 3" x 8"
(4 PIECES)

3/4" x 2-1/4" x 8"
(4 PIECES)

EVELER
SSEMBLY
)NE FOR
ACH LEG

3/4" x 2-1/4" x 2-1/4"
(4 PIECES)

3/8" TEE NUT

3/8" "LEVELER"

3/4" x 22" x 27"

10"

5"

29-1/2"

3"

8"

3/4" x 5" x 28-3/4"
(8 PIECES)

3/4" x 20-1/2" x 25-1/2"

3/4" x 3" x 20-1/2"
(4 PIECES)

3/4" x 3" x 24"
(4 PIECES)

Figure 4-6: Construction details of the all-plywood stand. The leveler assembly should be installed whether you use casters or the level screws that are shown.

The leveler assemblies shown in the drawing detail may be considered optional but they are a useful addition, for they can be used to adjust tool-table height to adjacent benches or to compensate for an uneven floor. The leveler screw is a commercial item available in hardware stores and do-it-yourself centers. Casters may be substituted, but use those with a locking device.

A DROP-LEAF EXTENSION. On its own movable stand, the radial arm saw requires very little floor space and not too much operating room at the front. However, to fully utilize the machine it is wise to consider extending its table surface on one or both sides. One way to do this without occupying more floor space than you may have is to equip the table with one or two hinged extensions of the type shown in Figure 4-7. This increases work-support area by 3' (6' if two are made) but can be swung down (Figure 4-8) when it is not required. Because the extension is hinged to the tool's table, it may be employed whether you have the saw mounted on a homemade stand, leg assembly, or cabinet stand.

Figure 4-7: The hinged extension provides an additional 3' of work-support surface. If one is made for each side of the saw there will be 9' of table area.

Figure 4-8: The hinged extension folds down out of the way when it isn't needed.

Construction details of the drop-leaf extension are shown in Figure 4-9. Bear in mind that the extension's top surface must be level with the tool's table surface. To assure this, first make the upper part of the extension, attach it with the two T-hinges, and use temporary braces to keep it on a level plane. Then attach the leg assembly using the area marked "A" on the drawing for height adjustment. If there isn't enough leeway here, you can shorten the legs slightly.

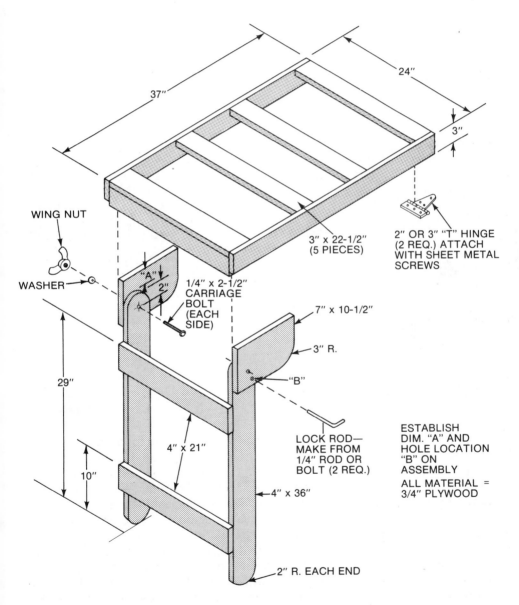

24"

37"

3"

WING NUT

WASHER

3" x 22-1/2" (5 PIECES)

2" OR 3" "T" HINGE (2 REQ.) ATTACH WITH SHEET METAL SCREWS

"A"

2"

1/4" x 2-1/2" CARRIAGE BOLT (EACH SIDE)

7" x 10-1/2"

3" R.

"B"

29"

4" x 21"

LOCK ROD— MAKE FROM 1/4" ROD OR BOLT (2 REQ.)

ESTABLISH DIM. "A" AND HOLE LOCATION "B" ON ASSEMBLY

ALL MATERIAL = 3/4" PLYWOOD

10"

4" x 36"

2" R. EACH END

Figure 4-9: This is how the hinged extension is made. The prototype is all plywood but lumber may be substituted.

The legs are secured in vertical position by the wing nuts and lock rods (Figure 4-10). Drill the holes for the lock rods while the extension is set up for use. These same rods are used to secure the legs when the extension is not in use (Figure 4-11). Here too, the holes for the rods should be drilled on assembly, that is, with the legs folded.

While the prototype is made entirely of plywood, there is no reason why solid lumber can't be used. Projects like this, including most of the homemade accessories shown in this book, are long-lived units and will see much use. Therefore, they should be carefully sanded and protected with several applications of penetrating sealer. The particular craftsperson might wish to add a coat of varnish.

Figure 4-10: A wing nut and a lock rod secure the legs when the extension is used. Drill the lock-rod hole on assembly.

Figure 4-11: The same lock rod is used to secure the legs when they are folded. This hole should also be drilled on assembly.

AN EXTENSION STAND. Another unit that can supply support for oversize work is the movable, adjustable, roller-top stand shown in Figure 4-12. Many workers have a similar stand on hand even when the tool is equipped with attached extensions or is placed between support surfaces. The stand will not only support long work but can also be placed in front of the machine to ease the chore of, for example, ripping large panels. Since the stand is adjustable vertically, it may be used for more than radial arm saw work.

The stand is made as shown in Figure 4-13. Make the lower part first, then the telescoping upper arm, and make sure the sliding action is smooth. The holes for the carriage bolts must be drilled and the carriage bolts installed **before** the upper arm is assembled. Carriage bolts have a shoulder that sinks into the wood and keeps the bolt from turning when the nut is tightened, so note that ordinary bolts can't be substituted.

Figure 4-12: A roller-top extension stand may be used on either side and in front of the machine. The height of this one is adjustable so it can be used for more than radial arm saw work.

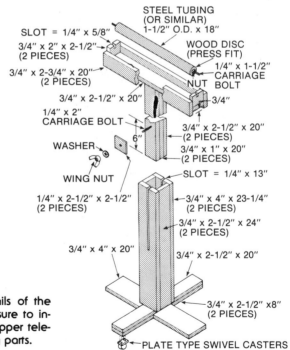

STEEL TUBING
(OR SIMILAR)
1-1/2" O.D. x 18"

SLOT = 1/4" x 5/8"

3/4" x 2" x 2-1/2"
(2 PIECES)

WOOD DISC
(PRESS FIT)

1/4" x 1-1/2"
CARRIAGE
BOLT

3/4" x 2-3/4" x 20"
(2 PIECES)

NUT

3/4" x 2-1/2" x 20"

3/4"

1/4" x 2"
CARRIAGE BOLT

3/4" x 2-1/2" x 20"
(2 PIECES)

WASHER

6"

3/4" x 1" x 20"
(2 PIECES)

WING NUT

SLOT = 1/4" x 13"

1/4" x 2-1/2" x 2-1/2"
(2 PIECES)

3/4" x 4" x 23-1/4"
(2 PIECES)

3/4" x 2-1/2" x 24"
(2 PIECES)

3/4" x 4" x 20"

3/4" x 2-1/2" x 20"

Figure 4-13: Construction details of the roller-top extension stand. Be sure to install the carriage bolts in the upper telescoping arm before assembling parts.

3/4" x 2-1/2" x8"
(2 PIECES)

PLATE TYPE SWIVEL CASTERS
(4 REQ.)

The closure discs for the roller can be formed with a coping saw or saber saw—the saber saw attachment for the radial arm saw can be used—but work carefully since the disc should fit tightly in the tubing. Be sure to install the 1/4" x 1-1/2" carriage bolts before you force the discs into place.

The casters on the stand are optional. If you add them, be sure they are the locking type. The stand must not move about when it is used to support work.

A SUPER SHOP. It's not difficult to design an ideal shop for the radial arm saw since the machine itself needs less than 3 square feet of floor space and is efficient even when placed against a wall. Ideally there should be room to the left and right of the tool, but little operating space is required at the front. The shop shown in Figure 4-14 is located against a wall in an oversize garage but with some modifications if necessary, it could be erected in a basement, an attic, an existing outbuilding, or one specially constructed for use as a woodworking shop.

The shop illustrated is complete, providing a good-sized workbench and storage room for radial arm saw accessories as well as other woodworking tools and equipment, and yet it is little more than 10' long and occupies only 31-1/2 square feet of floor space (Figure 4-15). A unique feature is the access door cut through the wall at the end of the bench, so that extra-long work just pokes through the building (Figure 4-16). With this setup it is easy, for example, to square off the end of a 16' or 20' board.

Figure 4-14: The super shop provides ample bench area plus storage space for all radial arm saw accessories and other tools.

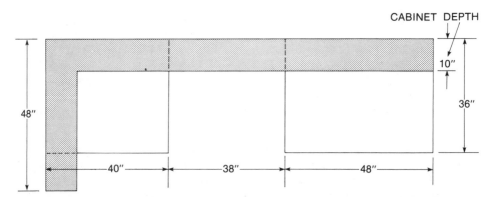

Figure 4-15: Floor plan of the super shop. This fits neatly against a side wall of an oversized garage but is suitable for just about any location.

Figure 4-16: A feature of the shop is the access door so that long work can poke through the wall of the building.

If the access door is included, the builder should remember that the outside wall of a building is a "bearing" wall so that the framing must be redone along the lines shown in Figure 4-17. This construction will prevent the wall's strength from being reduced.

The width of the access door is optional but should not be less than about 24". Figure 4-18 shows a door more than 4' wide incorporated in the wall of a small building that was specially constructed for a radial arm saw shop. Full-width plywood panels can pass through. When the opening isn't needed the door is swung up and latched on the inside (Figure 4-19).

If the work is carefully done, the siding that is cut away for the opening can be reused as the door. Whichever way the job is done, be sure that the bottom of the opening will be below the surface of the bench (Figure 4-20).

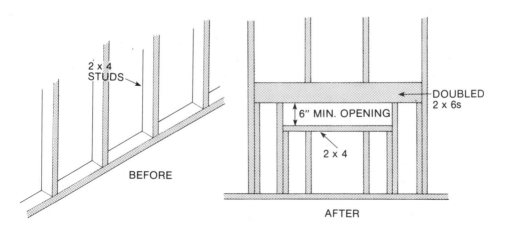

Figure 4-17: Cuts made through a wall must be done in line with building codes. The doubled 2 x 6s (called a "header") substitute for the strength lost when existing studs are cut.

Figure 4-18: This access door was incorporated in the wall of a small building erected specially for a radial arm saw shop. The door is more than 4' wide so even plywood panels can pass through.

Figure 4-19: When not in use, the door swings up and is secured with inside latches. Note that the door is made from the same material used in the siding.

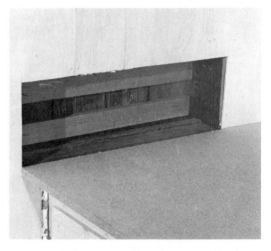

Figure 4-20: Be sure to locate the access door so its lower part will be below the top of the shop's bench.

Construction. Although making the shop is not a difficult task, it is not something that can be done in a weekend. Assuming the radial arm saw is on its stand, however, the tool will be useable for any chore, and the worker can devote time now and again to assembling the super shop.

Construction procedures consist mainly of erecting frames and then closing in. For example, the wall cabinets (Figure 4-21) can be set up in the following steps.

1. Place 1 x 2 or 1 x 3 strips on the wall, locating nails whenever possible so they will penetrate studs. The strips show the basic outline of the cabinets.

2. Attach a sheet of 1/8" or 1/4" perforated hardboard to the strips using 1" sheet metal screws along perimeter edges. The cabinet backs can be plywood but the hardboard is a ready-made means of hanging accessories and other tools.

3. Close in the cabinet by nailing the top, bottom, and sides to the wall strips and to each other. These pieces can be 1 x 10s which, less the thickness of the wall strips and hardboard, will provide a cabinet depth of about 8-1/2". Vertical dividers and shelves can be added now, but if you hold off until you know what you will be storing, it will be easier to custom-design the cabinet interiors for maximum use of space.

50

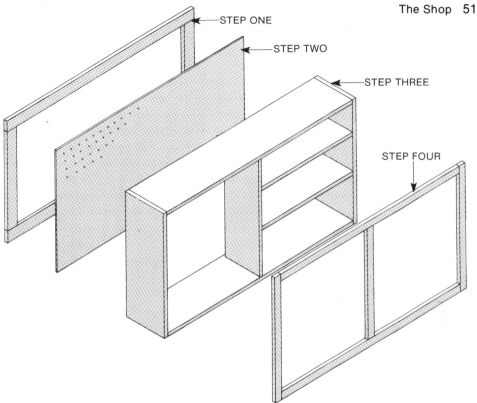

STEP ONE

STEP TWO

STEP THREE

STEP FOUR

Figure 4-21: Hanging the wall cabinets will be a simple procedure if you follow these steps.

4. Use 1 x 2s or 1 x 3s to face the cabinet. The facing adds a finishing touch and provides a surface on which to hang the doors. The doors can be sheets of plywood rabbeted or shaped on four edges to provide a lip and hung with kitchen-type, offset hinges, or the doors can have square edges so they will be flush with the facing and can be hung with surface hinges or mortised, butt hinges.

THE BASE CABINETS (BENCHES). Regardless of tool site, the benches can be constructed as shown in Figure 4-22. First establish a line across the wall that will indicate the height of the tool's table. This will serve as a guide for positions of bench components. The three back frame pieces (part No.1) are secured to the wall with 16d or 20d nails driven into studs. Establish the horizontal plane of these pieces by checking with a level. In fact, a level should be used throughout construction. Working with a square might cause problems since walls and floors of rooms generally are not square to each other.

Add other framing pieces using 16d nails as fasteners. Add the bottom shelf (part No. 6) when the frame is complete. It will be easier to install the shelf if you make it in two pieces. Cut the two pieces that form the bench's surface but just rest them in place at this time. Don't permanently attach them until all other work has been done. A bill of materials for one of the benches is shown in Figure 4-23. If these sizes are not exactly right (you may wish to modify to suit particular requirements), they will at least serve as a guide.

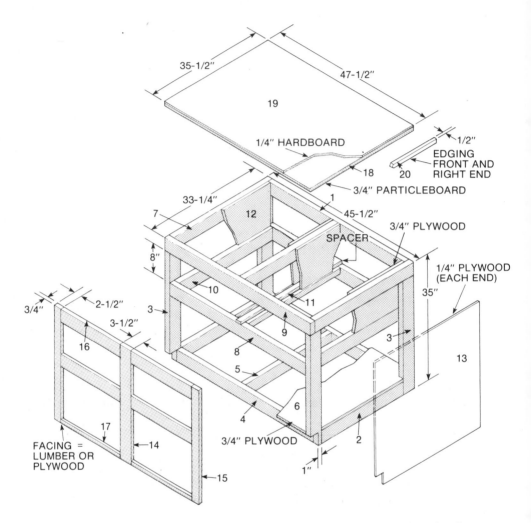

Figure 4-22: Assembly details of one of the cabinet benches in the super shop. It isn't necessary to change the construction design if you need a bench that is longer or shorter.

Drawers are constructed as shown in Figure 4-24. This is not an elaborate design but results in a sturdy project. If you are unfamiliar with the procedures involved in forming dadoes and rabbets, you will find the information in Chapter 11. Be sure to use glue in all joint areas when the drawer is assembled.

The drawer guides are attached to the inside of the case (Figure 4-25) and are positioned so the drawer will not scrape frame members when it is moved in or out. This guidance system is simple and economical since it doesn't require special hardware, and it will work efficiently if you are careful to size the dado and the guide for a good sliding fit (Figure 4-26). Sand the guide and the edges of the dadoes and then apply a coat of paste wax to mating surfaces.

Size the drawer heights to suit particular storage items. The top area of deep drawers is often wasted, but it can be used efficiently and at the same time create safe little nooks for accessories if sliding trays are installed (Figure

PART NO.	NO. PCS.	SIZE	MATERIAL
1	3	1-1/2" x 3-1/2" x 42-1/2"	Lumber
2	2	1-1/2" x 3-1/2" x 26-1/4"	Lumber
3	4	1-1/2" x 3-1/2" x 31-1/2"	Lumber
4	1	1-1/2" x 3-1/2" x 38-1/2"	Lumber
5	3	1-1/2" x 3-1/2" x 27-3/4"	Lumber
6	1	3/4" x 33-1/4" x 45-1/2"	Plywood
7	2	1-1/2" x 3-1/2" x 31-3/4"	Lumber
8	1	1-1/2" x 3-1/2" x 42-1/2"	Lumber
9	1	1-1/2" x 3-1/2" x 45-1/2"	Lumber
10	2	1-1/2" x 3-1/2" x 30-1/4"	Lumber
11	1	3/4" x 1-1/2" x 33-1/4"	Lumber
12	4	3/4" x 11-1/2" x 30-1/4"	Plywood
13	2	1/4" x 33-1/4" x 35"	Plywood
14	1	3/4" x 3-1/2" x 31-1/2"	Lumber or plywood
15	2	3/4" x 2-1/2" x 31-1/2"	Lumber or plywood
16	4	3/4" x 3-1/2" x 18-3/4"	Lumber or plywood
17	2	3/4" x 3/4" x 18-3/4"	Lumber or plywood
18	1	3/4" x 35-1/2" x 47-1/2"	Particleboard
19	1	1/4" x 35-1/2" x 47-1/2"	Hardboard
20	1 pc.	1/2" x 1" x 35-1/2"	Lumber
20	1 pc.	1/2" x 1" x 48"	Lumber

Note: Do not install the top covers until the drawers have been made and the drawer guides have been installed.

Figure 4-23: Bill of materials for the bench.

4-27). The tray doesn't have to be more than a simple, partitioned box that slides on strips of wood nailed to the sides of the drawer (Figure 4-28).

The bottom part of the bench is closed in with doors that are installed as shown in Figure 4-29. This type of door is hung with offset hinges and can be kept closed with a conventional magnetic catch. Flush doors are also possible. These can be hung with surface hinges or mortised butt hinges.

To install the bench top, first nail the particleboard securely to frame members. Then add the hardboard surface, either by nailing or with contact cement. The advantage of nailing is that the top can easily be replaced if it should become damaged. If you work with contact cement, be sure to read the instructions on the container. Some of the modern contact cements are water soluble and flameproof, and are therefore easier and more comfortable to work with than older products.

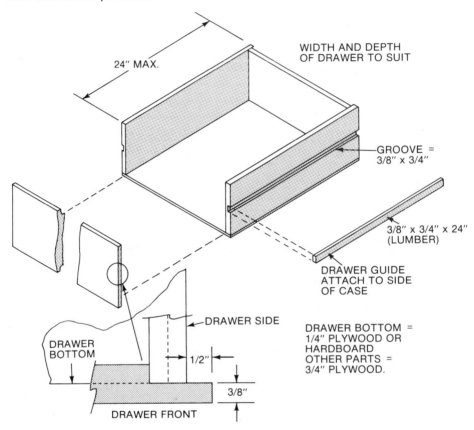

Figure 4-24: How the drawers are constructed. This is a simple design but will produce a strong project.

Figure 4-25: The drawers move on guides that are secured inside the case. Place them carefully so the drawers won't bind.

Figure 4-26: The dadoes in the drawer-sides and the guides must be
sized for a smooth sliding action.
Polishing the slides and the dadoes
with paste wax is helpful.

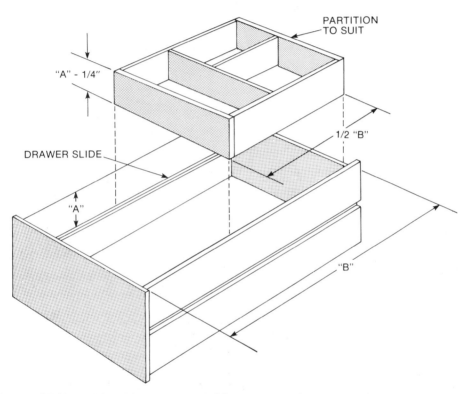

PARTITION
TO SUIT

"A" - 1/4"

1/2 "B"

DRAWER SLIDE

"A"

"B"

Figure 4-27: You will be able to use more of the space in a deep drawer if you add a sliding
tray. Partition the tray to suit particular items.

Figure 4-28: The tray moves on
guides that are nailed to the
drawer-sides. Be sure the top of
the tray is below the top edges
of the drawer. The arrow shows
the guide on which the tray
moves.

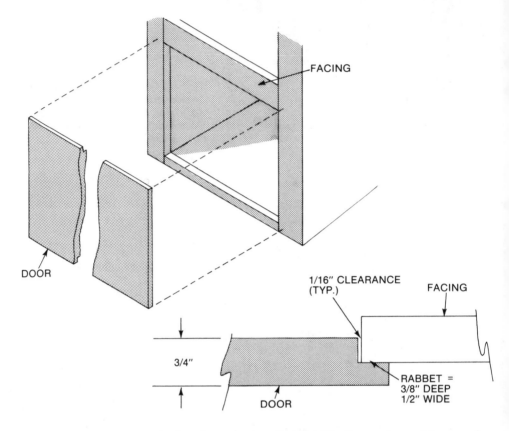

Figure 4-29: The doors in the bench can be installed like this. Be sure to provide enough clearance so the doors won't rub or bind.

WALL CABINET STORAGE. Figures 4-30 through 4-36 show some ways to make the most use of the wall cabinet space. Note that even the back of the doors were fitted with perforated hardboard so small accessories could be neatly stored in space that would otherwise be wasted. The hardboard is mounted on strips of 1/2"-thick plywood or lumber to provide space behind the hardboard for the hooks.

Figure 4-30: Adding perforated hardboard to the back of the doors provides neat storage for many small accessories.

Figure 4-31: The cabinet interiors should be fitted for storage of particular accessories. Be sure shelves are set back enough so they won't interfere with closing the doors.

Figure 4-32: Many accessories are easily stored on hooks that are specially made for use with perforated hardboard. Keep adequate space between accessories so they won't bang against each other.

Figure 4-33: Although this super shop is equipped with all radial arm saw accessories, there is still considerable room for additional equipment.

Figure 4-34: The cabinets also have space to store portable tools. The router on the lower shelf will be later shown in use on the radial arm saw.

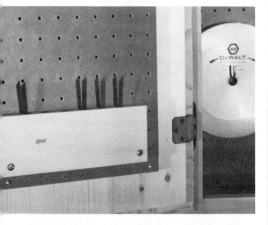

Figure 4-35: It is wise to make special holders for some accessories. This saber saw blade container is merely a block of wood with holes drilled in one edge.

Figure 4-36: Making special holders keeps tools safe and is a way to assure that all tools are where they should be.

The photographs also show various custom-made storage units specially designed for particular accessories. The construction details for the units are shown in Figure 4-37. Methods of using the radial arm saw for drilling holes, forming slots, and cutting curves are shown elsewhere in the book.

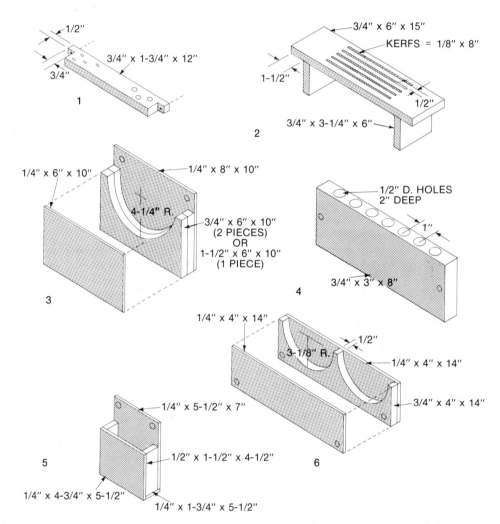

Figure 4-37: Some accessory holders you can make for the cabinets of the super shop: (1) for Allen wrenches, chucks, and so on; (2) rack for saw blades. The platform can be wider to accommodate more blades; (3) to hold an 8" sanding disc; (4) a container for saber saw blades; (5) to hold a drill case; and, (6) to hold two 6" grinding wheels.

CATCHING SAWDUST. Many operations done on a radial arm saw throw sawdust to the back of the machine, so a catcher, placed behind the column, is useful for clean-up chores. The accessory sawdust catcher shown in Figure 4-38 is easy to attach and is functional wherever the machine is placed. The unit consists of a translucent vinyl cover that is stretched over a heavy wire frame.

Figure 4-38: Sawdust catcher of translucent vinyl secured over a strong wire frame. It can be used regardless of the saw's location.

The sawdust catcher that was designed specially for the super shop is shown in Figure 4-39. Note the access hole for the tool's power cord through the back of the catcher. This places the cord behind the catcher so it can't interfere with work. Construction details of the catcher are shown in Figure 4-40. Follow the dimensions closely so the unit will fit without interfering with the table clamp screws.

Figure 4-39: A sawdust catcher designed specially for the radial arm saw shop. It is not attached to the wall or the tool so it does not interfere when a job calls for moving the saw from its shop location.

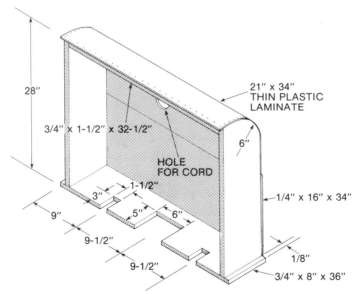

Figure 4-40: Construction details of the sawdust catcher. Install the plastic laminate by first nailing across the top front edge. Bend it to conform to the 6" radius as you continue to nail.

A SHOP VAC. Cleaning up around the saw and generally in the shop will be much easier if you add a shop-type vacuum cleaner (Figure 4-41).The accessory can be fitted with various nozzles for the floor, bench tops, cabinets and drawers, as well as nooks and crannies. A vacuum that is fitted with casters is especially useful.

Figure 4-41: A shop vacuum cleaner makes it easy to be a good housekeeper. A clean area is more pleasant and safer to work in.

Chapter 5
Accuracy Depends
on Alignment

The person who drives an automobile with front wheels out of alignment soon discovers the tires are wearing unevenly. The marksman who doesn't adjust his rifle's sights hits anything but the bull's eye. The craftsperson who works without making sure the components of the power tool have the correct relationship soon wonders why cuts are not square, edges are rough, joints don't mesh as they should, and so on.

Correct alignment is critical for accurate work and easier working. When the tool functions as it should, all operations go smoothly. Therefore it is very important to check the tool before you use it, even though it was probably aligned at the factory. The jars and knocks of shipping can throw things off. It is equally as important to make the same check periodically since use and abuse of everyday shopwork can cause changes; slight ones, perhaps, but enough to affect accuracy.

All good power tools are designed with adjustment features so corrections can be made to maintain a respectable degree of precision for the life of the machine. Only a few basic actions need to be checked on the radial arm saw. The following information tells what these are. For the actual procedure required to make a correction, consult the owner's manual that comes with the tool. Systems change so that the appropriate actions can vary from model to model.

TABLE FLATNESS. Since the table is wood or a wood product, it can be affected by changing humidity conditions. It's not likely that a change will be critical but it doesn't hurt to check by placing a straightedge in various positions across the table. If you do this with a strip of wood, be sure the wood is straight enough to be used as a gauge. A level will work, but remember that table flatness not levelness is being checked.

Obvious high spots can be reduced by rubbing them with a piece of fine sandpaper wrapped around a block of wood. However, don't be overly critical. Slight variations won't affect woodworking requirements.

Don't leave the saw plugged in when you are doing alignment chores.

THE TABLE SURFACE SHOULD BE PARALLEL WITH THE RADIAL ARM. To check, remove the saw guard and materials from the arbor. Raise the radial arm high enough so the motor can be tilted 90° down toward the table. Place a small block of wood under the arbor as shown in Figure 5-1 and lower the arbor until its end just touches the wood. You should be able to move the wood, using it like an oversized feeler gauge.

Figure 5-1: Using a block of wood as a feeler gauge to check whether the table is parallel to the radial arm. The check should be made at various places by swinging the arm and moving the motor.

Release the miter lock and then, by swinging the arm and by moving the motor to and fro, make the wood block test at various points on the table. If there is variation—that is, if the wood block won't move under the arbor or if there is clearance between the arbor and the block—the table requires adjustment. Usually, this is just a matter of loosening nuts that secure the table cleats to the tool frame.

The easiest solution is to find the table's highest point as close to a cleat nut as possible and to use the area as a guide for setting the table correctly.

THE SAW BLADE SHOULD BE SQUARE TO THE TABLE. When the saw blade is locked in vertical position the angle between it and the table must be 90°. Be sure the saw blade is correctly mounted and tightened and then use a try square or similar gauge, as shown in Figure 5-2. Set the gauge flat on the table and flush against the saw blade. If the saw blade has set teeth, be sure the square rests **between** teeth. This test will show if the blade has any amount of tilt. If so, adjustment is in order. When an adjustment is made, be sure to set the bevel scale so that it will read "0" when the blade is vertical.

Figure 5-2: When the blade is in vertical position it must form an angle of 90° to the table. The blade of the square should be at least almost as long as the diameter of the saw blade.

To be sure the adjustment is correct, loosen the bevel lock and tilt the blade up and down several degrees. Then return it and lock it in vertical position and make the square test a second time.

When the vertical position of a saw blade is correct, crosscut edges will check out as shown in Figure 5-3. The cut edge will be square to adjacent surfaces.

Figure 5-3: Crosscuts will check out like this when the saw blade's verticalness is correct. The cut edge will be square to adjacent surfaces.

CROSSCUT TRAVEL MUST BE 90° TO THE GUIDE FENCE. A common check method is shown in Figure 5-4. Place a large square, elevated on wood blocks, on the table so that one leg of the square is snug against the guide fence. Elevate the saw blade so its "bottom" teeth are slightly below the top surface of the square. Set the square so that it barely touches the blade and then very slowly move the saw blade through its full crosscut travel. If the saw blade moves the square or moves away from the square, adjustment is needed.

Figure 5-4: Using a large square to check crosscut travel. The tips of the blade's teeth should just touch the square throughout the crosscut path.

Here, too, a retest is important to be sure that a necessary adjustment was done correctly. Swing the radial arm to a miter setting and then return it to crosscut position. Repeat the checking procedure.

When crosscut travel is correct, the cut edge will be square to adjacent edges (Figure 5-5).

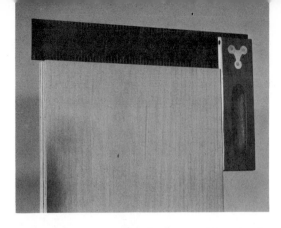

Figure 5-5: Work will check out like this when crosscut travel is accurate. The cut edge will be square to adjacent edges. This assumes the work had parallel sides to begin with.

Another way to check crosscutting is shown in Figure 5-6. A piece of wood or plywood, preferably about 12" wide, is marked for crosscutting with an accurate square. Actually making a cut will show if the saw blade is following the line. Marking crosscut lines should be common practice or, at least, should be done frequently, since it provides an ongoing checking procedure.

Figure 5-6: Another way to check cross-cut action is to mark the cut-line with a square. This should be done occasionally during routine working chores.

ELIMINATE "HEELING." "Heeling" occurs when the "back" teeth of the saw blade are not cutting on the same line as the "front" teeth. It can be compared to the rear wheels of an automobile moving parallel to the front wheels, but on a different line. If this misalignment were exaggerated and you made a scraping cut on the surface of a piece of stock, you would form a cove rather than a true kerf.

Checking is done as shown in Figure 5-7. Place a length of 2" material against the guide fence on the right side of the blade. Make a crosscut that just trims the end of the stock, but don't move the blade enough to clear the wood.

Figure 5-7: The arrow shows the area where scored radial marks will appear when a heeling adjustment is required. This test should be made on the left and the right side of the saw blade. When making the test, be sure that the wood is long enough so that your hand will not be near the blade or the motor.

Move the wood away from the blade and return the blade to its neutral position. Check the cut in the area indicated by the arrow in the photograph for pronounced radial marks—scored arcs that travel from the bottom to the top of the wood. Adjustment is required if the arcs are very obvious.

This test should be repeated with the wood positioned on the left side of the saw blade. If adjustment is needed, then you can judge in which direction the blade must be turned. Adjustments for heeling are made in the yoke area of the machine.

Heeling is often indicated by a drag on the blade as a cut is made, or by the quality of the cut. It can be felt because the blade isn't cutting as smoothly as it should.

THE 45° MITER SETTING. The best way to check this setting is to use a gauge to mark the 45° angle and to actually make a cut (Figure 5-8). If the blade doesn't follow the line, you know adjustment is required.

Always check the miter scale located on the arm above the column (Figure 5-9) after making a crosscut or miter adjustment. The miter scale should read "0" when the tool is set in crosscut position.

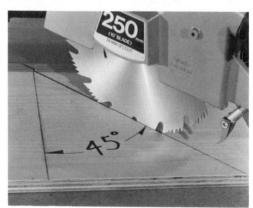

Figure 5-8: Test a miter setting, especially the auto-stops, by marking the work with an accurate gauge and then making a cut. You will know immediately if adjustment is needed.

Figure 5-9: Examine the miter scale after any crosscut or miter adjustment. The scale should read "0" when the tool is set for crosscutting.

Some of the common signs that might indicate a misalignment problem are listed in Figure 5-10.

WARNING SIGN	WHAT TO CHECK
Crosscuts not square.	Is the crosscut travel 90° to the guide fence?
Crosscuts have slight bevel.	Is the saw blade perpendicular to the table?
Blade drags in cut, kerfs wider than normal.	
Excessive splintering on plywood.	Heeling.
Rough cuts.	
Dado depths are not uniform.	Is table parallel to arm?
Cross bevels or rip bevels not accurate.	Bevel scale and auto-stops.
Miters not accurate.	Miter scale and auto-stops.
Work moves away from fence or binds between fence and blade when doing rip cuts.	Heeling or arm is not 90° to fence.

Figure 5-10: Some of the common signs that might indicate a misalignment situation.

Chapter 6
Saw Blades—
The Prime Cutters

Wood is called **hard** or **soft** but the terms can't be taken literally. They actually are botanical designations—hardwoods coming from broad-leafed deciduous trees, softwoods from cone-bearing or evergreen trees. Other tree characteristics, some general ones and some applicable only to a particular species, determine whether lumber will be **close-grain** or **open-grain**, whether the grain will be uniform, the texture smooth, and so on.

Add to these factors the properties of other nonwood and wood materials used in a workshop—for example, that plywood has opposing grain patterns and abrasive glue lines—and it is easy to see why a single saw blade design can't do everything.

That is why it is wise to know what blades are available and their applications even though you may not need a complete assortment of saw blades at the outset.

GOOD PRACTICE. Much engineering talent and knowledge of metallurgy, forestry, geometry, electronics, and physics go into making a saw blade, but it is all wasted if the blade isn't used correctly. A rip blade will cut cross-grain but the quality of the cut will not be acceptable. Using a hollow-ground blade or a special plywood blade to saw through timbers is like using a quality kitchen knife for pruning. A dull blade won't make good cuts and can be dangerous to use.

Probably the most common misuse of any saw blade is rushing the cut. The teeth are designed to remove just so much wood. Ideally, the feed speed should relate to the rpms of the blade, but since this can't be monitored in the average shop, the best rule is to feed conservatively. Forcing the cut will choke the teeth and cause rough cuts, gouges, and burns.

The test pieces shown in Figure 6-1 are the results of slow and fast feeds. Both cuts were made with the same blade but the one on the right, made with a slow, steady feed, is certainly the acceptable one.

When you mount a saw blade, be sure the blade, arbor, collars, and arbor nut are clean. Wood chips, lodged between blade and collars, can angle the blade so it won't turn on a true plane. The result will be something like the heeling marks that were described in Chapter 5.

CLEARANCE IN THE KERF. A saw blade will bind in a cut unless the kerf is wider than the gauge of the blade. Many saw blades are able to avoid this because they have "set" teeth—that is, alternate teeth are slightly bent away from the

Figure 6-1: How fast a saw blade is moved can make a great difference to the quality of a cut. The same blade made both cuts but feed-speed caused different results. The left sample resulted from cutting too fast.

body of the blade in opposite directions. Because the points of the teeth form the sides of the kerf, the kerf is wider than the thickness of the blade.

Another way clearance is obtained is by reducing the gauge of the blade from its teeth to a point closer to its center. This is called hollow-grinding and will be found on blades like the special plywood and the hollow-ground or planer blade. Since the blades work without set teeth, they produce smoother cuts.

COMBINATION BLADES. Most saws come equipped with a combination blade like the one shown in Figure 6-2. The design provides deep gullets needed for waste removal on ripping operations and sharp points that do a good job of severing wood fibers when crosscutting. The combination blade in Figure 6-3 works with banks of what are essentially crosscut teeth, plus a "raker" tooth that cleans out the kerf and deep gullets that help the blade cut more freely.

Combination blades are general purpose blades and may be used for ripping, crosscutting, mitering, and so on. Although they produce work of acceptable quality, when a particular type of sawing is required to a great extent, a blade specially designed for the purpose should be used.

Figure 6-2: Combination blade, often called a "chisel tooth," has deep gullets for ripping and sharp toothpoints needed for severing wood fibers when cutting across the grain.

Figure 6-3: Another type of combination blade has banks of crosscut teeth as well as a "raker" tooth immediately behind the deep gullet, which cleans out the waste wood in the kerf.

RIP BLADE. The rip blade (Figure 6-4) is designed for cutting **with** the grain of the wood. Each tooth works like a small chisel chipping out its own bit of wood. The teeth have considerable bulk behind the cutting edges and generous gullets to catch and spew out waste.

Because of its special design, the rip blade should not be used for general purpose cutting.

Figure 6-4: The rip blade has generous gullets and considerable bulk behind the cutting teeth. Each tooth works like a small chisel, removing its own chip of wood. A crosscut blade produces much finer sawdust than a rip blade.

CROSSCUT BLADE. The teeth of a crosscut blade are designed for a shearing action as opposed to the chiseling action of a rip blade. It has many small, spring-set teeth that sever wood fibers cleanly. Because the waste it produces is like a fine sawdust, the blade gets by with shallow gullets. Small teeth and shallow gullets mean the blade can easily choke if the cut is forced. Here, even more than with other blades, speed and pressure of feeding should be very slow and steady.

The crosscut blade can be used for miter work but never for ripping.

PLANER BLADE. The planer blade (Figure 6-5)—or hollow-ground blade—is reduced in thickness from the points of its teeth to the center area indicated by the arrow in the photograph. This gives it kerf-clearance without set teeth so it produces smoother cuts than other blade designs.

Figure 6-5: The hollow-ground or "planer" blade is reduced in thickness from its perimeter to the area indicated by the arrow. It cuts much smoother than a blade with set teeth.

In a sense it is a combination blade but not one to be left on the machine for general sizing cuts or work on timbers. It may pinch easily on some woods, leave burn marks on hard wood, and should be fed slowly. It can be used on plywood but may not be tempered to maintain sharpness for too long under the abrasive action of the glue lines. It is a fine blade to use, for example, when especially smooth crosscuts or miter cuts are needed.

PLYWOOD BLADE. The special plywood blade shown in Figure 6-6 is designed to cut smoothly through multidirectional grain and to withstand the abrasive action of plywood's glue lines. Many such blades are made specifically for cutting plywood that is 3/4″ or less in thickness. Thus hollow or taper grinding has a limited area, as indicated by the arrow in the illustration. The blade must never be used on cuts deep enough to put the full gauge of the blade in the kerf.

Figure 6-6: The special plywood blade is hollow-ground (sometimes taper-ground) in a limited area since it is designed for cutting plywood 3/4″ or less in thickness.

The test cuts in Figure 6-7 show what a plywood blade can do. The cut on the left, made with a conventional blade, is acceptable but the plywood-blade cut on the right is smooth enough to use as is. It looks and feels burnished.

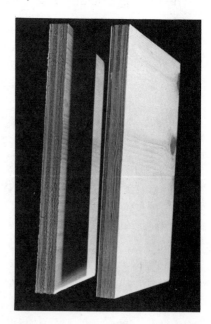

Figure 6-7: The plywood sample on the left was cut with a conventional blade. It is acceptable but doesn't have the cut-quality of the right-hand piece, which was cut with a special plywood blade.

THIN-RIM BLADE. The name of this blade is very appropriate (Figure 6-8). Its perimeter is ground down thinner than the blade's body so it cuts a fine kerf that wastes little wood. It is used extensively in industry where the savings in material can be significant considering the thousands of cuts that are made. This may not be so important in a small shop but the blade has other qualities. It's a fine blade to use when sawing veneers and when preparing delicate grooves for inlay work. Note that the gauge reduction is in a limited area. Like the plywood blade, the thin-rim blade should never be used on cuts deep enough to put the full gauge of the blade in the kerf.

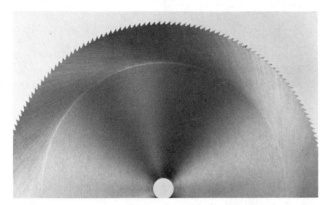

Figure 6-8: The thin-rim blade has many small teeth and cuts an extremely fine kerf. It cuts smoothly, saves material when expensive wood is being used, and is fine for cutting veneers.

BLADES WITH TEETH OF TUNGSTEN CARBIDE. Saw blades of this type, examples of which are shown in Figures 6-9 through 6-11, are often called the kings of saw blades. They are more expensive than conventional blades but because they have been shown to stay sharp ten times longer, on the average, than steel blades, they may prove to be more economical. One reason for long-lived keenness is that tungsten carbide, a man-made material, is extremely hard, even harder than the steel used in files.

Figure 6-9: Carbide-tipped blades with eight or 12 teeth are not expensive and can be used for many kinds of cutting. It can be used like a combination blade.

Figure 6-10: A carbide-tipped blade with 40 teeth is often chosen by crafts-people who do much work with hard-woods.

Figure 6-11: This carbide-tipped blade has 60 teeth—it is an excellent performer on all types of cutting. Treat carbide-tipped blades with special care. The tungsten-carbide is hard but also brittle.

Tooth sharpness stands up even under the abrasive actions that quickly dull other types of blades. They take in stride cuts through materials like hardboard, particleboard, high-pressure laminates, laminated panels, all types of plywood, even nonferrous metals.

Carbide-tipped blades do not have set teeth so they make smooth cuts, and since most are multipurpose or combination types, they can be used for crosscutting, ripping, mitering, chamfering, beveling, or whatever.

The number of teeth on a blade has a bearing on its function. Generally, the more teeth, the smoother the cut; but, the more teeth, the more expensive the blade.

In general, a blade with 8 or 12 teeth is acceptable for rough carpentry. A blade with 40 teeth is fine for general-purpose cabinetry and cutting hardwoods. A blade with 60 teeth is the smoothest cutter of all and does a particularly good job when cutting plywoods.

Blades of this type should be carefully handled. Tungsten carbide is hard but also brittle. Store the blades so they can't knock against other objects.

BLADES FOR NONWOOD MATERIALS. Some metals, like do-it-yourself aluminum, can be cut with regular wood-cutting blades (Figure 6-12), such as the combination blade, crosscut blade, hollow-ground blade, and even the special plywood blade. Remember, however, that any metal is harder than wood, so feed-speed should be very slow. Allow the teeth ample time to cut and use lubricant to prevent aluminum build up.

Some workers on jobs like this prefer to reverse the crosscutting action. That is, they pull the blade to the front of the machine before turning it on and then push the blade through the work instead of pulling it. Although this technique works and may be a personal preference for some operators, remember that is the exception and not the rule of crosscutting. Should you use this method of cutting, be certain the material is held securely or is clamped down against the table and back against the fence. When you reverse the action, the blade or cutting tool has a tendency to lift the material and could result in a kickback.

Figure 6-12: Conventional woodcutting saw blades can be used to cut material like do-it-yourself aluminum. This material is soft, but still harder than wood, so feed-speed should be very conservative.

A blade designed primarily for cutting nonferrous metals is shown in Figure 6-13. The metal is a special high-speed steel alloy so teeth will stay sharp under rigorous cutting conditions. In fact, the steel is so hard that it can't be touched with a file. Sharpening must be done by grinding.

Figure 6-13: Special blades are available for cutting nonferrous metals. Blades like this are usually hollow-ground and made of a high-speed steel alloy that can't be filed. Grinding procedures are required for sharpening.

The blade is hollow-ground and has 150 very small teeth. It is often used on plywoods and veneers because of the exceptionally smooth cut it makes. As is the case with all blades that have very small teeth and shallow gullets, feed-speed should be very conservative.

The blade shown in Figure 6-14 is designed for cutting plastics and will do a good job on phenolics, acrylics, and general types of plastics. The blade is made of a special alloy that is harder than the metal used in conventional blades so it will withstand the abrasion that results when cutting plastics.

A blade like this can be used to cut some nonferrous metals but not aluminum since a soft alloy can plug the gullets of the blade.

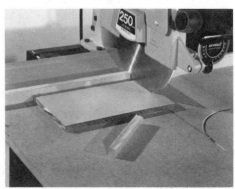

Figure 6-14: Plastic cutting blade is hollow-ground and made from an alloy plate that can withstand the abrasive action of plastic cutting better than the steel used for conventional blades.

73

Plastics are not easy to cut. The waste material of some types, heated by blade friction, can fuse in the kerf behind the blade as well as give off toxic fumes. Make shallow cuts when working on thick plastic, increasing the depth of cut for each pass until the material is severed.

A "toothless" blade, like the one shown in Figure 6-15, can be used to cut resistant, abrasive materials like synthetic marble, asbestos-cement, fiberglass, tempered hardboard, and so on. The blade is a steel disc with hundreds of particles of tungsten carbide permanently bonded to its perimeter. These particles, like the teeth on tungsten carbide-tipped saw blades, are extremely hard and stay sharp for long periods of time.

Figure 6-15: No-tooth blade is fine for cutting materials like synthetic marble. Hundreds of tungsten carbide particles that are permanently bonded to its perimeter perform the cutting.

The blade will give smooth cuts in plywood, although cut-speed is very slow, but it should never be used on softwoods and similar materials since they may gum up and clog the cutting particles. Should clogging occur, for whatever reason, use a stiff wire brush or a file card for cleaning.

The blade will cut in any direction. To extend cutting life, occasionally change the blade's direction of rotation.

CLEANING SAW BLADES. Saw blades are most efficient when they are clean and free of gummy deposits. After some jobs, cleaning can be done merely by soaking the blade in warm water and a detergent. This often does a good job on hardwood gum and deposits left by redwood. Rub the blade with a cloth while it is in the soapy water. Wipe it dry with a soft cloth before putting it away.

Obstinate deposits should not be removed by scraping with a screwdriver, knife, or chisel. Some workers use commercial pitch removers or rub on solvents with a discarded toothbrush or an old typewriter brush. Let the solvent soak in for a while before scrubbing, then wash the blade and dry it.

For tough, overall cleaning jobs, try one of the following methods. Mix about three tablespoons of a common household drain cleaner and about two quarts of water in a glass container that is large enough to hold a blade flat. With a wire that is looped through the blade's arbor hole, lower the blade into the solution and let it soak for about five minutes. Then hose it off and thoroughly dry it.

A second method calls for spraying the blade with a household oven cleaner, allowing the cleaner to soak in for five minutes or so and then hosing the blade before thoroughly drying it. Part of the blade shown in Figure 6-16 was cleaned using the oven cleaner method.

Figure 6-16: Half of this blade shows the results of a cleaning job done with a spray-type household oven cleaner. Obey the cautions on the container when using any such product.

When using any of the above products or any solvent, be sure that you follow the instructions, and obey the cautions that will be on the container. Some oven cleaners should not be used on chrome surfaces.

When you put a blade away, coat it with a very light film of oil or paste wax that is rubbed to a polish.

BLADE STORAGE. The easiest way to store blades is on hooks spaced so the blades can't touch, or on a homemade rack such as that shown in one of the cabinets in the super shop.

A more elaborate case, one that provides maximum protection for blades and that can even be used for carrying blades about, is shown in Figure 6-17. It will store six blades with adequate space between them and can be fitted with a carrying handle and a lock.

Figure 6-17: A deluxe case for saw blades that makes it easy to store blades safely. The case can be fitted with a carrying handle and a lock.

Construction details are shown in Figure 6-18. The kerfs needed in the bottom and end pieces must be in line. To ensure accuracy, form the kerfs in a long piece of wood and then crosscut the wood into the lengths needed.

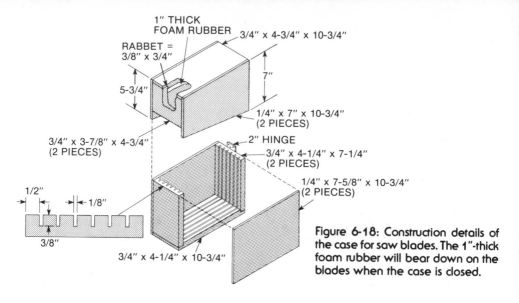

1" THICK
FOAM RUBBER

3/4" x 4-3/4" x 10-3/4"

RABBET =
3/8" x 3/4"

7"

5-3/4"

1/4" x 7" x 10-3/4"
(2 PIECES)

3/4" x 3-7/8" x 4-3/4"
(2 PIECES)

2" HINGE

3/4" x 4-1/4" x 7-1/4"
(2 PIECES)

1/4" x 7-5/8" x 10-3/4"
(2 PIECES)

1/2"

1/8"

3/8"

3/4" x 4-1/4" x 10-3/4"

Figure 6-18: Construction details of
the case for saw blades. The 1"-thick
foam rubber will bear down on the
blades when the case is closed.

SHARPEN BLADES YOURSELF? It is not recommended. It takes experience and special equipment to do a professional job of sharpening. An inadequate effort will certainly do more harm than good. Working by hand with files and improvised setups requires time—know-how and skill can come only with experience.

The cost involved in having blades sharpened by an experienced, competent craftsperson who is equipped to work on any style of blade is small and, in the long run, economical.

However, some craftspeople do some touch-up filing on saw teeth to extend the original keenness of the blade. The blade is held in a special clamp or merely between discs of wood so it will be snug and chatter-free as the filing is done (Figure 6-19).

The files required are an 8" "cant" file, an 8" "mill" file with two round edges, and a 6" or 8" "slim-taper" file. The tapers are for blades with small teeth, the cant file for blades with larger teeth.

The objective is to place the file on the top of a tooth so it duplicates the original angle of the tooth. Then take two or three firm strokes to reshape to the original point. It's very important to take the same number of strokes on each tooth because the height of each tooth should be the same. Filing removes metal and shortens the tooth.

Remember that even this interim chore must be done correctly. Don't try it on blades with special tooth designs like the plywood or thin-rim blade. Certainly don't attempt to touch up blades with carbide-tipped teeth. These can be sharpened only with special equipment.

Figure 6-19: Blades must be tightly gripped to keep them from chattering when filing is done. Let the original angle of the tooth guide the file. Take the same number of strokes on each tooth.

Chapter 7
The Basic Cuts

Basic cutting refers to the initial operations that bring stock to a particular dimension—that is, the sizing cuts that are the starting point for any project. These will always be **crosscuts,** made across the grain of the wood, and rip cuts, made **with** the grain of the wood (Figure 7-1). The majority of other cuts are variations or combinations of these simple techniques. For example, a miter cut made across the grain is a crosscut but is made with the blade tilted. A miter done on the long edge of stock is a rip cut but is made with the blade tilted.

The difference in the action of the radial arm saw in making the two types of cuts is that for crosscutting, the work is held down firmly on the table and against the guide fence while the blade is pulled through the work, whereas for ripping, the blade is locked in a position parallel to the fence and the work is moved to make the cut.

CROSSCUTTING

Operator's Position. Crosscutting can be considered a "right-hand" operation. That is, the operator's right hand should grip the control handle while the left hand secures the work (Figure 7-2). This is a convenient way to work and is easily adopted even by left-handed people. Keep the work-holding hand well away from the path of the saw blade. Use four fingers on the surface of the work, the thumb against the edge of the work.

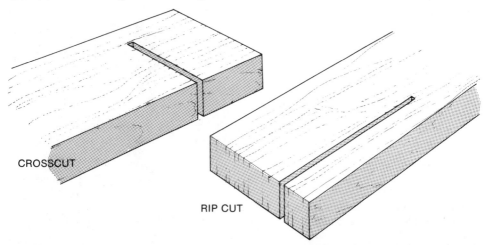

CROSSCUT

RIP CUT

Figure 7-1: All projects start with sizing cuts—crosscutting stock to length, and ripping it to width.

Don't grip so tightly with either hand that you feel awkward and strained. The left hand is used in general to steady the work rather than to lock its position. The action of the saw blade tends to keep the work flat on the table and against the fence. Your hand merely aids this action.

Remember that while the cut is complete as soon as the wood is severed, the "pass," the crosscut operation is not finished until you have moved the blade back to its neutral position behind the fence (Figure 7-3). At this point, the switch is turned off and the blade is allowed to come to a full stop before the work is removed.

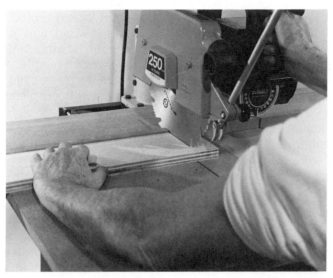

Figure 7-2: Normal operating position when crosscutting. The left hand is on the work well away from the saw blade, the right hand is on the control handle. As in other illustrations in the book, guarding has been removed for photographic purposes.

Figure 7-3: The crosscut procedure is not complete until the blade has been moved to neutral position behind the fence and has stopped turning. Then it is safe to remove the work.

The Fence Kerf. The cut that is made through the guide fence (Figure 7-4) not only allows the blade to pass through, but also serves as a gauge point when work is placed for crosscutting. Remember that different blades may cut different-width kerfs. One fence may not be suitable for all blades; especially not if the fence kerf will be used as a guide for crosscutting.

Figure 7-4: A kerf is needed in the fence so that the saw blade can pass through but it also serves as a guide for placing work.

Marking stock is not critical if you are only squaring the end of a board. In such a case, the wood is placed so that the blade can do a trim cut. But if you are cutting to a particular length, then it is wise to mark the cut line with a square so you will have a point to line up with the fence kerf and can make a visual check of cutting accuracy (Figure 7-5). For maximum accuracy, the blade should just remove the pencil line.

Figure 7-5: Marking the cut-line with a square, even if done occasionally, is a good way to keep track of tool alignment as you work.

Extra-Wide Cuts. Crosscuts that are longer than the basic capacity of the machine are accomplished as follows.

Place the work and pull the blade forward to its maximum crosscut position (Figure 7-6). Push the blade back to neutral position and turn off the motor. Use a square to mark an extension of the kerf that was formed and then turn the stock to the position shown in Figure 7-7. Now make a second cut to meet the first one.

Another possibility is to work with a stop block (to be shown later) on the guide fence. The work, positioned by the stop block, is placed against the fence and the first cut is made. The work is turned over and is again positioned against fence and stop block. Then the saw is pulled through until it meets the first kerf. This system makes it unnecessary to mark the work for the second cut so long as you remember that the same edge of the work must be against the stop block for each cut.

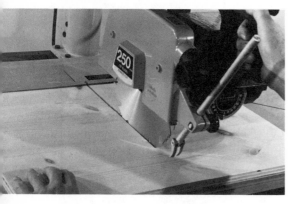

Figure 7-6: The first step in making an extra-wide crosscut. Place the work and pull the blade out as far as it will go. Then return the blade to neutral position and turn off the machine.

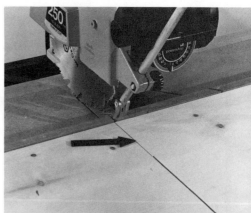

Figure 7-7: The second step. Use a square to mark an extension of the kerf. Then place the work and make a second cut just far enough to meet the first one.

Extra-Thick Cuts. Heavy stock (whose thickness is more than the depth-of-cut capacity of the saw blade can handle) can be crosscut by making two passes. Raise the blade to a position that will allow it to cut through slightly more than half the stock's thickness. You will be cutting through the top surface of the wood. For example, if the stock is 4" thick, the distance from the table to the blade should be about 1-3/4".

Make the first cut and then, as shown in Figure 7-8, flip the work and make a second cut to meet the first one. For accuracy you can line up the kerf in the work with the kerf in the table, or mark the line for the second cut with a square.

Cutting to Length. It is often necessary to cut many pieces to the same length. To do this accurately, use a stop block on the guide fence as shown in Figure 7-9. The distance from the stop block to the blade determines the length of the pieces. Be sure not to spoil accuracy by allowing sawdust to accumulate against the fence or the stop block.

The unit shown can be locked at any point on the fence and has fine-adjustment screws on each side so it can be used on either side of the blade.

Figure 7-8: This is the second step of the technique used to crosscut extra-thick stock. The arrow indicates the first cut. Note the guide lines that were marked with a square.

Figure 7-9: A stop block, locked to the guide fence, makes it easy to cut any number of pieces to the same length. The screws may be used to make a final adjustment after the stop is secured.

Stop blocks can take many forms. Some workers simply use a small piece of wood as a stop, securing it to the fence with a clamp. It is more advisable to make a unit to keep on hand like any accessory. A workable design is shown in Figure 7-10. It does not have fine-adjustment screws but can be used on either side of the blade. The stop can be used so the eye bolt, which serves as a lock, will be behind the fence. The stop block is made as shown in Figure 7-11.

Figure 7-10: A stop block you can make. It can be situated so the eye bolt is behind the fence and it can be used on either side of the saw blade.

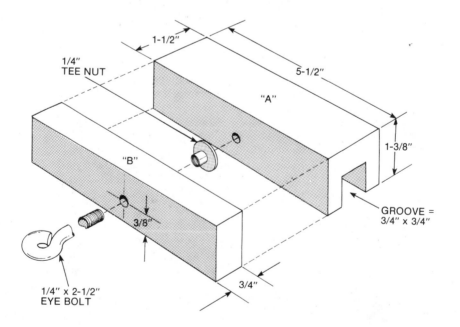

Figure 7-11: When you make the stop block, be sure to install the tee nut before attaching part B to part A.

Gang Cutting. This is another way to cut many pieces to the same length. Instead of cutting pieces individually, several pieces of stock are **ganged,** positioned by a stop block, and cut in one pass as shown in Figure 7-12. This method speeds up work and assures accuracy.

Note that a stop block of different design is used (Figure 7-13). Its extra length makes it easier to align multiple pieces. Construction details are shown in Figure 7-14.

Figure 7-12: Gang cutting is another way to cut many pieces to the same length.

Figure 7-13: This stop block design is especially useful for gang cutting because of its long support leg.

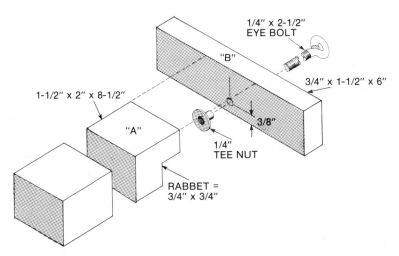

Figure 7-14: Construction details of the long stop block. Install the tee nut before attaching part A to part B.

RIPPING

Operator's Position. The saw is organized for ripping by locking the blade in a position that is parallel to the guide fence. The operator's position will depend on whether the setup is that commonly used for the in-rip position, or the out-rip position needed for extra-wide cuts. The worker will be at the right of the machine when in-ripping, at the left of the machine when out-ripping. In all cases, the hands must never come close to the saw blade.

In-Ripping. Loosen the yoke lock and rotate the blade 90° toward the tool's column so it will click into the position shown in Figure 7-15. Tighten the yoke lock and then situate the blade so the distance from it to the guide fence will equal the width-of-cut needed. The reading can be taken directly from the rip scale but if you choose to check, and the blade has set teeth, be sure to measure from a tooth that is set toward the fence.

Adjust the antikickback assembly (at the opposite end of the guard) so that the ends of the fingers will be approximately 1/8" **below** the surface of the work. Also, be sure to check the dust spout. It should be turned to point toward the back of the machine.

Basically, the left hand, kept a good distance away from the saw blade, is used to hold the work against the fence while the right hand moves the work forward. Work-feed direction, when in-ripping, is from right to left—**against** the direction of rotation of the saw blade. Keep feed-speed slow and steady so the work will move easily and sawed edges will be as smooth as they should be.

Figure 7-15: The setup needed for in-ripping. The arrows indicate the width of the cut. The guard can be tilted even further.

Push Sticks. A rip cut is not complete until the work has cleared the saw blade. Many operators will hand-feed the work along those final inches, but this technique really is not good practice, especially on narrow cuts, since it can bring hands too close to the saw blade. It is more professional and certainly safer to complete the pass with a special device called a "pusher."

The one shown in Figure 7-16 and detailed in Figure 7-17 can be used on rip cuts of various widths. It is designed so that when the vertical part—in front of the operator's hand—contacts the guard, the work will have passed the saw blade. Then the pusher is pulled back and the machine shut down before the work is removed. The pusher is made with spaced legs so the saw blade won't cut into it.

Figure 7-16: A pusher that can be used for many in-ripping operations. When the vertical part hits the guard, the work will be past the saw blade. Then the pusher is pulled straight back.

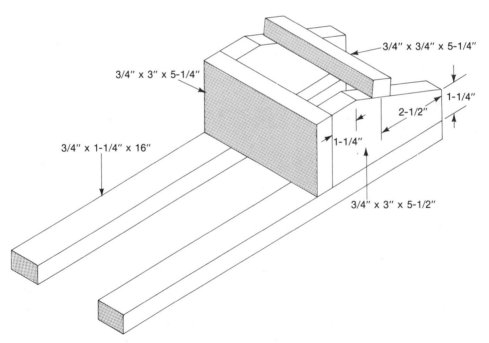

Figure 7-17: Construction details of the general-use pusher.

Another pusher design is shown in Figure 7-18 (construction details in Figure 7-19). This one straddles the guide fence and should be used to complete passes on narrow rip cuts. The groove in the body of the pusher should be sized so the tool will move easily on the fence.

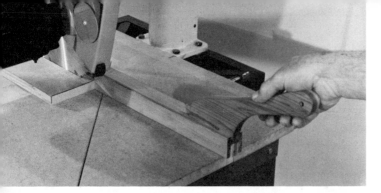

Figure 7-18: This type of pusher straddles the guide fence and should be used to move narrow work past the saw blade.

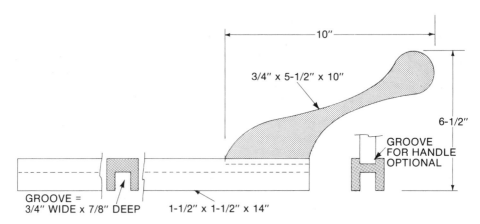

10"

3/4" x 5-1/2" x 10"

6-1/2"

GROOVE
FOR HANDLE
OPTIONAL

GROOVE =
3/4" WIDE x 7/8" DEEP

1-1/2" x 1-1/2" x 14"

Figure 7-19: This is how the fence-straddling pusher is made. The profile of the handle is not critical but follow the overall length and height dimensions.

A third design, one which may not be needed by all workers, is shown in Figure 7-20. This one also rides the guide fence but is made so that thin pieces of work can be fed past the saw blade (Figure 7-21). Like the first pusher that was shown, this one is sized so that when the vertical part contacts the guard, the work will be free of the saw blade. Figure 7-22 shows how the pusher is made.

A Special Splitter. One of the problems that can arise during ripping, especially if the work is long, is that the kerf might tend to close. This can bind the blade and allow the work to move back toward the operator. A splitter keeps the kerf open so the blade can cut freely. This means easier feeding, less possibility of kickback, and smoother cuts. An adjustable splitter you can make is shown in Figure 7-23.

The splitter, made of hardboard or a similar material, can be locked anywhere on the threaded rod so that it can be positioned for various cut-widths. The tool is secured between the guide fence and the movable table board. Use a strip of 1/4" plywood as a spacer between fence and board across the remainder of the table. In this way, the table clamp screws will provide adequate pressure against the fence throughout its length.

The splitter is made as shown in Figure 7-24.

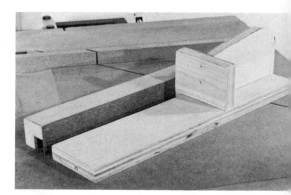

Figure 7-20: A third pusher is designed specifically for ripping very thin pieces.

Figure 7-21: The third pusher also straddles the guide fence and is designed so work will be past the saw blade when the vertical part contacts the guard.

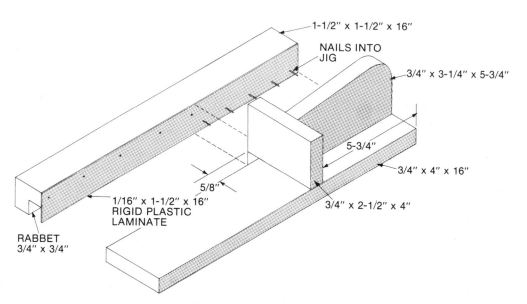

1-1/2" x 1-1/2" x 16"

NAILS INTO JIG

3/4" x 3-1/4" x 5-3/4"

5-3/4"

3/4" x 4" x 16"

5/8"

1/16" x 1-1/2" x 16"
RIGID PLASTIC
LAMINATE

3/4" x 2-1/2" x 4"

RABBET
3/4" x 3/4"

Figure 7-22: Construction details of the pusher for very thin ripping. When assembling, nail the laminate to the jig before attaching it to the rabbeted piece.

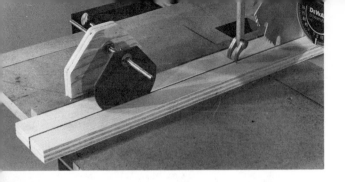

Figure 7-23: The homemade splitter is adjustable for various cut widths. It is locked between the guide fence and the movable table board.

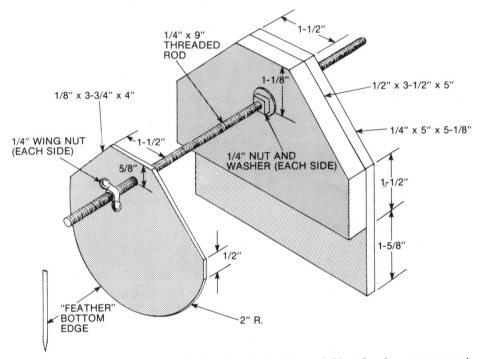

Figure 7-24: How the splitter is made. The threaded rod is available in hardware stores and similar supply centers.

Out-Ripping. The out-ripping technique is used for extra-wide cuts. The saw blade, from its normal crosscut position, is rotated 90° **away** from the tool's column so that it can be locked in the position shown in Figure 7-25. Settings are made as they are for in-ripping—either by measuring from the blade to the fence, or by reading the scale on the radial arm. Make sure, however, that you read the **out-rip** scale.

The guide fence can be used in its normal position, but when extremely wide cuts are required, it may be locked at the back of the machine so the movable boards are between it and the main table.

The guard and the antikickback assembly must be organized as they would be for any rip cut. Work-feed direction is from left to right.

Ripping Extra-Thick Stock. When the stock thickness is more than the depth-of-cut capacity of the saw blade, ripping can be accomplished by working somewhat along the lines described for crosscutting extra-thick material. Raise the blade above the table so the first cut will be deeper than half the

Figure 7-25: The saw set up for out-ripping. The arrow indicates feed direction of the work which is from left to right.

stock's thickness. There must, of course, be clearance between the top of the work and the motor.

Make the first pass as you would for any rip cut but remember that the saw blade is buried and feed-speed will have to be gentle. Make the second pass after flipping the stock and placing **the same surface** against the fence (Figure 7-26). This makes it unnecessary to mark the work for the second pass since the fence controls cut-width.

Figure 7-26: This is the second of two passes needed to rip through extra-thick stock. Be sure the same side of the work is against the guide fence for each pass.

Ripping Stock with Irregular Edges. When it is necessary to rip a piece of stock that does not have an edge straight enough to bear against the guide fence, the cut can be accomplished by tack-nailing or clamping the work to a guide strip that rides the outboard edge of the table (Figure 7-27). The saw is set up in the out-rip position so work-feed direction is from left to right. How much material is removed will be determined by placement of the guide strip and the locked position of the saw blade. Make the cut in normal fashion but be sure the guide strip is snug against the table's edge throughout the pass.

This same technique is used for certain kinds of taper cuts. The procedure will be demonstrated in another chapter.

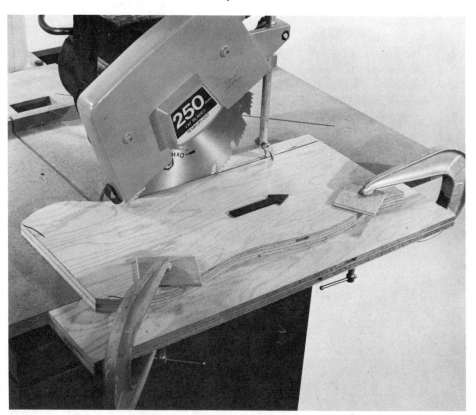

Figure 7-27: This is the technique used to rip stock with irregular edges. The work is tack-nailed or, as shown here, clamped to a guide strip that rides the edge of the table.

Chapter 8
Getting More
from Basic Cuts

All the cuts shown in Figure 8-1 can be made with a regular saw blade. In some cases a saw blade is the only tool to use because of the kerfing required. In other cases, like the dadoes and rabbets, the saw blade technique is shown so that it may be used whenever one or two are needed and you choose not to switch to a special accessory (which will be shown later) that can do the job faster.

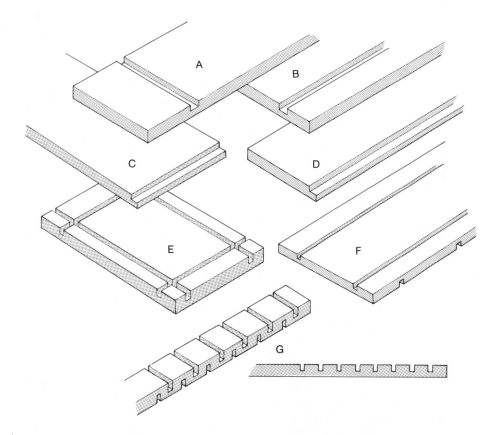

Figure 8-1: This chapter tells how the illustrated cuts are made with a regular saw blade: (A) dado; (B) groove; (C) end rabbet; (D) edge rabbet; (E) decorative kerfing; (F) piercing; and (G) kerfed moldings.

REPEAT-PASS DADOES AND GROOVES. If you make a crosscut with the blade elevated above the table so the stock is not severed, you form a kerf-wide slot. If you repeat the cuts so each removes an additional amount of material (Figure 8-2) you can form a dado as wide as necessary to accommodate the insert piece. This applies to grooves as well (Figure 8-3).

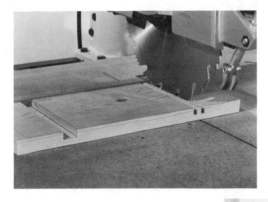

Figure 8-2: When doing a repeat-pass dado, make the shoulder cuts first and then clean out the waste stock between them. Cuts should overlap slightly.

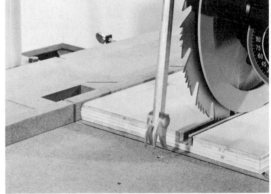

Figure 8-3: Making a repeat-pass groove is like making a series of rip cuts, but with the saw blade raised above the table. Follow all the rules that apply to regular ripping operations.

The depth of the dado or groove depends on how high you raise the blade above the table. For example, for a dado 1/2" deep in 3/4" stock, the blade should be 1/4" above the table. You can set blade height by using the elevation control handle to raise or lower the radial arm (one full turn equals 1/8" of adjustment), or you can make a height gauge like the one in Figure 8-4.

Figure 8-4: The height gauge is used to set, or to check, the saw blade's height above the table. The teeth of the saw blade should just touch the correct step on the gauge.

To use this gauge, raise the blade an arbitrary amount, then place the gauge under the blade. Lower the blade until it just touches the correct step on the gauge. The gauge is made as shown in Figure 8-5 from strips of 1/8" thick hardboard and 1/4" thick plywood. It can be used to set the height of other cutting tools—for example, a dado assembly.

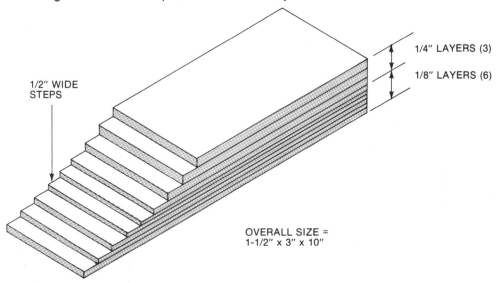

1/4" LAYERS (3)

1/8" LAYERS (6)

1/2" WIDE STEPS

OVERALL SIZE = 1-1/2" x 3" x 10"

Figure 8-5: Construction details of the height gauge. Parts can be put together with glue, contact cement, or nails.

REPEAT-PASS RABBETS. End and edge rabbets (Figures 8-6 and 8-7) can be formed using the same technique described for dado cuts. The only difference is that the rabbet has one shoulder—it is L-shaped instead of U-shaped.

When doing repeat-pass rabbets, dadoes, or grooves, you can work more accurately if you make the shoulder cuts first, then clean away the waste stock.

Don't rush the cuts simply because you have many to make. A slow, steady feed is still the best way to do quality work.

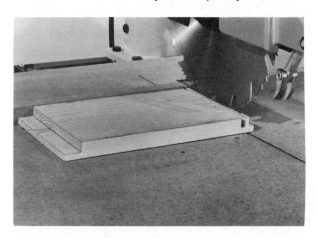

Figure 8-6: Repeat passes can be used to form rabbets as well as dadoes. Do the shoulder cut first.

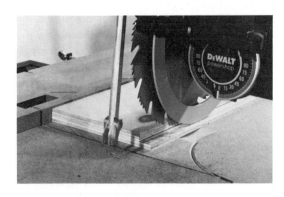

Figure 8-7: The repeat-pass technique was used to form this edge rabbet. Don't rush just because you have a few passes to make. Working quickly is never good practice.

DECORATIVE KERFS. Shallow kerfs, no more than 1/16" or 1/8" deep and cut to form a particular pattern, are often used to add a decorative detail to furniture components. This is, for example, a popular treatment for drawer fronts (Figure 8-8).

Almost any blade can be used as long as it is sharp and will produce clean kerfs. Many operators do this kind of work with a hollow-ground or carbide-tipped blade.

Figure 8-8: Shallow kerfs that form a pattern can add a decorative detail to many furniture components. The part shown here is a drawer front.

PIERCING. Piercing is a highly effective technique for making decorative panels for cabinet doors, or screens, and similar projects. The objective is to kerf one surface of the stock to a particular pattern with depth-of-cut being slightly more than half the stock's thickness (Figure 8-9).

Then the stock is turned over and the opposite surface is kerfed but to a different pattern. The cuts on opposite surfaces must not be in line. Because the depth of the cuts is more than half the stock's thickness, the wood is completely removed wherever the kerfs cross each other and openings are formed through the work like those shown in Figure 8-10.

By experimenting with the technique, you can create very interesting designs. The sample in Figure 8-11 was made by combining straight cuts on one surface of the stock with angular cuts on the opposite surface. Remember that the kerfs are part of the design, so plan patterns carefully.

Figure 8-9: Piercing begins by cutting kerfs in one surface of the stock. Kerf-depth should be slightly more than half the stock's thickness.

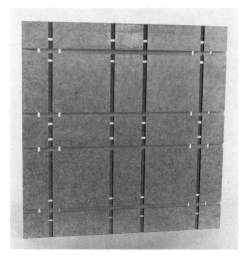

Figure 8-10: After the stock is kerfed on the opposite side, there will be openings through the work where the kerfs cross.

Figure 8-11: Many variations are possible. This design is the result of straight kerfs on one side, angled kerfs on the other side.

KERFED MOLDINGS. Only a brief comment is made here about kerfed moldings for we will have more to say about them later. One approach is to kerf a strip of wood as shown in Figure 8-12 and then to strip-cut the wood into slim pieces that can be glued to a backing to form a type of dentil molding. Spacing and width of the kerfs is optional. Use a hollow-ground blade for this kind of work.

Figure 8-12: Many types of moldings can be created by kerfing material, then cutting it into strips, and gluing these to a backing. More illustrations of kerfed moldings will be shown in another chapter.

Chapter 9
Horizontal Sawing

Horizontal sawing is a unique feature of the radial arm saw that has many practical applications, as you can see by the typical shapes shown in Figure 9-1. The technique is possible because the tool's motor may be tilted to a vertical position which puts the cutting tool parallel to the table. We say "cutting tool" since the idea can be used with accessories other than saw blades.

In this chapter we'll briefly discuss procedures and describe the custom-designed tables that are needed to fully utilize the technique. Other chapters will provide additional information.

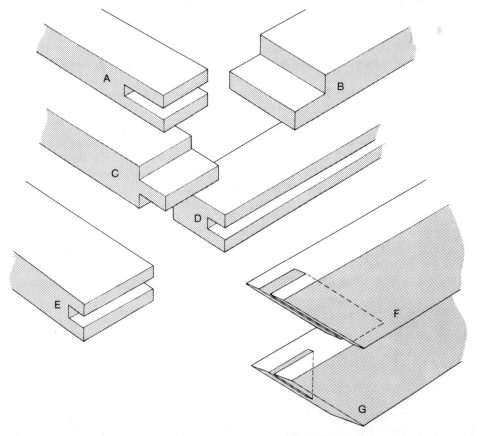

Figure 9-1: Typical cuts that can be made in horizontal sawing positions: (A) open mortise; (B) end rabbet; (C) tenon; (D) edge groove; (E) end groove; (F) miter groove; and (G) feather slot (a miter joint reinforcement).

TOOL SETUP. There are two ways to set up the saw, depending on whether it will be used in a fixed position so the work is moved to make the cut, or whether the saw is moved along the radial arm (as in crosscutting) and the work stays put.

The Fixed Position—Raise the radial arm until the blade is well above the table; then swing the blade toward the column to the in-rip position. Tilt the blade downward 90° so that it will be parallel to the table, and then move it as far back toward the column as it will go. Secure the position with the rip lock.

The Movable Position—Raise the radial arm until the blade is well above the table; then, with the blade in crosscut position, tilt it downward 90° so that it will be parallel to the table. Since this is the position where the blade will be moved along the radial arm, the rip lock is not used.

Be sure, as always, that the guard is correctly placed and that all lock levers and knobs are tightened.

HORIZONTAL SAWING TABLE NO. 1. In the fixed position, the bulk of the saw guard will not permit the blade to be lowered enough to be useful for all applications. Also, some to-and-fro adjustment of the saw must be possible to allow depth-of-cut settings. Therefore, a table like the one shown in Figure 9-2 is needed. This provides a higher work surface and adjustment room behind the fence so only the business end of the blade pokes through.

The guard, of course, is in place behind the fence. Be sure to secure the rip lock after the blade is set for the cut and to turn the dust spout so waste will be directed toward the back of the machine.

The construction of the table is shown in Figure 9-3. How the slot can be made is shown in Chapter 11 on dadoing tools. Be sure the bottom of the slot is above the table so there will be bearing surface for the work.

A typical application is shown in Figure 9-4, where grooves are being formed by repeat passes. The projection of the blade determines the depth of the groove; height adjustment of the blade controls the width of the groove. The most accurate way to work, especially if the groove must be centered in the stock, is to first set the blade's height for a shoulder cut. For example, for a 1/4"-wide groove in the center of 3/4" stock, the bottom of the blade should be 1/4" above the table.

Make the first pass; then flip the stock so the opposite surface is down on the table and make a second pass. The waste material between the two cuts is removed by adjusting the height of the blade and making additional passes.

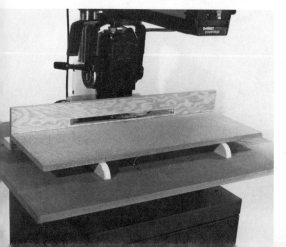

Figure 9-2: Horizontal sawing table No. 1. It provides a necessary, higher table surface and room behind the fence so depth-of-cut adjustments can be made. It locks in place by using the table clamp screws as you would to secure the regular guide fence.

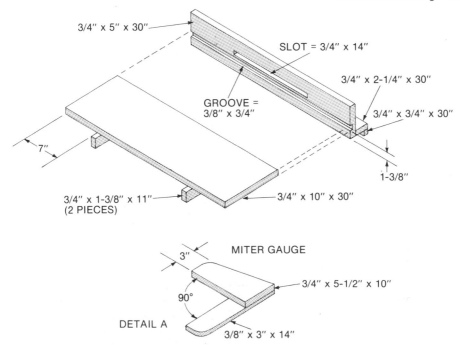

3/4" x 5" x 30"

SLOT = 3/4" x 14"

3/4" x 2-1/4" x 30"

GROOVE = 3/8" x 3/4"

3/4" x 3/4" x 30"

7"

1-3/8"

3/4" x 1-3/8" x 11" (2 PIECES)

3/4" x 10" x 30"

MITER GAUGE

3"

3/4" x 5-1/2" x 10"

90°

DETAIL A

3/8" x 3" x 14"

Figure 9-3: Construction details of horizontal sawing table No. 1. Detail A shows how a miter gauge is made.

Figure 9-4: Feed direction when using the No. 1 table is from right to left, against the blade's direction of rotation. Depth-of-cut is controlled by blade projection, width-of-cut by blade height.

SPRING STICKS. Work like the grooving operation just described will be more accurate and easier to do if you provide a means of holding the work snugly against the fence. This can be done by making a "spring stick" and using it as shown in Figure 9-5. The spring stick is clamped to the table so that it bears against the work just enough to keep the work from moving away from the fence as the cut is made.

Position the spring stick at a point just before the work contacts the blade. It is helpful to have several of these tools. In the grooving operation, for example, having one placed before the cut and one after the cut would provide good support throughout the pass.

Spring sticks are made as shown in Figure 9-6. Straight-grain fir is a good material to use but pine or a similar wood will serve.

Figure 9-5: Spring sticks you can make help to keep the work snug against the fence. The spring stick should bear against the work before the work contacts the blade.

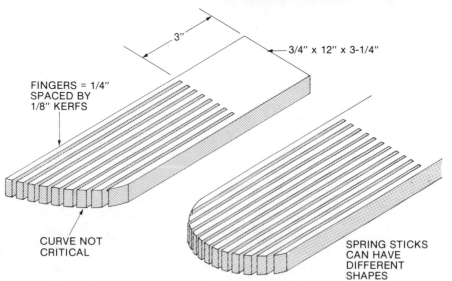

Figure 9-6: Typical spring stick designs.

A MITER GAUGE. Cuts can be made on the end of narrow stock but never without providing adequate support for the work. Narrow ends won't bear sufficiently against the fence and the work can swing out of position if you try to hold it only with your hands. The miter gauge shown in Figure 9-7 is more accurate and safer. Its construction is shown in Figure 9-3A. Be sure the angle between the two parts is 90° and that the edges that will bear against the table-edge and the work are smooth and straight.

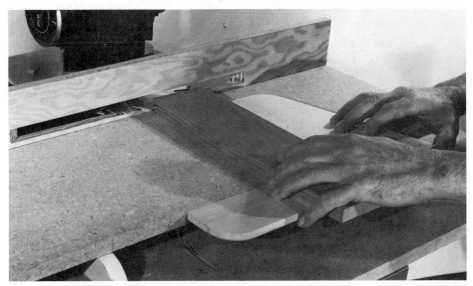

Figure 9-7: Work can be done on the end of narrow stock but never by using only your hands to move the work past the blade. Work will be more accurate and you will be safer if you use a "miter gauge."

HORIZONTAL SAWING TABLE NO. 2. The special table that is needed when horizontal sawing is done by moving the blade to and fro on the radial arm is shown in Figure 9-8. Like table No. 1, this one is secured by using the table clamp screws as you would to lock the guide fence. The table, as a unit, is movable so adjustments can be made between it and the cutting tool. Be sure to retighten the table clamp screws after any table-position change. The table is made as shown in Figure 9-9.

A typical application, forming an end groove, is shown in Figure 9-10. As you can see, the work stays put, the blade is pulled through for the cut. If the groove must be centered, follow the procedure that was outlined for forming edge grooves. That is, make one shoulder cut, flip the stock and make the second shoulder cut, then make repeat passes to clean out the waste. In this and similar operations, depth-of-cut is controlled by the position of the work. When repeat passes are required, a stop block should be used to make sure the work doesn't move.

Figure 9-11 shows the second stage of a two-pass operation often used to form end rabbets. The first pass forms the shoulder of the rabbet and is made in normal crosscut position. The second pass, as shown in the photograph, completes the job.

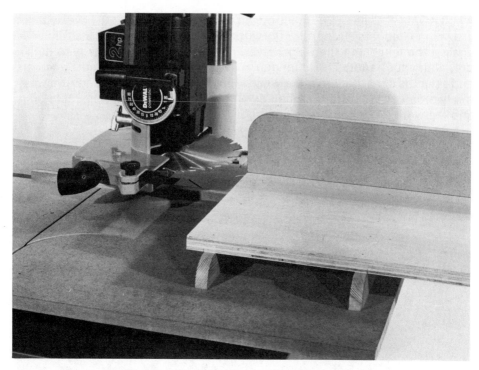

Figure 9-8: Horizontal sawing table No. 2. With this table the work stays put; the saw blade is moved to make the cut. The table is movable longitudinally for adjustments between it and the saw blade.

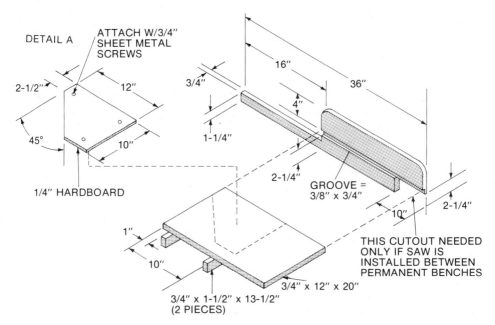

Figure 9-9: Construction of horizontal sawing table No. 2. Detail A describes the miter-cut guide.

Figure 9-10: Cutting an end groove. The shoulder cuts are made and then the waste between them is removed by making repeat passes. Note the clamped "stop block," in this case, just a small piece of wood.

Figure 9-11: The second pass of a two-pass rabbet cut. The first pass (or cut) was done in normal crosscut position to form the rabbet's shoulder.

MITER WORK. Work that has been miter-cut can be accurately positioned for horizontal sawing when the table is equipped with a guide like the one shown in Figure 9-12. This is simply a small sheet of 1/4" hardboard with a corner cut off at a precise 45° angle (see Figure 9-9A).

A typical example of work that can be done with it is shown in Figure 9-13 where a groove is being cut in a mitered edge. Operational procedures are normal but the guide makes it easier to position the work for accurate cutting. Other uses for the setup will be shown elsewhere.

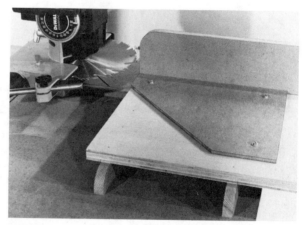

Figure 9-12: The guide used to position work that has been miter-cut. The angular cut in the guide must be exactly 45° to the path of the saw blade.

Figure 9-13: A typical operation using the miter guide to position the work. Using a clamp will assure that the work does not move during cutting operations. The clamp also makes it unnecessary to use hands close to cutting areas.

Chapter 10
The Many Angles
of the Radial Arm Saw

Angular cutting can be done four ways:

Cross Bevels (or Cross Miters)—In crosscut position but with the saw blade tilted.

Rip Bevels (or Rip Miters)—In rip position but with the saw blade tilted.

Simple Miters—By swinging the radial arm to the left or right with the saw blade in vertical position.

Compound Miters—With the radial arm in simple-miter position but with the saw blade tilted.

Figure 10-1 shows examples of angular cuts. The chamfer and the V-cut (or V-groove) are just variations of the rip-bevel procedure. Both these cuts can also be made across the grain by using the cross-bevel setup.

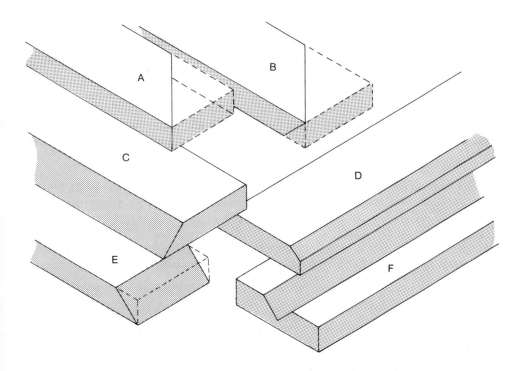

Figure 10-1: Typical angular cuts: (A) simple miter; (B) compound miter; (C) rip bevel (or miter); (D) chamfer; (E) cross bevel (or miter); and (F) V-cut (or groove).

ACCURACY IS CRITICAL. When woodworkers, especially beginners, experience difficulty with power sawing, it usually occurs with angular cuts and most often when a particular tool setting is not controlled by the tool's built-in automatic stops.

If a project requires 35° miters or bevels and the tool is set at 34-1/2°, the total error when a number of pieces must be assembled can be substantial.

A picture frame actually requires eight cuts. If each is not precisely 45°, there will be a considerable gap at the last joint and frame parts will not be square to each other. The accuracy factor applies to all cuts even if only two pieces are involved (Figure 10-2). If the parts are to form a particular corner angle, the miters or bevels must be right.

Figure 10-2: Examples of miter joints. The cuts must be accurate and smooth in order to obtain a clean joint-line.

It isn't more difficult to make angular cuts than it is to make straight ones. You just have to be extremely careful with arm-swing or blade-tilt settings. It is good practice to check the first piece that is cut with a gauge or to make a test cut on scrap wood. Then any necessary adjustment can be made before the error is repeated on other pieces.

RIGHT AND LEFT MITER POSITIONS. The setup for a right-hand miter is shown in Figure 10-3. The arm, in this case, has been swung 45°, a setting that does have an auto-stop. As in crosscutting, the pass starts with the blade in neutral position behind the guide fence. The motor is started after the work is positioned. Then the blade is pulled through to make the cut, returned to neutral position, and allowed to come to a stop before the work is removed.

Figure 10-3: A right-hand miter is made with the saw blade swung to the right. Here, the saw is set for a 45° cut, but any angle between zero and 45° is available.

When the stock has plain surfaces, opposing miters can be cut with the saw in the same position by turning the stock over for each cut. The cuts will be left- and right-hand miters.

When, for example, the stock is a piece of molding and turning it over for successive cuts won't work, left-hand miters are cut with the saw in the position shown in Figure 10-4. When the miter angle is extreme, the guide fence should be placed and locked behind the wide, movable table board. This will provide "extra" table surface for work-support.

This kind of work calls for changes in the tool's setting in order to make opposite cuts. You can see why the operator should check the setting very carefully before making cuts.

Figure 10-4: A left-hand miter is made with the saw in this position. This setting is needed for opposing cuts when the stock (as explained in the text) can't be flipped for consecutive cutting with the saw kept in the right-hand position. Notice that the fence is set back to provide more table room.

DUPLICATE PIECES. When many pieces of equal length are required and the stock can be turned over for successive cuts, a stop block may be used as shown in Figure 10-5 to assure accuracy. The procedure is to make a cut at one end of the stock and then flip it and position it so the cut end butts against the stop block. Make the second cut and then repeat the actions until you have the number of pieces that are needed. On operations like this, be sure not to allow sawdust to accumulate against the fence or the stop block. Also avoid the tendency to speed up production. A calm, steady procedure is safer and will result in smoother cuts. Remember to move the blade completely back to neutral position after each cut.

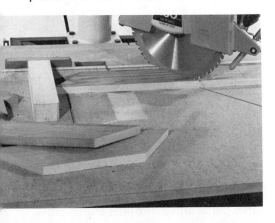

Figure 10-5: When the stock is plain, the length of similar pieces can be gauged by using a stop block. The stock is turned over for each cut. Don't allow sawdust to accumulate against the fence or the stop block.

A SPECIAL MITERING JIG. A reason for making a jig like the one shown in Figure 10-6 is to minimize the possibility of human error when organizing the tool for miter cuts. The jig provides the correct angle for the work. The cut is made with a simple crosscut action.

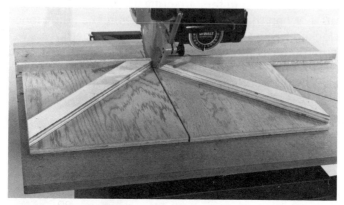

Figure 10-6: The mitering jig makes miter cuts more accurate because it minimizes the possibility of human error.

There are several ways the jig can be used. Parts, for example, for a frame can be precut to the lengths required and then placed for cutting in the jig as shown in Figure 10-7. One end is cut, then the stock is flipped so the opposing cut can be made. This procedure wastes some material but is followed by many operators because accuracy is easier to achieve than by making successive cuts along one length of wood.

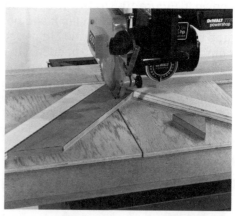

Figure 10-7: Parts can be precut to the lengths required and then placed in the jig like this. The miter cut then becomes a single crosscut procedure.

When the stock is shaped so that it can't be turned over to accomplish opposing cuts, the pieces can still be precut because the second guide arm of the jig can be used to position the work (Figure 10-8).

The jig is a two-piece structure so the worker can, if he chooses, set it up as shown in Figure 10-9 and can make consecutive cuts along one length of stock. It doesn't matter whether the stock is plain (so it can be turned over for opposing cuts) or whether it is contoured; either guide arm of the jig is still useable.

Figure 10-8: Either guide arm of the jig may be used. This is important when the shape of the stock makes it necessary to change its position for opposing cuts.

Figure 10-9: The parts of the jig can be separated to provide a path for the work. In this way, miter cuts can be made consecutively along one length of material.

In consecutive cutting, the worker has to pay attention to length accuracy. Each cut-line must be carefully marked and the work placed so the saw blade will follow the line.

CUTTING DISCS. Figure 10-10 shows an unusual application of the mitering jig. When it is necessary to halve or to quarter a disc, the guide arms of the jig serve as a "V" to position the work for accurate cutting. Cutting the disc in half is easy. Just be sure the work bears against both guide arms. If the half pieces must then be quartered, remember that the work must be positioned so the first diameter cut will be at right angles to the cut-path of the saw blade.

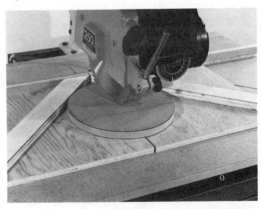

Figure 10-10: Using the mitering jig to bisect a circular piece of work. When the work is held snugly against the guide arms, the cut will be exactly on the disc's diameter.

MAKING THE MITERING JIG. Although the jig consists of two pieces (Figure 10-11), its construction will be more accurate if it is initially assembled as a single unit. This means, first, that the table will be 28" long and the fence will be 36" long. These two pieces are assembled and then secured to the tool's table, so that the jig's fence is sitting in place of the guide fence.

109

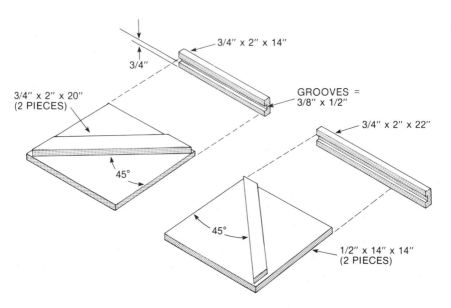

3/4" x 2" x 14"

3/4"

3/4" x 2" x 20"
(2 PIECES)

GROOVES =
3/8" x 1/2"

3/4" x 2" x 22"

45°

45°

1/2" x 14" x 14"
(2 PIECES)

Figure 10-11: Construction details of the mitering jig. Follow the assembly procedure that is outlined in the text.

Locate the jig so that the center of a crosscut kerf will be 14" from the left side of the jig. Then, with the jig secured and preferably with a hollow-ground blade mounted on the arbor, cut a kerf across the jig. Locate the guide arms so each will form a 45° angle with the kerf. Then make a crosscut to sever the jig.

CROSS BEVEL (OR MITER). This is a crosscut operation except that the blade is tilted to whatever angle is needed (Figure 10-12). Whenever it is necessary to tilt the blade, first raise it well above the table; then, after tilting, move the blade back to neutral position. Lower the blade until it almost touches the table; then, with the motor on, lower the blade slightly so that it will take the necessary bite in the table.

Be careful when setting the blade's angle. The machine has an auto-stop for a 45° cut but other tilt-angles must be judged by reading the bevel scale.

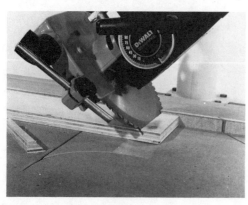

Figure 10-12: A cross bevel is made with the tool set in crosscut position but with the blade tilted to the angle that is needed.

Figure 10-13: Rip bevels are made with the tool in ripping position but with the blade tilted. Here, work-feed direction is from right to left. Use pushers!

RIP BEVEL (OR MITER). This is a rip cut made with the blade tilted to the necessary angle (Figure 10-13). Be sure to raise the blade a sufficient amount above the table before tilting it. Secure the bevel lock and then lower the blade for the cut. Be sure to tighten the rip lock after you have established the correct distance between fence and blade.

Follow all the rules that apply to normal ripping operations. Correctly set the guard and antikickback assembly. Use a pusher. Feed the work slowly and steadily.

SEGMENT CUTTING. When a number of segments are cut at a particular joint angle, the pieces can be assembled to form a circle. As shown in Figure 10-14, segments can be formed by making rip-bevel cuts or simple miter cuts. The more segments you have and the narrower they are, the closer you approach a true circle.

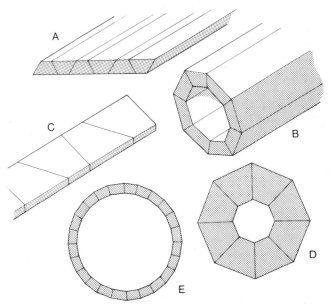

Figure 10-14: Examples of segment cutting. The project in B is made by rip-beveling stock as in A. As shown in E, the greater the number of pieces and the narrower they are, the closer to a true circle the project will be. D results from miter cuts as in C.

The technique can be used in many areas of woodworking. Projects can range from table pedestals and lamp bases to posts for a porch. Often, a segmented construction used in place of a solid component results in savings on material costs and definitely cuts down on weight.

Other times, especially on barrel projects like those shown in Figure 10-15, this is the only method that is feasible.

Of course, the angle of the cuts can't be determined arbitrarily. The formula shown in Figure 10-16 must be followed. It is important to understand that the **cut-angle** for the joints is one-half the **included angle** of the segments.

The cuts required are simple rip bevels or miters but accuracy is especially critical because of the number of joints involved. Imagine what the total error will be if the cut is just slightly off on each of 20 pieces.

Figure 10-15: Examples of projects that were made using the segment-cutting technique.

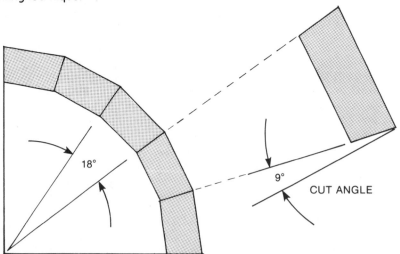

Figure 10-16: The formula used to determine the correct cut-angle for segments: (1) Determine the number of segments; (2) divide 360 (degrees in a circle) by the number of segments; and (3) divide the answer by two.

COMPOUND MITERS. Compound miters, examples of which are shown in Figure 10-17, are required on any frame or open structure with sloping sides, such as a peaked figure with any number of sides, a shadow-box picture frame, a square or rectangular planter box with sloping sides, or almost any kind of hopper construction.

Figure 10-17: Examples of compound angle joints.

How the slope angle of the work (Figure 10-18) affects the cut can be more readily seen by performing the following test. Hold together two pieces that have been cut on a 45° cross bevel. Then tilt the pieces outward to an arbitrary angle and you will see that a miter cut is required in addition to the bevel if the parts are to join while still forming a 90° corner.

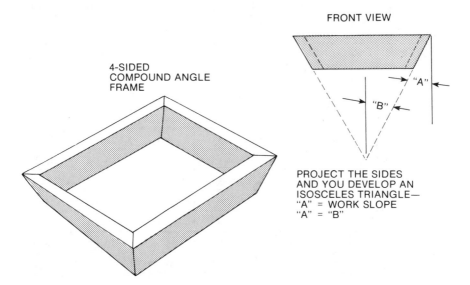

FRONT VIEW

4-SIDED
COMPOUND ANGLE
FRAME

"A"

"B"

PROJECT THE SIDES
AND YOU DEVELOP AN
ISOSCELES TRIANGLE—
"A" = WORK SLOPE
"A" = "B"

Figure 10-18: The slope angle on some projects makes it necessary to make compound angle cuts.

It is no more difficult to make or set up compound angles than it is to make any other cut. While a simple miter calls for swinging the radial arm, and a cross bevel calls for tilting the saw blade, the compound miter requires both these settings at the same time. Once the tool is set, sawing proceeds in routine fashion (Figure 10-19).

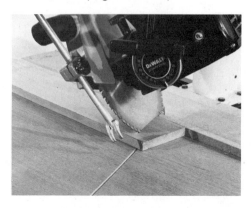

Figure 10-19: Making a compound angle cut is not difficult but because both blade tilt and arm swing are needed, attention to settings is mandatory.

Any difficulty factor has to do with the accuracy of settings when the work must have a particular slope angle. The chart in Figure 10-20 shows the blade-tilt and arm-swing settings for four-, six-, or eight-sided figures that must have a specific work slope. As you can see, some of the settings are in 1/4°, 1/2°, and 3/4°, and they should indicate the care needed to ensure the tool is organized correctly.

RADIAL ARM SAW SETTINGS FOR COMPOUND ANGLE CUTS

WORK SLOPE ANGLE (in degrees)	4-SIDED FIGURE		6-SIDED FIGURE		8-SIDED FIGURE	
	Blade Tilt	Arm Swing	Blade Tilt	Arm Swing	Blade Tilt	Arm Swing
10	44-1/4	9-3/4	29-1/2	5-1/2	22	4
15	43-1/4	14-1/2	29	8-1/4	21-1/2	6
20	41-3/4	18-3/4	28-1/4	11	21	8
25	40	23	27-1/4	13-1/2	20-1/4	10
30	37-3/4	26-1/2	26	16	19-1/2	11-3/4
35	35-1/2	29-3/4	24-1/2	18-1/4	18-1/4	13-1/4
40	32-1/2	32-3/4	22-3/4	20-1/4	17	15
45	30	35-1/4	21	22-1/4	15-3/4	16-1/4
50	27	37-1/2	19	23-3/4	14-1/4	17-1/2
55	24	39-1/4	16-3/4	25-1/4	12-1/2	18-3/4
60	21	41	14-1/2	26-1/2	11	19-3/4

Figure 10-20: Radial arm saw settings for compound angle cuts. These can be used when the slope angle of the work must be exact.

Check each setting twice before cutting. Make test cuts on scrap stock. Start cutting good material only when tests indicate the settings are correct. Also, it is a good idea to work on compound angles with a hollow-ground or carbide-tipped saw blade.

When the shape of the work permits and parts are of similar length, you can make consecutive cuts on one long board using a stop block as shown in Figure 10-21 to gauge the length of the pieces. First cut one end of the stock, then flip it and place the stop block where it is needed. The stock must be turned over for each of the cuts that follow.

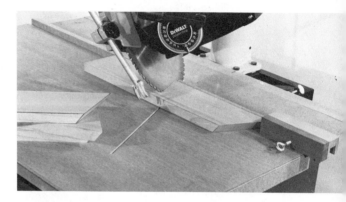

Figure 10-21: Compound angle cuts can be made this way if the stock is plain so it can be turned over for consecutive cuts. Place the stop block on the end of the work after one cut has been made.

EASY WAYS TO FORM COMPOUND ANGLE JOINTS. A commonly overlooked factor in compound-angle cutting is that the slope angle, as far as the appearance of the work is concerned, is seldom critical. No one will judge, for example, a shadow box picture frame on the basis of whether the slope angle needs to be moved a few degrees one way or the other. The same is true for a nut bowl, a humidor, a taper-sided plant container, and so on.

If, instead of keeping work flat on the table when sawing a simple miter, you support the work by some means at the desired slope angle, the job will still be as easy as cutting a simple miter, but the result will be a compound angle. This will occur regardless of the slope angle the work is held at.

Another method is to set the machine for crosscutting but to position the work at a 45° angle to the cut-line and to prop it up at the slope angle wanted. A compound angle will result by doing a simple crosscut. An example of this latter method is shown in Figure 10-22, where the mitering jig is being used to support the work. The block tack-nailed to the table braces the work so that it can be held at the slope angle. The position of the block, closer or moved away from the jig's guide arm, determines the slope angle.

Figure 10-22: The mitering jig can be used this way to support work when the slope angle is not critical. The tack-nailed block holds the work at the slope angle the worker considers to be visually pleasing.

Figure 10-23 shows a special jig that can be made for doing compound angle cuts in this fashion. The support block, centered on the kerf line, is secured with clamps in the position needed to maintain the work's slope angle. The work, placed as shown in Figure 10-24, is cut at a compound angle even though the action is a simple crosscut.

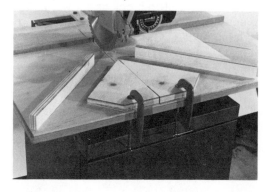

Figure 10-23: A special jig that can be used to position work for compound angle cuts when the slope angle is arbitrary.

Figure 10-24: The clamps that secure the position of the support block also lock the jig to the table. It's also permissible to use one or two brads at the back edge of the jig's table to be sure it stays flat.

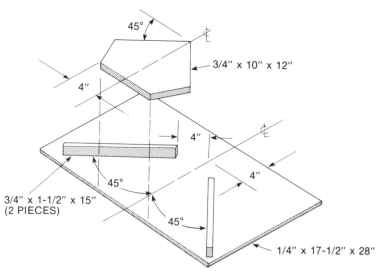

45°

3/4" x 10" x 12"

4"

4"

4"

45°

45°

3/4" x 1-1/2" x 15"
(2 PIECES)

45°

1/4" x 17-1/2" x 28"

Figure 10-25: How to make the special jig that is used to position work for compound angle cuts.

Construction details of the special compound angle jig are shown in Figure 10-25. Like all jigs, it should be carefully and accurately made and then sanded smooth and protected with several coats of sealer.

ANOTHER EASY WAY. When the work is held at a slope angle as in Figure 10-26, and the saw is set for a simple miter cut, the result will be a compound angle. The slope-guide block is clamped to the table so its forward edge is parallel to the fence. The distance between the block and the fence determines the slope angle.

Guides of this type can be made as shown in Figure 10-27.

Figure 10-26: A height block, attached to a platform so it can be secured to the table, can be used to set the slope angle. With this technique, a simple miter cut produces a compound angle.

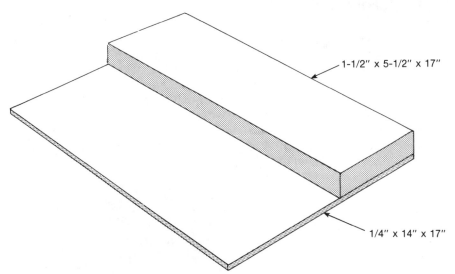

1-1/2" x 5-1/2" x 17"

1/4" x 14" x 17"

Figure 10-27: How the height block can be made.

IN SUMMARY. If it is necessary for the project to have a particular slope angle, then blade-tilt and arm-swing settings must be made to the degrees shown in Figure 10-20. If the slope angle is not critical, which is generally the case, then the operator can decide which one is visually acceptable and can make cuts by following one of the easier procedures.

CHAMFERS. A chamfer is a partial bevel made across the end or along the edge of a board or panel to remove the top corner. Usually, it is a decorative cut and is common on drawer fronts and cabinet doors.

When the cut is required along stock edges, the saw is set up as for ripping but with the blade tilted and elevated above the table as in Figure 10-28. Chamfers are usually cut at a 45° angle, but this is not critical.

Be sure the bevel clamp is secured and that the rip lock is tightened. Adjust the guard, use pushers, and follow all the rules that were outlined for ripping operations.

A chamfer that is across the end of stock is made with the saw organized as it should be for making cross-bevel cuts but with the blade above the table.

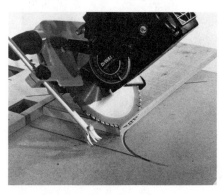

Figure 10-28: Chamfers are made with the tool in rip position but with the blade tilted. This is like a rip-bevel cut but with the blade raised so that only a corner of the stock's edge is removed.

V-CUTS (OR GROOVES). V-cuts are made with the saw set up as it should be for rip-bevel cuts but with the blade elevated above the table to provide the cut-depth that is required (Figure 10-29).

If the V must be centered, the saw should be situated for the first cut so the bottom of the kerf will be on the work's center line. Then the V-form can be finished merely by turning the stock end-for-end and making a second pass. If the V is not centered, then the saw blade position will have to be changed for the second cut in order for it to mate with the first one.

Deep or shallow V-cuts are often used for decorative purposes but can have practical applications as well. A length of 2 x 4 with a V-cut down its center is called a "V-block." Uses for such a tool will be shown as we progress.

Figure 10-29: V-cuts, or grooves, result when two matching rip-bevel cuts are made but with the blade raised above the table. A cut like this down the center of a 2 x 4 produces a V-block. Later we'll show how a V-block is used.

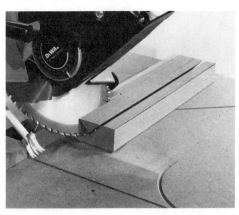

Chapter 11
What You Can Do
with Dadoing Tools

One of the first accessories usually acquired by the power-tool woodworker is a dadoing tool. Several types are available but all are designed to make cuts of various widths in a single pass—cuts, as we have shown, that can be made with a saw blade only by repeat passes. Being able to form dadoes or grooves from 1/8" up to 13/16" wide in a single pass lessens the time required to form many joint shapes. As shown in Figure 11-1, the dadoing tool can be used to accomplish many cuts in addition to the standard ones.

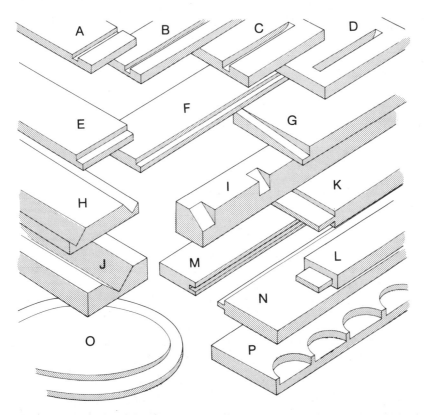

Figure 11-1: A dadoing tool speeds up much of the work involved in forming joints. It can also be used for decorative cuts: (A) Dado; (B) groove; (C) stopped dado (also stopped groove); (D) blind dado (also blind groove); (E) end rabbet; (F) edge rabbet; (G) tapered rabbet (also applies to dado); (H) angled rabbet; (I) corner dado and rabbet; (J) V-cuts; (K) tenon; (L) tenon; (M) groove; (N) tongue; (O) disc rabbeting; and (P) scallops.

TYPES OF DADOING TOOLS. A popular design is shown in Figure 11-2. This unit, called a "dado assembly," consists of two 1/8"-thick outside saw blades and a set of five "chippers," four 1/8"-thick and one 1/16"-thick. The chipper thickness is the gauge of the metal. The cutting edges of the chippers are actually wider, being "swaged" so the cutting path of each one will overlap that of the adjacent chipper or saw blade (Figure 11-3).

Figure 11-2: A dado assembly consists of two outside blades and a set of chippers. The number and size of chippers placed between the blades determines the width-of-cut.

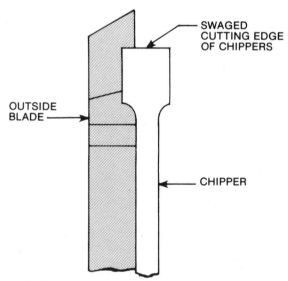

Figure 11-3: The chippers are placed so their cutting edges—which are broader than the body-gauge—fall in the gullet area of the outside blades.

Chippers are **always** used between the blades; the number of chippers mounted plus the thickness of the saw blades determine the width of the cut. For example, three 1/8" chippers plus the saw blades will make a cut 5/8" wide. Chippers must be mounted so the swaged ends are in the **gullets** of the saw blades, not against the teeth, and their placement should be staggered so cutting-teeth are not on the same line. For example, if two chippers are used, consider them the diameters of a circle, one being perpendicular to the other.

For precise cut-widths, often made necessary because of slight variations in lumber and even plywood thicknesses, paper washers may be used between the saw blades and chippers. Most dado-assembly packages include some of these washers, but if not, they are easily cut from wrapping paper or bond paper, even very thin cardboard. They should be 3" to 4" in diameter.

The outside blades of a dado assembly can be either **flat-ground** or **hollow-ground**. The latter type is used on more expensive units, and because they cut with minimum friction, they produce smoother cuts and there is less chance of burn marks on the shoulders of dadoes and grooves.

A dado assembly is mounted on the tool's arbor in almost the same way as a saw blade. First, an arbor collar is mounted with its recessed surface facing the end of the arbor; then, the assembly is mounted so direction of rotation is correct. Then, the second arbor collar with recessed side facing the assembly is mounted, followed by the lock nut. When the dado assembly's width-of-cut is extreme, the second arbor collar may be omitted; that is, the lock nut can bear directly against the blade. Always be sure enough arbor length remains for the lock nut to be fully seated.

All dadoing work is done with the saw guard correctly mounted as it would be when using a regular saw blade.

OTHER DADOING TOOLS. The "Quick-set" dadoing tool shown in Figure 11-4 works by means of a flat core studded with eight tool-steel cutters that is mounted between matched, tapered outside plates. It does not work with chippers because rotating the outside plates puts the cutting knives on a particular width-of-cut path. In essence, the knives are "spread" from the minimum cut of 1/4" to the maximum cut of 13/16".

Figure 11-4: The Quick-set dado cuts with eight tool-steel blades. Settings can be varied infinitely between minimum and maximum cuts.

Adjustments should be made while the tool is on the arbor but before the arbor nut is completely tightened. Hold the center core steady and make certain you can see the black arrow that is stamped on it. Rotate the outside plates until the dimension you want (width-of-cut settings are marked on the plates) is in line with the arrow, and then tighten the arbor nut.

Adjustments can't be made while the arbor nut is tight. If a test cut is slightly over or under, loosen the arbor nut just enough to permit the plates to rotate. Retighten the nut after making the correction.

An advantage of this tool, and of the more economical version shown in Figure 11-5, is that settings are infinite between minimum and maximum. Cut-widths can be extremely accurate; and fine adjustments can be made without the use of paper washers.

Figure 11-5: Economy version of the Quick-set dado also permits infinitely variable settings.

DADOING PRACTICE—IN GENERAL. A dadoing tool is not used to sever stock; therefore, it is always elevated above the table. The distance between tool and table depends on the depth-of-cut that is required. When cutting a 1/2"-deep dado in 3/4" stock, the tool will be 1/4" above the table. This height can be achieved by using the elevating handle (two full turns equal 1/4") or by working with a height gauge like the one described in a previous chapter.

The cut-depth can also be gauged by marking one end of the stock to indicate how deep to cut and then adjusting dado height so it matches the mark on the work.

Dado work requires a cut through the guide fence (Figure 11-6), and this can be used to accurately position work. It is impractical to have a special fence for each cut-width. A single one will serve if you work this way. Adjust the fence so the left side of the cut bears against the outside blade of the assembly or against the extreme left-hand "swing" of the cutters if a Quick-set is mounted. This side of the fence-cut is then used as an alignment point for the work.

Figure 11-6: A dado "kerf" through the guide fence will help to accurately position work for the cut. This is useful mainly when stock thickness is not higher than the fence.

Dadoing tools are moved like saw blades; however, they remove considerably more material, so hold back on the piece to prevent too fast a feed. If you try to force the cut, the tool's teeth will not function correctly and the cutter will try to climb like a wheel. Fast feeds are very poor practice. They produce rough cuts, can burn the wood or the cutter, and can even stall the machine.

Very deep cuts, especially in hardwoods like maple and birch, should be accomplished by making more than one pass. What is a very deep cut? This factor is controlled by the operation, the cutter, width-of-cut, wood density, and so on. Two alert signals are: (1) the cutting tool tends to slow up, and (2) the pass is calling for more feed pressure than you normally use.

THE SIMPLE DADO. This is done with the machine in crosscut position as shown in Figure 11-7. The operation starts with the cutter moved back to neutral position after its height has been adjusted. With the work placed, the cutter is slowly pulled forward until the cut is complete. Then it is moved back to neutral and allowed to stop before the work is removed.

Figure 11-7: A dado is cut across the grain of the wood. Feed action is like a crosscut but feed-speed should be even more conservative because of the amount of material the tool removes.

Some operators, especially when making a deep cut in a single pass, reverse the pass procedure (Figure 11-8) because they feel this eliminates any tendency of the cutter to "climb." The cutter is positioned near the end of the radial arm before the tool is turned on and before the work is placed. Then the pass is made by moving the cutter to the back of the machine. It works, but if it is used, remember it is the exception not the rule of radial arm work. As explained previously, the normal action of the blade has a tendency to pull the

Figure 11-8: Some workers will occasionally push instead of pull the cutter. This might be helpful on a deep cut in hardwood but it is the exception not the rule of radial arm saw work.

material down against the table and back against the fence. When you "reverse the pass," the blade has a tendency to lift the material. Therefore, the material should be clamped or securely held down against the table and back against the fence.

DUPLICATE DADOES. It is often necessary to form dadoes with the same edge distance on several pieces of stock. The most accurate way to do this is to use a stop block as shown in Figure 11-9 to gauge the distance from the end of the work to the dado. Any number of pieces can be dadoed with the assurance that all cuts will exactly match.

Figure 11-9: The position of similar cuts can be gauged by using a stop block. Don't allow sawdust to accumulate against the fence or the stop block.

Sometimes it is necessary to cut matching dadoes on opposite ends of similar pieces of material. One way to assure that the dadoes on all pieces will be the same distance apart is shown in Figure 11-10. After the first dadoes are cut—by the stop-block method—the parts are aligned for the second cut by using a small piece of the insert material, as shown in the photograph.

Figure 11-10: This is an accurate way to work when the distance between dadoes on similar pieces must be the same. A sample of the insert piece is placed in the first dadoes to align the parts for the second cut.

EXTRA-WIDE DADOES. A dado-width that is beyond the maximum capacity of the cutting tool can be made by repeat passes. If the dado is needed only on one piece, the easiest way to work is to mark the stock and then visually gauge the cuts. If the cut is required on several pieces, work with a stop block.

Make the first cut with the stop block set to gauge one side of the dado (Figure 11-11). Then relocate the stop block to gauge the opposite cut (Figure 11-12). Always make the first cut on all pieces before changing the stop block's position. After the second cut is made, and assuming that the dado needed is wider than you can accomplish by making two adjacent passes, there will be two separate dadoes. The last step is to remove the waste stock between them by making additional passes.

Figure 11-11: The first step when cutting extra-wide dadoes. Place the stop block to position the work for one side of the cut. When several parts are needed, make this first cut on all of them.

Figure 11-12: The second step for extra-wide dadoes. The stop block positions the work for the second cut. When necessary, the waste between the cuts is removed with additional passes.

DADOES AT AN ANGLE. When you organize the radial arm saw for a simple miter cut with a saw blade, you swing the arm away from normal crosscut position and lock it at the miter-angle position required. You do the same to cut angular dadoes (Figure 11-13), a procedure called "gaining."

The cut has many uses in cabinetmaking, construction work, and general woodworking. For example, it can be used in cutting recesses for treads in stair construction, cutting narrow slots to receive louvers, or for making slanted slats in shutters.

Figure 11-13: The tool is set in simple miter-cut position when dadoes must be cut at an angle. When spacing must be similar, make a mark on the fence as an alignment guide.

SIMPLE GROOVES. The groove, like the dado, is a U-shaped cut but is made parallel to the grain of the wood. The cutting operation is commonly called "ploughing."

The major difference between ripping and grooving is that a dadoing tool is used in place of a saw blade. Most grooving is done with the saw in the in-rip position so that work-feed is from right to left (Figure 11-14). Be sure to adjust the guard correctly so that the tines of the antikickback assembly ride on the work and the dust spout points toward the back of the machine. Tighten the rip lock after the cutter has been adjusted. Use pusher sticks to complete passes.

Figure 11-14: Grooves are cut with the tool in the ripping mode. This is the in-rip position so work-feed is from right to left. Remember that there is a lifting action when ploughing. Therefore, a pusher should be used to hold down the workpiece as well as push it through. The anti-kickback fingers are high only for photographic purposes.

EXTRA-WIDE GROOVES. The procedure is the same as the one outlined for simple grooves. After the first groove is formed, the position of the cutter is changed and a second groove is cut (Figure 11-15). The first grooves indicate the total width of the cut that is required. The waste stock between them is removed by making repeat passes. Don't forget to tighten the rip lock after each change in cutter position.

Be careful on this and similar jobs. Because repeat passes are required, there may be a tendency to hurry—which is never good practice.

Figure 11-15: Make the outside cuts first when forming extra-wide grooves. Then make repeat passes to remove waste. Be sure to tighten the rip lock after every cutter-position adjustment.

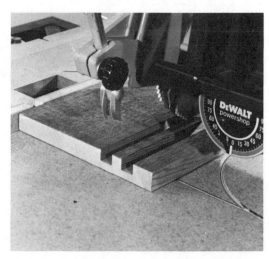

RABBET CUTS. An end rabbet is formed by following the same procedure outlined for cutting dadoes. The only difference is that the rabbet, formed on the end of the stock as shown in Figure 11-16, is L-shaped instead of U-shaped.

An edge rabbet is done following the procedure outlined for grooving. Again, the difference is that the rabbet is L-shaped, having one shoulder instead of the dado's two (Figure 11-17).

Figure 11-16: End rabbets are cut like dadoes but the cutter removes an entire corner of the material so the result is L-shaped.

Figure 11-17: Edge rabbets are cut like end rabbets but the work is done with the machine in ripping position. The arrow tells the pass direction, which is from right to left.

The width of the rabbet is determined by the thickness of the part that will be joined to it. The rabbet should be 3/4" wide if the insert piece is 3/4" thick, 1/2" wide if the insert piece is 1/2" thick, and so on.

Organize the dadoing tool for a maximum-width cut regardless of how wide the rabbet should be so that the cuts will be smooth to the end of the stock. Often, rabbets are cut 1/32" or 1/16" wider than necessary. The extra amount is sanded off after assembly to assure a smooth joint-line.

Extra-wide rabbets are made like extra-wide dadoes, by repeat passes. Make the shoulder cut first; then clean away the remaining material.

"STOPPED" AND "BLIND" DADOES AND GROOVES. A stopped dado is made exactly like a regular dado except that it does not go completely across the stock (Figure 11-18). The length of the cut can be controlled by pulling the cutter to a mark that is made on the work. But, a better way is to use a "roller head stop" which is secured to the radial arm, as shown in Figure 11-19. The stop,

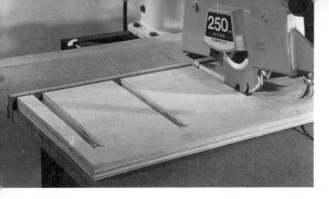

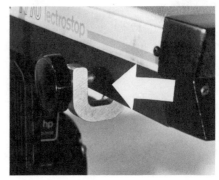

Figure 11-18: A stopped dado does not completely cross the stock. Length of the cuts is easily controlled by using a roller head stop on the radial arm.

Figure 11-19: The roller head stop, which resembles a C-clamp, is used this way. The roller head, which supports the motor, can't move past it.

which is shaped like a C-clamp, can be placed anywhere on the radial arm to limit crosscut travel. The stop is better than a mark on the work simply because it eliminates the possibility of human error.

Why stopped dadoes? For one reason, the shape of the dado can't be seen when a shelf is joined to a vertical member. Since the dadoing tool is a circular cutter, any stopped cut will end in a radius. Therefore, the insert piece must be shaped in one of the ways shown in Figure 11-20. A corner can be rounded to match the dado's arc, or it can be notched back far enough to clear the arc.

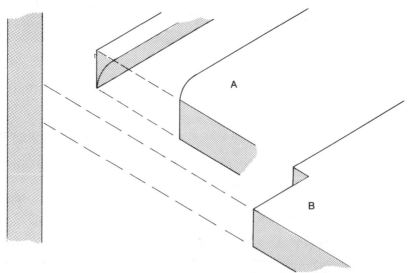

Figure 11-20: A stopped dado ends in an arc. The insert piece can be set back and shaped as in A, or, if it must be full width, can be notched back far enough to clear the arc as in B.

128

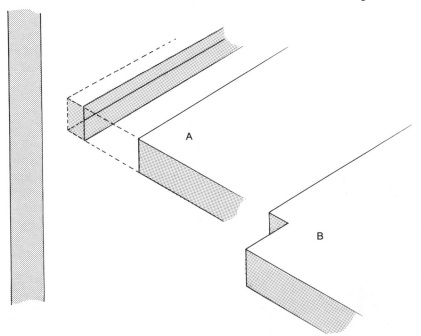

Figure 11-21: Another system calls for cleaning out the arc with a chisel. Then a set-back shelf can have a square corner; a full-width one can be notched only to the point where the dado ends.

Another way to work is shown in Figure 11-21. Here, the arc left by the dado is cleaned out with a wood chisel. Then the inserts can have square corners.

This is an appearance factor. If the project will have a front facing or frame, these pieces will hide the dado-shapes and stopped cuts will not be necessary.

Blind grooves or dadoes differ from stopped ones because they start and finish within the ends of the stock. A blind groove is done in rip position; however, the cutter is elevated above the work to start. After the work is correctly positioned against the guide fence and at a point where the groove should start, the cutter is slowly lowered to the desired depth of cut. Then the work is moved, as in ripping, until the cut is the correct length (Figure 11-22). At this point the machine is shut down and the cutter is elevated so the work can be removed.

Figure 11-22: Stopped and blind grooves are done with the tool in ripping position. The length of a blind groove is controlled with two stop blocks. A stopped groove (marked A) needs one stop block.

Cuts can be made to marks on the work but it is more advisable to use stop blocks as controls. If the groove is blind, use one stop block at the in-feed end to position the work for the start of the cut, a second one at the out-feed end to halt the work at the end of the cut.

The part marked "A" in Figure 11-22, a stopped groove, required a single stop block placed at the out-feed end of the guide fence.

VARIABLE DEPTH DADOES AND RABBETS. This technique is handy when a slight slope is required on opposite sides of a frame and on similar applications. A strip of wood which acts as a height block is tack-nailed under one edge of the work so its top surface is no longer parallel to the table. Since the dado assembly moves on a plane that is parallel to the table, it will cut deeper at one end of the stock than at the other. The difference in cut-depth is controlled by the thickness of the elevating strip.

The idea can be used on dadoes (Figure 11-23) and on rabbets (Figure 11-24).

Figure 11-23: A variable depth dado is cut by using a height block under one edge of the work. The tool cuts on a plane parallel to the table; but because the work is tilted, the dado will be deeper at one end.

Figure 11-24: With a height block under one edge, the work is positioned for cutting a variable depth rabbet. The slope of the cut is controlled by the thickness of the height block.

CORNER DADOES. This is one of those situations mentioned earlier in which a V-block comes in handy (Figure 11-25). The work, in this case a square piece, is positioned by the V-block so that corner dadoes can be formed. If the operator wishes, he can secure the V-block to the guide fence with a pair of clamps.

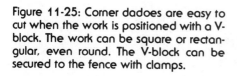

Figure 11-25: Corner dadoes are easy to cut when the work is positioned with a V-block. The work can be square or rectangular, even round. The V-block can be secured to the fence with clamps.

This same setup can be used to cut dadoes in a cylinder, but in no case should work be done on parts that are not large enough or long enough to be safely handled.

The design for a typical V-block is shown in Figure 11-26.

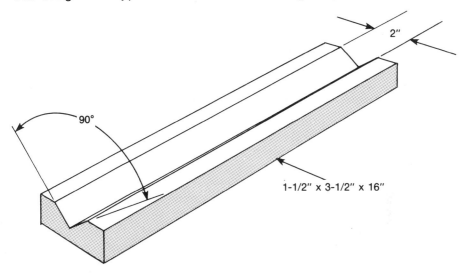

Figure 11-26: A typical V-block. Other uses for it will be shown in later chapters.

V-CUTS. V-cuts can be made in a single pass with a dadoing tool when the machine is set up as shown in Figure 11-27. This is exactly the same position used for a 45° rip bevel, except that a dado tool is used in place of a saw blade. Depth of cut is variable, controlled by the height above the table at which the dado is situated.

Figure 11-27: A dadoing tool can make a V-cut in a single pass. The tool is in rip-bevel position—the pass is from right to left.

You can produce fluted panels by making a series of parallel V-cuts as shown in Figure 11-28. The spacing between the cuts is accurately controlled by using the rip scale on the radial arm. Be sure the rip lock is tightened after each change in setting.

Figure 11-28: A series of parallel V-cuts produces a "fluted" surface. Use the rip scale to determine spacing. Tighten the rip lock after each adjustment.

Parts like this can be used to add a decorative touch to projects. Often, the fluted piece is strip-cut across the V's to produce slim moldings.

Jobs like this are done like rip cuts, so the operator should follow all the rules that govern ripping operations. The illustrations show the antikickback assembly higher than it should be for photographic purposes only. Situate the device as it should be for any rip cut.

DECORATIVE CUTS. The technique used to produce decorative surface kerfs with a regular saw blade can be used with a dadoing tool (Figure 11-29). The difference is that a dadoing tool makes it easy to control the width of the cuts. Designs are controlled by the width, spacing, and direction of the cuts.

Figure 11-29: A dadoing tool can be used to make decorative surface cuts—like kerfs made with a saw blade. Design possibilities are unlimited. Angular cuts can be combined with straight cuts.

Often, the idea is used to provide grooves for inlay strips. One procedure to consider, assuming the inlay strips will cross each other, is as follows. First, cut the longitudinal grooves (with the saw in rip position) and then glue in the inlay strips. When the glue is dry, make the crossgrain cuts and then glue in the second set of inlay strips. The joints where the strips cross will be perfect. Of course the inlay will be more effective if the strips are of a contrasting wood.

Some quite fancy cuts that resemble intricate chip carvings result when intersecting cuts are made with the dado tilted so that V-grooves can be made with and across the grain.

V-cuts made across the grain will produce stock that can then be strip-cut for moldings (Figure 11-30). Much variation is possible by controlling the depth of the cuts and the spacing between the cuts. A special fence with a V cut through it will help to accurately position the work.

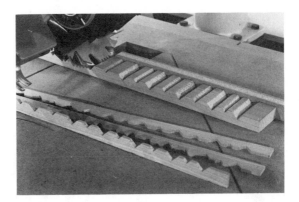

Figure 11-30: V-cuts across the stock can produce decorative parts. Often, the finished work is strip-cut to make slim moldings.

Figure 11-31: Half-arch shapes are the result of stopped V-cuts. Control the length of the cut by using a roller head stop on the radial arm.

Attractive half-arch shapes are formed in similar fashion if the length of the cuts is controlled by a roller head stop on the radial arm (Figure 11-31). Mark the work carefully so the cuts will have uniform spacing. The marks on the work can be aligned with the V in the fence.

A full arch with an inverted V down its center can be produced by following a very special procedure. One side of the arch is formed as described above. Then the work is turned so the edge that was against the fence is facing the operator. The second side of the arch is formed by pushing the cutter instead of pulling it. This means that at the start of the second step, the cutter will be on the operator's side of the work. Remember that this method of cutter-feed is the exception not the rule of radial arm saw work.

Very careful alignment of cuts is necessary for full-arch cuts to be successful. A sample is shown in Figure 11-32.

Figure 11-32: A full arch shape with an inverted V down its center is also feasible. Read the text for the special procedure that is required.

Pierced panels like those shown in Figure 11-33 can be produced with dado cuts by following the same procedure described for doing such work with a saw blade. Depth-of-cut is slightly more than half the stock's thickness. Cuts are made on both sides of the stock and will form openings wherever they cross. The openings can be square, rectangular, or diamond shaped, depending on whether all cuts are straight, or whether straight cuts on one side are combined with angular cuts on the other side.

Figure 11-33: Pierced panels result when cuts are made on both sides of the stock. Since the cut-depth is a little more than half the stock's thickness, openings appear wherever the cuts cross.

HORIZONTAL DADO OPERATIONS. A dadoing tool can, just like a regular saw blade, be positioned parallel to the table and used for horizontal cutting operations. The setup procedure is as follows. After the dadoing tool is secured on the arbor, rotate it 90° toward the back of the machine until it clicks into the in-rip position. Loosen the bevel lock and tilt the cutter 90° downward so it will be parallel to the table, and then tighten the bevel lock. Move the motor back as far as it will go.

The setup is completed by installing a special fence with an elongated "kerf" and a special guard (Figure 11-34). The guard is one that was designed specifically for shaping operations, but it is ideal in this application because it doesn't interfere with cutter adjustments as much as the regular saw guard.

Figure 11-34: A simple way to set up for horizontal dado work. The special fence has a cutout so the dado can poke through. The guard that is shown is designed for shaping operations but should also be used when dadoing tools are in horizontal position.

The guard is mounted and locked in place like a saw guard, but the protective section of the guard may be raised or lowered to accommodate the job being done. More will be said about this guard in other chapters.

EDGE RABBETS. Edge rabbets (Figure 11-35) are easy to do when the dadoing tool is organized for horizontal cutting. The distance the cutter projects from the front of the fence determines the width of the cut; its height above the table determines the depth of the cut. The height adjustment follows the principles outlined for dado cuts. For example, if the rabbet must be 1/2"-deep in 3/4" stock, then its height above the table must be 1/4".

Lower the guard as close to the surface of the work as possible. Work-feed direction is from right to left.

Figure 11-35: Edge rabbets are easy to form. The size of the cut is controlled by the cutter's projection in front of the fence and its height above the table. Set the guard as close to the work as possible. Work-feed direction is from right to left.

BEVELED RABBETS. The only difference between this cut and a conventional rabbet is that the cutting tool is tilted to the necessary angle (Figure 11-36). Cuts like this one are usually made with the tool positioned between automatic stops. The angle can be established by reading the bevel scale. Be sure the bevel lock is secure before cutting. If the degree of the angle is very critical, make a test cut in scrap stock before cutting good material.

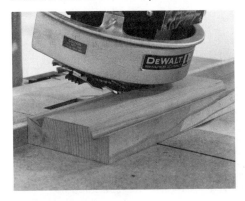

Figure 11-36: The only difference between cutting a regular rabbet and an angled one is that the dadoing tool is tilted.

DECORATIVE SCALLOPS. In this case, a scallop is a circular cut made into the edge of material as shown in Figure 11-37. The radius of the scallop depends on the distance the cutter projects from the front of the fence. The depth of the scallop is controlled by the cutter's height above the table.

Figure 11-37: Scallops are formed by moving the work into the turning cutter. Stop blocks must be used, not only to control spacing but also to provide a brace-point for starting the cut (see text).

Jobs like this one can be done safely and accurately only if stop blocks are used as brace-points. An example procedure is to secure a stop block to the guide fence at a particular distance from the cutter. Place the work flat on the table, clear of the cutter, and with one corner bearing against the stop block. Start the machine and, using the stop block as a pivot point, swing the work very slowly into the cutter until it contacts the guide fence.

Shapes and sizes of scallops are controllable by cutter height, cutter projection, and spacing of cuts.

A SPECIAL TABLE FOR HORIZONTAL DADO WORK. A special table, like the one shown in Figure 11-38, can broaden the scope of horizontal dado cutting. This one is made in almost the same way as the one designed for horizontal sawing, but with a slot that is right for a dado-cutting tool and with a relief area for the bottom of the motor to increase depth-of-cut capacity. Without the relief area, depth-of-cut would be limited because the motor would hit the back surface of the fence.

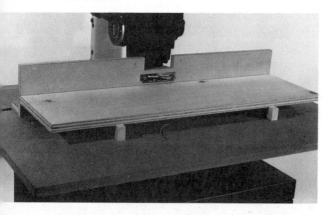

Figure 11-38: You can broaden the scope of horizontal dado work by making this special table.

Construction details of the special table are given in Figure 11-39. An extra detail, wise to make, is the L-shaped guard shown in Figure 11-40. This guard, made as shown in Figure 11-41, is vertically adjustable to accommodate various thicknesses of stock.

136

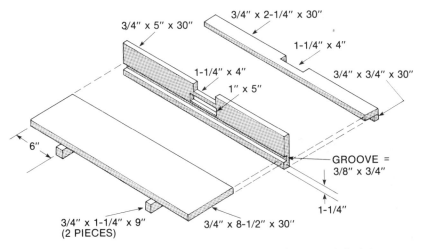

3/4" x 2-1/4" x 30"

3/4" x 5" x 30"

1-1/4" x 4"

1-1/4" x 4"

3/4" x 3/4" x 30"

1" x 5"

6"

GROOVE =
3/8" x 3/4"

1-1/4"

3/4" x 1-1/4" x 9"
(2 PIECES)

3/4" x 8-1/2" x 30"

Figure 11-39: Construction details of the special table for horizontal dadoing.

Figure 11-40: This is a guard
that is part of the special table.
It is adjustable vertically to
accommodate various stock
thicknesses. It isn't shown
in all the in-work illustrations
but should be used whenever
possible.

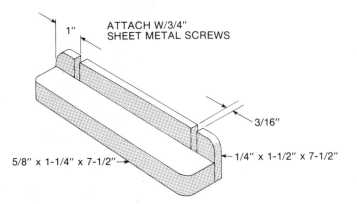

1"

ATTACH W/3/4"
SHEET METAL SCREWS

3/16"

5/8" x 1-1/4" x 7-1/2"

1/4" x 1-1/2" x 7-1/2"

Figure 11-41: Construction details of the guard for the special table.

TYPICAL USES FOR THE SPECIAL TABLE. Edge grooves are cut as shown in Figure 11-42. The dadoing tool is organized for the width of the groove, and its projection determines the depth of the groove. When the groove must be centered in the edge of the stock, it is helpful to set the dadoing tool for a cut that is less than the groove's width. After the first cut is made, turn the stock over, place end for end, and make a second pass.

Figure 11-42: An edge-grooving operation. The size of the groove is controlled by cut-width of the dado and its projection from the front of the fence. Work-feed direction is from right to left.

For example, if a 1"-wide groove must be centered in the edge of 1-1/2"-thick stock, set the dado for a 5/8"-wide cut and elevate it 1/4" above the table. Make the first pass, then, after flipping the stock and turning it end for end, make the second pass. The groove will be centered and it will be 1" wide.

Grooves that are needed close to stock edges (for sliding doors) can be cut into the surface of the material by working as shown in Figure 11-43. Here, the pass is made with the stock on edge. Be careful, when feeding the work, to keep it snug against the fence throughout the pass. The only restriction, as far as the width of work that can be handled, is the distance from the table to the radial arm.

When similar cuts are required parallel to opposite edges, the second cut is made by turning the stock over but keeping the same surface against the fence.

Figure 11-43: Grooves may also be cut into surfaces when the stock is held on edge this way. Be sure the work is held firmly against the fence throughout the pass.

RABBETING. The procedure for cutting edge rabbets is the same as for edge grooving. The cutter's height is set for the depth of the rabbet, and its projection is set for the width of the rabbet. If the same cut is required on opposite edges, the second pass is made by turning the stock end for end while the same surface is down on the table (Figure 11-44).

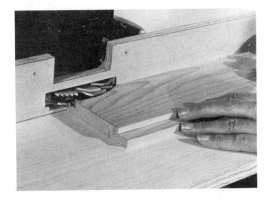

Figure 11-44: Edge rabbets are formed in normal fashion. Cutter projection controls width; cutter height controls depth.

End rabbets are cut the same way but should not be fed past the cutter using only hands unless the work is large enough to be safely handled. A back-up block may be used when the work is narrow, but a better way is to work with a "miter gauge." The one shown in Figure 11-45 was also described in Chapter 9 on horizontal sawing.

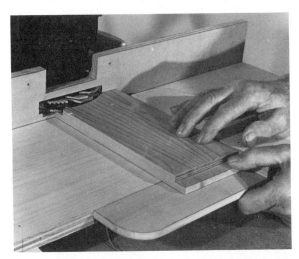

Figure 11-45: End rabbets should never be cut by feeding the work only with hands. A backup block may be used but a better way is to work with the miter gauge that was described in the chapter on horizontal sawing.

STOPPED EDGE-GROOVES. Narrow pieces that are joined edge-to-edge to form a large slab are often reinforced with "splines" that do not run the full length of the pieces. A procedure that can be used to form the limited-length grooves is shown in Figure 11-46.

The dado is set to cut the groove's width and is elevated above the table so the groove will be centered in the stock's edge. Stop blocks, which in this case are merely small pieces of wood, are clamped to both the infeed and outfeed sides of the fence to control the length of the cut.

Figure 11-46: Blind edge grooves are often formed so that hidden splines may be used to reinforce edge-to-edge joints. Two stop blocks are used because the cut must be controlled at its start and its finish.

Start the cut by placing the work flat on the table away from the cutter but with a corner braced against the infeed stop block. Swing the work in until it is snug against the fence and then move it until it contacts the outfeed stop block.

When making cuts like this, always work so the top surface of each piece will be down on the table. In this way, the grooves will match on assembly even though they may not be perfectly centered.

CIRCULAR RABBETS. Rabbet cuts on the perimeter of discs are made as in Figure 11-47. V-blocks, made like those shown in Figure 11-48, are clamped to the fence to provide a safe means of rotating the work against the cutter. The position of the blocks and the projection of the cutter determine the width of the cut. The depth of the cut is controlled by the height of the cutter above the table.

Start the cut by placing the work flat on the table and slowly easing it forward until it is firmly against both sides of the V. Rotate it slowly against the tool's direction of rotation (counterclockwise feed direction) until the cut is complete.

On operations like this, since the cutter is over the work, the worker must be careful not to tilt the work during the pass. Such an action can result in gouges in the cut area.

Figure 11-47: Rabbets can be formed on circular pieces when the V-block technique is used. The work is rotated in a counter-clockwise direction.

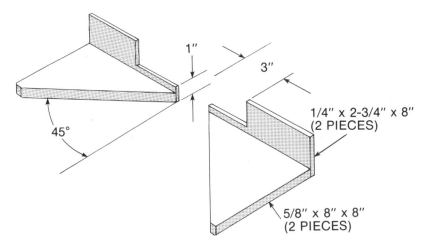

Figure 11-48: The V-blocks are made like this. They will also be shown in use in other chapters.

HORIZONTAL WORK BY FEEDING THE CUTTER. On operations like this, the horizontal sawing table No. 2 that was described in Chapter 9 is used. The machine is organized as for pull-through horizontal sawing but with a dadoing tool mounted and covered with the special shaper guard.

The end-grooving operation shown in Figure 11-49 is typical of work that can be done in this mode. The cutter's height is adjusted so the groove will be centered in the stock. Then the cutter is moved back to the neutral position. The width of the cut is controlled by the cutting tool; the depth of the cut is controlled by the position of the stock. Hold the stock very firmly, or clamp it in position, and very slowly pull the cutter forward to form the groove. Once the cutter has cleared the work, move it to the neutral position and shut down the machine before moving the work.

If the same cut is required on many pieces, the work position should be controlled by clamping a stop block to the table's fence. If the groove must be exactly centered, set the dadoing tool for a cut that is less than the groove's width. Make one pass and then a second one after the stock has been turned over.

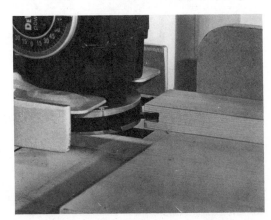

Figure 11-49: Horizontal dadoing operations can also be accomplished with the No. 2 horizontal sawing table shown in Chapter 9. Here, an end groove is being formed.

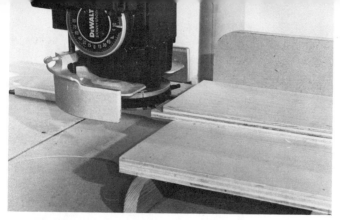

Figure 11-50: Forming an end rabbet. The work must be securely held throughout the pass. When the same cut is required on many pieces, use a stop block on the table's fence to control work position.

Rabbet cuts are accomplished the same way (Figure 11-50), the difference being that the cutter removes an entire corner of the stock to produce the rabbet's L-shape. This is a very good way to form rabbets on the end of narrow pieces.

A unique operation is shown in Figure 11-51 where a dado assembly has been organized to cut both sides of a tenon (or tongue) in one operation. Assuming that a 1/4"-thick tenon is required in 3/4"-thick stock, the dado assembly is set up as follows: an outside blade and a 1/8" chipper, followed by a 1/4"-thick spacer and then another 1/8" chipper, and finally the second outside blade. The total width of the dado will be 3/4" but the center 1/4" section will not do any cutting—that is why the tenon is produced.

Spacers can be heavy washers; many are available that have 5/8" diameter holes that will fit the tool's arbor. A set of washers will let you organize for various cuts of this type. Do remember that no matter what you mount, there must be sufficient arbor length so the lock nut can be fully seated.

Figure 11-51: In this application, a dado assembly has been organized so it will form a tenon in a single pass. Read the text for a full explanation.

Chapter 12
The Radial Arm Saw
as a Shaper

Shaping operations on the radial arm saw can be accomplished in various ways—among them, straight-edge shaping by moving the work along a fence, "freehand" shaping on curved edges, or surface shaping with the machine in rip or crosscut position. In some cases, work scope can be increased because the cutter may be tilted. This alters the cutter's relationship with the work so shapes other than the one the cutter was designed for can be produced.

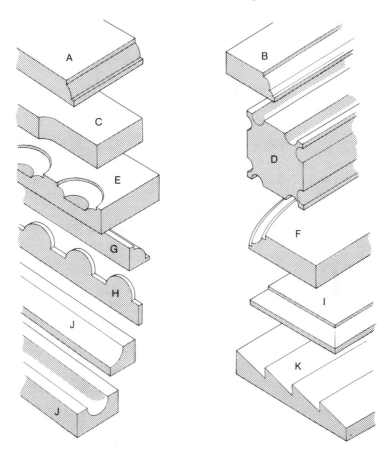

Figure 12-1: These forms represent the kind of work that can be done with shaping operations: (A) End shaping; (B) edge shaping; (C) jointing; (D) fluting (on round or square stock); (E) scalloping; (F) shaping curved or round edges; (G) slim moldings; (H) strip moldings; (I) panel raising; (J) coving; and (K) surface shaping.

The forms that are shown in Figure 12-1 are merely representative. Thousands of others are possible and do not require a thousand knives. In addition to machine position, controls include knife height and projection, work position, combination cuts with different knives, special techniques, and so on.

Shaping on the radial arm saw is not done with the three-lip shaper cutters used on conventional shaping machines, but with the special shaper head that is shown in Figure 12-2. The head itself is but a carrier, designed to securely grip the three matched knives that do the cutting.

Figure 12-2: The shaper head is a carrier that is slotted to receive matched sets of knives. The knives can only fit a certain way and this assures that each will cut on the same plane.

To be sure the knives will cut on the same plane they are grooved so they slip into slots in the head in a certain way. The knives are installed so the cutting edge (the sharp edge) points forward in the direction the head must rotate. Correct direction of rotation for the head is indicated by the arrows that are printed on it.

Follow this procedure to set knives correctly: Be sure the knife and the slot in the head are clean; slip the knife into place until it bottoms in the slot; then tighten the holding screw.

The shaper head mounts on the arbor in the same way as a saw blade. Obey the specific instructions that come with the accessory. On some operations the unit is used with the saw guard. When this is so, hand-turn the head before you turn on the machine. Check to be sure the head and knives have clearance inside the guard. Don't use extra-wide knives or create a setup that can cause knives to bite into the guard.

SHAPER KNIVES. The shape a knife produces will be the reverse of the knife's profile (Figure 12-3). For example, when matched sets of knives are used to form tongue-and-groove joints, the knife with the projection that looks like a tongue will form the groove. The mating knife, with the cutout that looks like a groove, will form the tongue. A good way to judge the cut a knife will make is to hold it against the edge of the stock as shown in Figure 12-4. Be sure to view it at eye level.

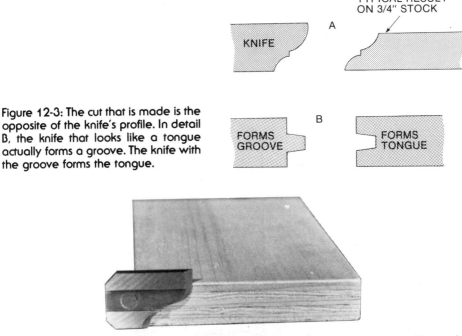

Figure 12-3: The cut that is made is the opposite of the knife's profile. In detail B, the knife that looks like a tongue actually forms a groove. The knife with the groove forms the tongue.

Figure 12-4: To preview what a cut will look like, hold the knife against an edge of the stock. Be sure the cutting edge of the knife is against the wood.

Some knives are designed for partial cuts. That is, a particular shape is produced when only part of the knife's profile is cutting. The knife shown in Figure 12-5, a combination bead and quarter-round, is such a unit. The cuts that are shown result from using only the top, the bottom, or the center section of the knife. This does not mean that such a knife can't be used in other ways. It can be used for a full profile cut, if the shape is applicable, or for any of the shapes that are shown in Figure 12-6. It all depends on the mode the tool is in, the number of cuts that are made, and the position of the work in relation to the cutter.

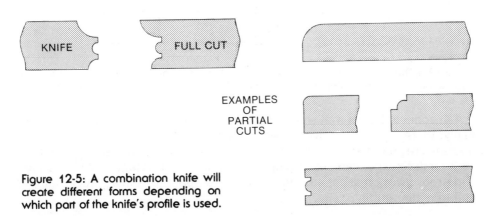

Figure 12-5: A combination knife will create different forms depending on which part of the knife's profile is used.

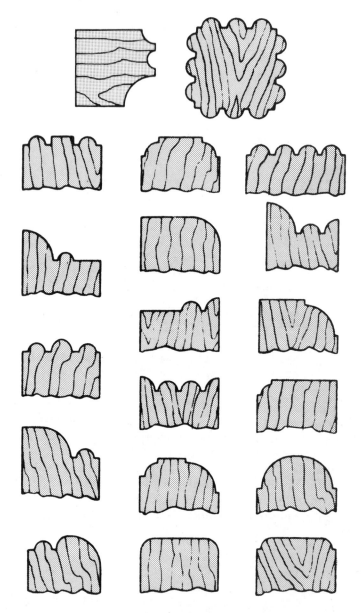

Figure 12-6: The shapes shown here were created with the combination quarter-round and bead knife. It all depends on the cutter-work relationship, height of cutter, and so on.

A misconception is that shaping is done only for decorative purposes. Actually, there are many knives designed for a particular, practical use. Some of these are included in the basic assortment of knives that is shown in Figure 12-7. Units like the "cabinet door lip," "glue joint," and matched sets for tongue and groove work make it easy to do standard operations in a precise manner and in minimum time.

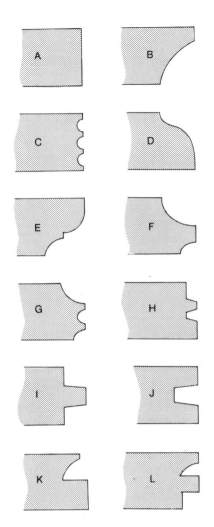

Figure 12-7: This assortment of typical shaper knives will prove useful in any woodworking shop: (A) Blank knives (often called "straight"); (B) base mold knives; (C) triple bead knives; (D) casing knives "ogee" shape; (E) bead and cove knives; (F) 1/4" and 1/2" quarter round knives; (G) combination bead and quarter round; (H) glue joint knives; (I) groove knives; (J) tongue knives (mate with groove knives); (K) cabinet door lip knives; and (L) cupboard door knives (provide a groove for a panel insert).

GENERAL PRACTICE. Shaping knives, like dado cutters, remove considerable material, so the work should be moved at a speed that allows the knives to operate correctly. Deep cuts, especially on hardwoods, may require several passes. A reasonable cut-depth and a conservative feed-speed will always produce the smoothest results. Some of the warning signs that indicate the job isn't being done correctly are: the work has to be forced to keep it moving, the work chatters, the cutters spew out large splinters, burn marks appear, and the cut is not as smooth as it should be.

Best results are obtained when cuts are made **with** the grain of the wood. Decrease feed-speed whenever it is necessary to cut **against** the grain. Cuts that are made **across** the grain will result in some amount of splintering where the cutter leaves the work. This can be minimized, but not always eliminated, with feed-speed. One way to work is to make the shaping cut on a piece that is a bit wider than necessary. A saw cut to bring the work to size will also remove any imperfection.

Some parts must be shaped on all four edges, for example, a lipped cabinet door. This calls for a particular pass procedure like the one shown in Figure 12-8. The final cuts that are made parallel to the grain of the wood will remove any crossgrain end imperfections.

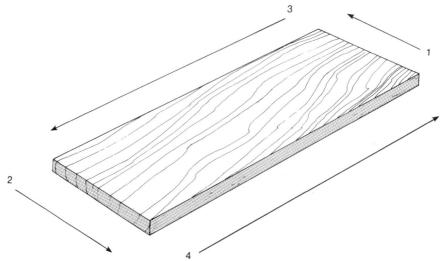

Figure 12-8: The correct sequence of passes when all four edges of work must be shaped. The arrows indicating direction assume the pass will be made from right to left.

Never, and this is a general woodworking caution, try to shape material that is too small to hold safely. If, for example, a narrow strip of molding is needed, do the shaping on a wide piece of wood and then saw off the part that is needed.

Always feed the work against the direction of rotation of the knives. It's not wise to back up work during a pass. The cutter might gouge the work or grab it hard enough to throw it from your hands. When you think that the cut isn't as it should be, remove the work and start from scratch.

The work must always be between you and the cutter. Hold the work in such a way that a slip won't cause your hands to move toward the cutter.

Always remember to use the guards even though they may not be shown in all the illustrations.

Check for wear between the radial head bearings and the arm tracks. Adjust for wear as described in the owner's manual to minimize chatter.

After the shaper head has been mounted on the arbor, organize the tool in the manner outlined for horizontal dadoing. Be sure the yoke lock, bevel lock, and miter lock are secured. The cutter's height is adjusted with the radial arm's elevating handle. Depth-of-cut is controlled by moving the motor along the arm. Be sure to tighten the rip lock after all depth-of-cut adjustments. Check rip lock tightness if several cuts are made.

STRAIGHT SHAPING. Straight shaping is always done with the work bearing against a fence. The radial arm saw's guide fence is not adequate for this purpose, so a special unit like the one shown in Figure 12-9, which is not difficult to construct, should be installed. Unit assembly is shown in Figure 12-10.

Figure 12-9: The special shaper table is designed so it can be secured with the table clamp screws. The arrow indicates feed direction.

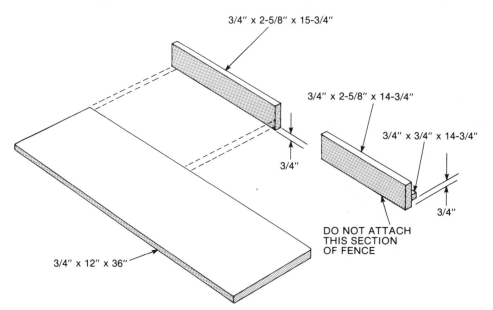

3/4" x 2-5/8" x 15-3/4"

3/4" x 2-5/8" x 14-3/4"

3/4" x 3/4" x 14-3/4"

3/4"

3/4"

DO NOT ATTACH
THIS SECTION
OF FENCE

3/4" x 12" x 36"

Figure 12-10: Construction of the shaper table. Only the left-hand fence is permanently attached.

Notice that the fence is a two-piece structure and that the **infeed** section (Figure 12-11) is not attached to the project's table. Actually, only the fences, used in place of the regular guide fence, would serve nicely for many shaping operations. The major reason for including a table is that often, to fully utilize a knife's profile, it is necessary for the bottom edge of the knife to be below the table surface. This is done by allowing the knife to cut into the table. An auxiliary surface eliminates the need to cut into the tool's standard table.

The reason that the infeed fence must be adjustable can be understood from two basic procedures. The surface of the fences must be on the same plane when a shaping cut removes only part of the stock's edge (Figure 12-12). The part of the stock's edge that remains intact will bear against the fences both before and after the cut.

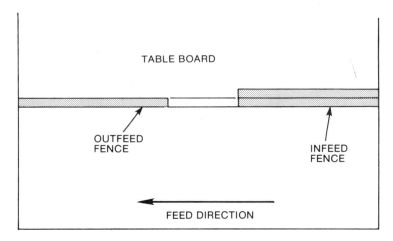

Figure 12-11: The infeed fence is where a cut starts. The outfeed fence supports the work after it has passed the cutters.

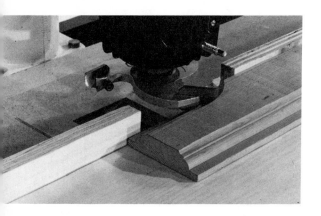

Figure 12-12: The surface of the fences must be on the same plane when the cut removes only part of the stock's edge.

When the shaping cut removes the entire edge of the stock, as shown by the jointing cut in Figure 12-13, the infeed fence must be set back a distance equal to the depth of the cut or, in other words, the thickness of the material that will be removed. In this way, the work will be supported by the outfeed fence after the cut, even though the width of the stock has been reduced.

Figure 12-13: When a cut removes all of the stock's edge, the infeed fence must be set back a distance that equals the thickness of the material that is removed. Here, 1" wide blank knives are being used to joint the edge of 3/4" thick stock.

Figure 12-14 shows how to offset the infeed fence. A shim, whose thickness equals the knives' depth-of-cut, is placed between the infeed fence and the table. A similar shim is placed between the outfeed fence and the tool's removable table board. The second shim is needed to equalize pressure when the table clamp screws are tightened to secure the fence. Shims can be made of plastic laminate, hardboard, plywood, and even stiff cardboard. They do not have to be very thick. For example, on a jointing cut, it usually isn't necessary to cut deeper than 1/32" or 1/16". To remove more material, make more passes. Once the shims are made, they should be stored for future use.

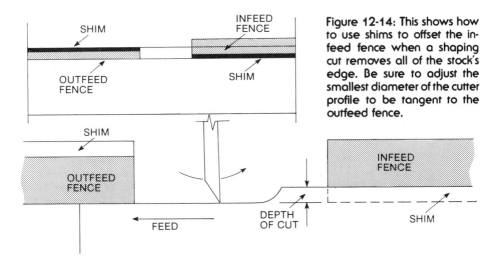

Figure 12-14: This shows how to use shims to offset the infeed fence when a shaping cut removes all of the stock's edge. Be sure to adjust the smallest diameter of the cutter profile to be tangent to the outfeed fence.

Because it consists of two pieces, the fence may be adjusted longitudinally. This makes it possible to set the fences for a minimum opening at the cutting area.

The cut is made by placing the work flat on the table and firmly against the infeed fence and then slowly advancing it until it is clear of the knives. Edges to be shaped must be straight, smooth, and square. Irregularities will result in poor work. Figure 12-15 shows a correct procedure. Work is fed from right to left; the special shaper guard is situated as close as possible to the surface of the work.

Figure 12-15: Although other photographs don't show it, the special shaper guard should be mounted like this— secured in place of the saw guard and as close to the work as possible.

END CUTS. Because narrow work will not have sufficient bearing against the fence, a backup support must be provided. Some workers use merely a block of wood, but a better system is shown in Figure 12-16. This is the same "miter gauge" illustrated in Chapter 9. The accessory keeps the work square and allows a firm grip without endangering the hands.

The procedure following should be used when a very narrow piece must be end-shaped. Assuming the part must be only 1" wide, work with a piece that is 4" or 5" wide. Use a backup to feed the work, but stop when the cut is slightly longer than 1". The strip needed can then be removed by sawing.

Figure 12-16: End shaping must be done with adequate support for the work. The "miter gauge" shown here permits a firm grip and ensures that the work will be square to the fence throughout the pass.

A PROFESSIONAL SHAPER FENCE. A sophisticated shaper fence (Figure 12-17) is available as an accessory for the radial arm saw. Like the homemade version, the fence consists of two pieces; an outfeed fence of heavy hardwood, an infeed fence made of metal. The fence is placed in the slot normally occupied by the machine's regular guide fence. Since both parts of the fence may be moved longitudinally, the opening around the shaper head can be kept to a minimum.

Figure 12-17: A sophisticated shaper fence is available as an accessory for the radial arm saw. The outfeed fence is hardwood, the adjustable infeed fence is metal.

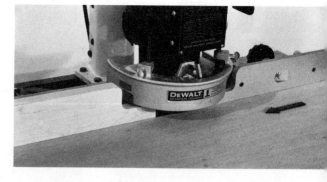

A major advantage of the accessory is that the adjustability of the infeed fence makes shims unnecessary. The infeed fence is mounted on two guide pins and can be set for any cut from zero to 1/2" by turning a large knob (Figure 12-18).

Figure 12-18: An advantage of the shaper-fence accessory is that the infeed fence is infinitely adjustable to a maximum setting of 1/2". Full-edge cuts can be made without the use of shims.

When using the shaper fence, you should consider installing an auxiliary table cover. With this cover, it won't be necessary to cut into the regular table when the bottom edge of a shaper knife must be below the work surface. The cover can be the slide-on unit that was described earlier, or simply a table-size sheet of 1/4" plywood tack-nailed in place.

STRIP MOLDINGS. There are two ways to produce slim moldings:

1. Shape the edge of a wide piece of stock that is easily handled and then rip off the shaped edge.

2. Make a special setup so that the pre-ripped pieces can be fed through easily and safely.

When only one piece of molding is required, the shape-and-rip procedure is the way to go. But if many feet of the same molding are required, the jig technique should be considered.

The jig is nothing more than a length of heavy stock which has a rabbet-cut sized to suit the dimensions of the precut strips. The jig is clamped to the shaper fence as shown in Figure 12-19 so strips can be fed through it for shaping. The rabbet cut should hold the work firmly while allowing just enough freedom for the work to be moved. Move the work into the jig at the infeed end; pull it at the outfeed end when the cut nears completion. Try to make this one continuous movement. Stopping the pass at any time may result in a gouged area.

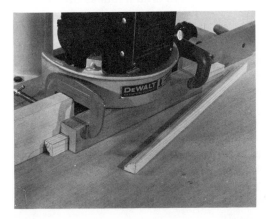

Figure 12-19: Precut, small strips can be safely shaped when this technique is used. The jig is just a large piece of stock with a work-size rabbet cut into it.

CIRCULAR WORK. The V-block technique described for rabbeting discs and performed with a dadoing tool can be adopted for shaping the perimeter of circular work. The amount the shaping knives project from the front of the fence and the position of the V-blocks determine how deep the cut will be.

Start the cut by easing the work into the V very slowly until contact with the knives is established. Then turn the work counterclockwise (against the shaper head's rotation) while maintaining contact with both sides of the V-block (Figure 12-20).

Figure 12-20: Circular edges can be shaped by using a set of V-blocks to position and guide the work. The work is slowly turned counterclockwise while it is held snugly in the V.

Figure 12-21: Decorative scallops are formed in this way. The stop (a clamp is used here) acts as a brace point for swinging the work into the cutters and as a guide for spacing the cuts.

SCALLOPING. Shaped scallops are formed when the work is moved directly into the cutters. A stop, which can be a clamp (Figure 12-21), is used as a brace point and helps to gauge spacing between cuts. Place the work flat on the table, clear of the cutters, and with a corner snug against the stop. Using the stop as a pivot point, slowly swing the work into the cutters until it makes full contact with the fence. Then pull the work away.

SURFACE SHAPING. Surface shaping may be accomplished on the radial arm saw because the shaper head can be used with the machine set for ripping. All rules for ripping should be followed—the guard and antikickback fingers should be in correct position, push sticks should be used, and so on. Always use a slow feed and position the work so the knives will be cutting **with** the grain of the wood. If a deep cut is required, which is unusual for this kind of work, obtain full depth-of-cut by making repeat passes.

Often, this shaping system is useful for producing many feet of similar molding. Figure 12-22 shows a triple-bead knife being used across the full width of a piece of stock, but the spacing between cuts is such that the wood can later be rip-cut into individual strips of molding. Correct spacing is easy to

Figure 12-22: Surface cuts, with the grain of the wood, are possible when the machine is set up in rip position. Parts that are surface cut like this can then be sawed to form individual strips of molding.

establish by using the rip scale. Be sure to tighten the rip lock after each adjustment.

Figure 12-23 shows a sample of the work that can be done when the cutter is tilted. Base-mold knives are being used to produce an unusual corrugated surface. Cut-spacing is critical on this kind of work, so make adjustments for successive cuts very carefully.

Figure 12-23: Tilting the cutter makes it possible to achieve many surface shapes. Make the settings for each pass very carefully so cuts will have uniform spacing.

CROSSGRAIN CUTS. Some shaping cuts can be made with the machine in crosscut position (Figure 12-24), but such work should be accomplished with a very slow feed-speed and by making repeat passes to reach full depth-of-cut. In cases like this, it may not be necessary to make a cutter-height adjustment for each pass if you proceed as follows.

Figure 12-24: Cuts across the grain can be made this way but results will be satisfactory only if you reach full depth-of-cut by making repeat passes. It is also essential for feed-speed to be very slow.

Set knife-height for the cut required, but position the work on the left side of the cutting path so that the first pass will just scrape the top corner of the wood. Then, for each pass, move the work further into the cutting path until you have obtained the desired shape. **Don't rush** just because you have several passes to make. Haste not only makes waste, it can also cause you to become careless.

Crossgrain surface cuts are often done to shape stock which can then be rip-cut into slim moldings (Figure 12-25). This kind of work must be done very carefully if the cuts are to be uniformly spaced. It is advisable to mark the center line **between** cuts on the stock. These marks can then be aligned with a gauge point on the guide fence. Correct position of work for each cut is even more critical when repeat passes are required.

Figure 12-25: Similar cuts, spaced uniformly, will produce stock that can be rip-cut into slim moldings. Patience is required for this kind of work.

SHAPING CURVED EDGES. The procedure for working on curved edges is often called "freehand shaping," a term that should not be taken literally. It merely describes a shaping system that is used when work can't be guided by a straight fence. On a conventional shaping machine, the depth-of-cut for freehand shaping is established with collars that are placed on the spindle along with the cutter. In order to make it easier to contact the cutter, a fulcrum pin is used as a brace-point for the work. A similar system, like the one shown in Figure 12-26, must be set up for the radial arm saw.

Figure 12-26: The setup that is required for "freehand shaping."

The semicircular piece is the guide against which the work bears during the cut. The position of the guide in relation to the shaper knives determines the depth of the cut. The pointed piece acts like a fulcrum pin; that is, as a brace-point for the work before contact is made with the knives.

The point of the fulcrum should be on the same plane as, or slightly in front of, the front edge of the guide. A cut is started by placing the work firmly against the fulcrum (Figure 12-27) and then very slowly advancing the work until it bears solidly against the front edge of the guide. At this point, the work may be swung free of the fulcrum, but this is not mandatory. Many workers allow the fulcrum to provide support until the very end of the pass.

Figure 12-27: The pass is started by placing the work so it is against the fulcrum but free of the cutters. Then the work is very slowly advanced until it bears solidly against the front edge of the guide.

Work like this must always be done with the shaper guard correctly positioned, as shown in Figure 12-28. Keep hands on the outside edges of the work, with fingers hooked against edges to guard against slipping. Remember that the work must bear against the guide throughout the pass. Also, be sure to tighten the rip lock after the knives have been set for the cut.

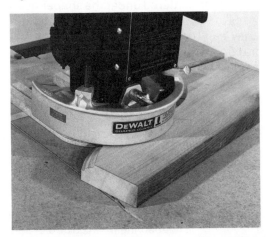

Figure 12-28: Once the work is bearing against the guide, it may be swung away from the fulcrum if the operator wishes. This photograph is also a reminder that a guard is made to be used.

Construction details of the guide and fulcrum are shown in Figure 12-29. The parts are made adjustable so depth-of-cut can be varied and so there can be some flexibility in guide-to-shaper head setups.

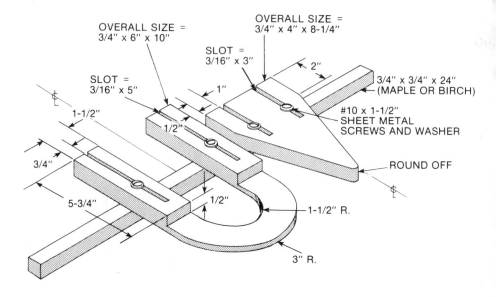

OVERALL SIZE =
3/4" x 4" x 8-1/4"

OVERALL SIZE =
3/4" x 6" x 10"

SLOT =
3/16" x 3"

2"

SLOT =
3/16" x 5"

1"

3/4" x 3/4" x 24"
(MAPLE OR BIRCH)

1-1/2"

#10 x 1-1/2"
SHEET METAL
SCREWS AND WASHER

1/2"

3/4"

5-3/4"

1/2"

ROUND OFF

1-1/2" R.

3" R.

Figure 12-29: Construction details of the guide and the fulcrum. The unit is locked in the slot normally occupied by the guide fence.

Because the shaper head can't be set below the guide, it isn't possible to make a full-edge cut unless you work as shown in Figure 12-30. Here, the work is elevated by means of a piece of plywood tack-nailed to its underside so that more of the shaper knives' profile can be used.

Another way that freehand shaping can be accomplished is as follows. Instead of using the adjustable guide, a disc whose diameter is less than the shaper head's cutting diameter is fastened to a strip of wood that fits the slot ordinarily used by the guide fence. The disc is centered under the shaper head and thus acts as a guide for the cut. Discs of various diameters may be required for particular cuts; but once made, they can be stored for future use like any accessory. The discs will be more practical if the center section is cut out (so you have a ring) to permit the motor's arbor to extend below the guide's surface.

Figure 12-30: When a full-edge cut is needed, the work can be elevated on a similarly shaped piece of plywood which is tack-nailed in place. This allows more of the shaper knife to be used.

PATTERN SHAPING. This is a system that can be used when a number of similar pieces must be shaped. A pattern, which is a smaller version of the work, is tack-nailed to the underside of the work so that it acts as a cut-guide as shown in Figure 12-31. The pattern can be made of plywood or hardboard, but its edges must-be sanded smooth. Any irregularity in the pattern will be duplicated on the work. It is advisable to rub the edges of the pattern with a candle or to polish them with paste wax so there will be a minimum amount of friction between the pattern and the guide.

Often, a pattern is used even if the shaping is done in a limited area, as in a table top that requires some shaping at the ends of perpendicular diameters.

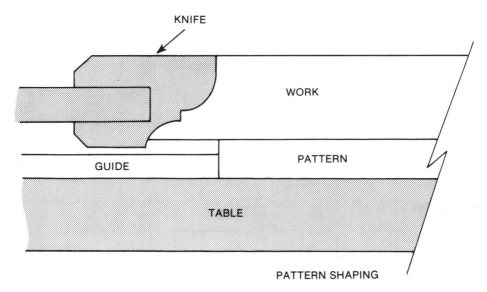

KNIFE

WORK

GUIDE

PATTERN

TABLE

PATTERN SHAPING

Figure 12-31: This cross-sectional view shows how pattern shaping works. The pattern, which is a smaller version of the work, rides against the guide.

FLUTING AND REEDING. Round or square stock and pieces that have been turned in a lathe can be further embellished with reeds or flutes by means of the system shown in Figure 12-32. The work is mounted between centers in a cradle which then serves as a carrier for making the pass. The height of the shaper head is set so the center line of the cutting portion of the knife will be on the work's horizontal center line. The depth of the cut is established by the position at which the motor is locked on the radial arm.

Figure 12-32: A simple cradle will hold work so a shaping operation will form flutes or reeds. The text describes the procedure. Be sure the work is clamped for each pass.

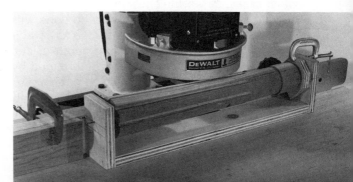

The cradle is held against the infeed fence and then moved forward until it hits a clamped stop block, which determines where the cut will end. The work is turned in the cradle the required number of degrees after each pass depending on the spacing between cuts.

The length of the cradle, which is made as shown in Figure 12-33, depends on the length of the work. The guide block must be attached to the work as shown in the drawing since it is clamped to one end of the cradle to secure the work for each pass. The guide block is turned 90° if cuts require 90° spacing, 45° if cuts will be 45° apart, and so on. Be sure the guide block is securely clamped before making each pass.

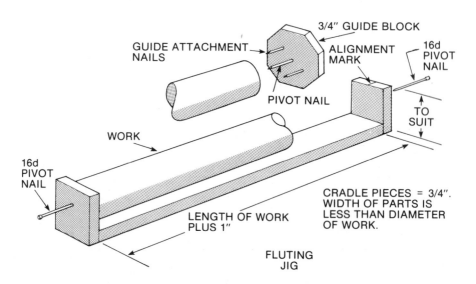

Figure 12-33: How the fluting and reeding cradle is made. The guide block is a very important component. Note that it is nailed to the end of the work. Clamping the block to the cradle also secures the work.

The knife making the flat-bottom flute in the photograph (Figure 12-32) is the groove cutter of a tongue-and-groove set. To form reeds, either the triple bead knives or the combination bead-and-cove knives can be used.

COVING WITH SHAPING KNIVES. A cove is a concave cut that can be made along stock-edges, as in Figure 12-34, or into stock surfaces, as in Figure 12-35. In most cases, as we will show in a later chapter, this type of work is done with a regular saw blade, but it can also be done with shaper knives.

All coving cuts should be regarded as scraping cuts. That is, repeat passes are used with a slight increase in depth-of-cut after each pass.

The shape of the cove will be determined by the knife that is used and by how the tool is organized. For the edge cove, the shaper head was rotated toward the column about 15° and then tilted about 15°. For the surface cove, the cutter was kept in level position but rotated toward the column about 45°. The greater the swing toward the column, the narrower the cove will be.

Figure 12-34: Coving an edge. The shaper head is swung toward the column about 15° and also tilted about 15°. This setting is just representative. The tool may be set at other angles for different cove shapes.

Figure 12-35: Here, the cutter is in level position but swung about 45° toward the column. All coving is done by combining small cuts with many passes.

All passes are made with depth-of-cut adjusted to remove about 1/16" or 1/8" of stock. For smoothest results, the cutter should just barely scrape the stock on the final pass. Two shaping knives frequently used for this type of work are the blank knives and the ogee-shaped casing knives.

More information about coving and the method of previewing the width and the depth of the cut will be presented later.

TWO KNIFE SHAPER HEAD. This accessory is used like the three-knife shaper head, but because of its heavy body construction, it can handle, for example, jointing knives that are 2" wide and almost 1/4" thick (Figure 12-36). This means that the tool can be used to make perfect jointing cuts on stock up to 2" thick (Figure 12-37).

The knives are not grooved, but the mounting system assures that each knife will cut on the same plane. Be sure the knives and the slots in the head are clean and that the knives are bottomed in the slot before tightening the lock screw.

Figure 12-36: The two-knife shaper head is a husky piece of steel which, like the three-knife head, is slotted to receive shaper knives. The blank knives, shown here mounted in the head, will prove extremely useful.

Figure 12-37: The blank knives are 2" wide and will easily joint 2" stock (which has a real thickness of 1-1/2"). Jointing cuts do not have to be deep. Remove only as much material as is necessary to produce a smooth edge.

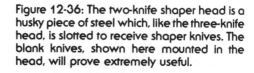

Figure 12-38: Because the ends of the jointing knives also are sharpened, they may be used efficiently for surfacing operations. Cuts don't have to be deep; 1/16" is usually enough to smooth stock.

Figure 12-39: The blank knives also do a fine job when used for panel raising. The tilt can be about 10° or 15°. Make the crossgrain cuts first. The guard is elevated to show the knives. It can be set much closer to the work.

An advantage of the jointer knives is that they are sharpened on side edges as well as the main, front edge. This allows them to be used for surfacing operations like the one shown in Figure 12-38. The tool is organized as for straight shaping with the jointer knives elevated above the table to cut about 1/16" into the stock. The pass, made slowly and steadily, is from right to left. Several passes can be made, with cutter position adjusted after each, in order to surface wide stock. This permits each pass to be made so the cutters work **with** the grain of the wood. Note, in the photograph, that a conventional-type fence may be used. A fence-cutout is required only when the stock's thickness is more than the height of the fence.

PANEL RAISING. The two-knife head, equipped with the jointer knives, is an ideal tool for panel raising operations (Figure 12-39). A conventional fence may be used as long as it has a relief area for the knives. The movable table board may not permit the shaper head to be used in tilted position. If this happens, substitute a board of similar size but with a more generous cutout.

Most panels are "raised" at an angle of 10° to 15°. When the angle is set, position the cutter so its projection in front of the fence will equal the width of the cut. Raise the knives above the table so the cut will leave a slight shoulder. Remember to make the crossgrain cuts first.

LOUVERS. To form louvers in the surface of solid stock, set the tool up as shown in Figure 12-40. This is like a horizontal shaping position but with the shaper head tilted from 5° to 15°, depending on the desired slope for the louvers. Set the knives above the table so the depth-of-cut will be about 1/4". Passes are made as in ripping operations with pusher sticks used when hands might come too close to the cutters.

Make each pass slowly and steadily from right to left. Be sure to tighten the rip lock after the tool is set for each louver-cut.

The louvers don't have to be back-to-back. Different effects can be achieved by leaving a flat area between the cuts.

Figure 12-40: Louvers are formed by tilting the shaper head and making parallel cuts. Cutter-tilt can be 5° to 15°; depth-of-cut can be about 1/4". These settings are not mandatory. Working with less tilt and a shallower cut can also be effective.

Chapter 13
Routing—Another Phase
of Woodworking

Many radial arm saws provide for routing operations by using a chuck that mounts on an auxiliary spindle. Chucks can serve the purpose, but they are usually limited in what they can grip, and a standard sawing speed doesn't approach the high rpms that are required for optimum router results.

The system we will discuss is unique in that it combines true router capability with radial arm saw flexibility. The setup is possible because of a special attachment that mounts on the arbor end of the motor, as shown in Figure 13-1. Basically, the attachment consists of two clamps. One, on a vertical plane, locks behind the motor's cover plate; the other, on a horizontal plane, grips a portable router (Figure 13-2). Because the router clamp is adjustable, it can hold almost any standard portable routing tool. Also, the clamp on the motor can be rotated, so there is no problem in placing the router perpendicular to the table.

Before using the router, be sure both parts of the attachment are locked and that the router's cord is situated so it won't interfere with the work. One way to do this is to feed the cord through the yoke area of the saw and then to an outlet. Be sure the router switch is in the "off" position before plugging it in. It is advisable to keep the radial arm saw unplugged, since its motor will not be used for routing operations.

Figure 13-1: This special clamping attachment makes it possible to use a standard portable router on the radial arm saw.

Figure 13-2: The clamp that secures the router is adjustable, so routers of various diameters may be used. Note that only the motor part of the router is used. The router's base, always a detachable part, is removed.

Cutting bits are locked in the router's chuck in normal fashion. Usually, the chuck is the collet-type; and two wrenches, turned in opposite directions, are used to secure bits and cutters. It is still important to check the owner's manual supplied with the tool you own or buy and to follow its instructions.

The shapes shown in Figure 13-3 represent the kind of work that can be accomplished by routing. Note that the results can be practical as well as decorative. It all depends on the bit or cutter that is used.

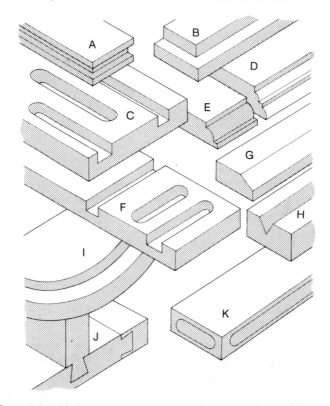

Figure 13-3: Typical shapes that can be produced with a router that is mounted on the radial arm saw: (A) End and edge grooves; (B) end and edge rabbets; (C) grooves—through, blind, and stopped; (D & E) decorative edges; (F) dadoes—through, blind, and stopped; (G) chamfers; (H) V-cuts; (I) grooves parallel to curved edges—also circular grooves; (J) dovetails; and (K) mortises. Note: Dovetails and mortises are shown in the chapter on "Wood Connections."

ROUTER BITS AND CUTTERS. Router bits, exclusive of the shapes that are available, are designed in one of two ways. The examples shown in Figure 13-4 are "pilotless" types. When a bit like this is used, the control of the cut—its depth, width, and so on—depends on how the radial arm saw is used and how the work is positioned. Generally, there are two procedures. In one, the work remains stationary and the router, controlled because of its position in the radial arm saw, is moved to make the cut. In the second procedure, the router is in a fixed position and the work, guided, for example, by a fence, is moved against the bit to make the cut.

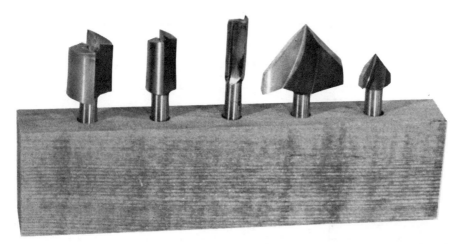

Figure 13-4: When "pilotless" bits like this are used, the control of the cut depends on how the radial arm saw is used and how the work is situated for the pass.

The router bit on the left in Figure 13-5 has an integral "pilot." The pilot, which is like an extension of the bit's shaft, rides against part of the work's edge and so controls the width of the cut. The maximum cut-width, not its depth, will be from the outer edge of the bit's profile to the outer surface of the pilot.

A problem with an integral pilot is that its rpms are the same as the bit's cutting edges and this can result in burn marks and indenting. It is good practice to keep the cutter moving and not try to cut too deeply in order to minimize and even eliminate the imperfections. Other types of piloted bits, like the one on the right-hand side in Figure 13-6, are available. These are equipped with ball bearings that rotate independently of the cutting edges. They turn only in relation to the feed-speed of the tool or the work. The result is zero friction, so there is no chance of indenting or burning the work.

Typical bits and cutters and the shapes they produce are listed in Figure 13-7.

Figure 13-5: This illustrates the difference between two basic types of router bits. The one on the left has an integral pilot which can ride against part of the work's edge to control the cut.

Figure 13-6: The cutter on the right has a ball bearing pilot. Since the bearing rotates independently of feed-speed, there is no chance that the pilot will indent or burn the wood.

SHAPE PRODUCED BY BIT	NAME OF BIT	TYPICAL SIZES
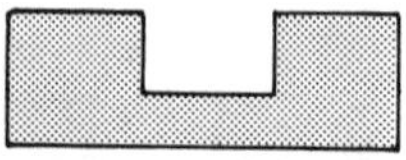	Straight	1/4" to 3/4"
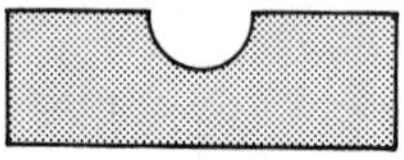	Veining	1/16" to 7/32"
	V-grooving	3/8" and 7/8"
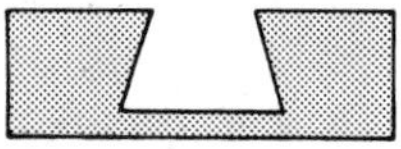	Dovetail	1/4" and 1/2"
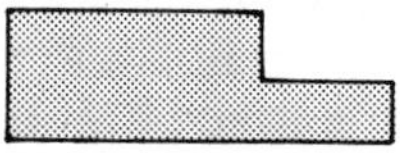	Rabbeting	1/4" and 3/8"
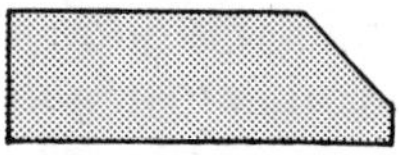	Chamfering	5/8"
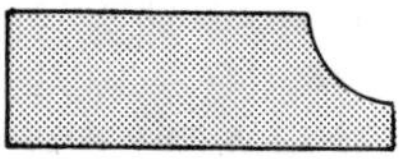	Cove	3/16" to 1/2"
	Beading	1/8" to 3/8"
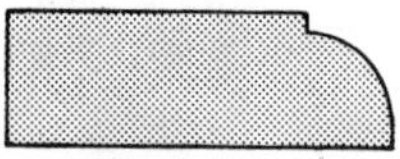	Corner rounds	3/16" to 1/2"
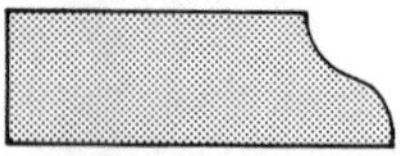	Ogee	3/16" and 9/32"
	Roman ogee	5/32" and 1/4"

Note: Only a sampling shown, other types and sizes available. Most common bits have 1/4" shanks.

Figure 13-7: Typical router bits and cutters.

GENERAL PRACTICE. When moving the work to make a cut, feed direction should be **against** the cutter's direction of rotation. The cutter rotates in a clockwise direction when the operator's viewpoint is above the router and downward.

Excessive feed-speeds, whether the work or the router is being moved, will result in inferior cuts and may even cause undue wear on the cutter. On the other hand, a feed-speed that is too slow can cause the bit's cutting edges or a pilot to burn the wood.

Because wood densities vary, a correct feed-speed must be judged by how well the cut is progressing. If you find that the cutter chatters or stalls, you are probably cutting too deeply or too fast. If a cutter remains too long in a given area so that it does more burnishing than cutting, then you are feeding too slowly. A few practice cuts will acquaint you with how the tool should "feel," sound, and move.

STRAIGHT CUTS. Cuts made across the grain to produce, for example, rabbets and dadoes, are done with the tool set up in crosscut position (Figure 13-8). The pass procedure is the same one used for doing a crosscut with a saw blade. Cut-depth is determined by the cutter's height above the table; cut-width, by the size of the bit that is used. The cut-width, however, does not have to be limited by bit-size. Any cut can be made wider, regardless of the bit's diameter, simply by making repeat passes.

It is most advisable, if an assortment of straight bits is available, to use one that will produce the correct cut-width in a single pass. How **deep** you can cut in a single pass—and this is a general rule—will depend on the density of the wood. Try a 1/8"-deep cut to start; let the results guide you. Judge by how smoothly the cutter works and by the quality of the cut.

STOPPED CUTS. Stopped and blind dadoes are also made in crosscut position (Figure 13-9). The length of a blind dado is controlled by using two roller stops; one is placed between the roller head and the column, the other between the roller head and the forward end of the radial arm. The stopped dado requires a single roller head stop.

Figure 13-8: Dadoes and rabbets can be formed with router bits when the tool is used in crosscut position. Feed the cutter slowly—make repeat passes on deep cuts.

Figure 13-9: The length of stopped or blind dadoes is controlled with roller head stops. Use two stops for blind dadoes, one stop for stopped dadoes.

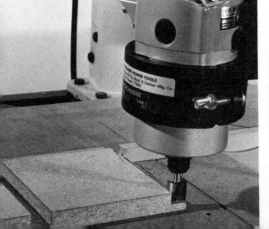

Start the operation with the cutter raised to clear the workpiece. Slowly lower the cutter until it bites into the work and then pull the cutter forward. It is advisable to secure the work with a clamp when repeat passes are required. This will assure accuracy since the work will stay put during any number of cuts.

Cuts like this, done with a router bit, will have semicircular ends, so the insert piece must be shaped to fit, or the insert can be notched to clear the rounded portion of the dado.

GROOVING. Grooves are formed with the tool set in rip position as shown in Figure 13-10. The router's position is secured with the rip lock. The work, guided by the fence, is moved to make the cut. General rules apply—move the work slowly, don't cut too deeply, use pushers.

Stopped or blind cuts are made as described for dadoing except that stop blocks on the fence, instead of roller head stops, are used to control the length of the cuts.

SHAPING WITH A FENCE. Edges can be shaped by using the shaper table described in Chapter 12 (Figure 13-11). The router is moved as far back as possible and the table is situated so its fences can be positioned to provide clearance for the cutter. The cutter's height is controlled with the radial arm's elevating handle, the cutter's projection in front of the fence by moving the motor along the arm. Be sure to tighten the rip lock.

When the router is used this way, the work feed-direction is from left to right. The router bit being used in the photograph is a "roman ogee."

Figure 13-10: Grooves or edge rabbets can be formed with the tool set in rip position. Move the work against the cutter's direction of rotation. Use pushers to complete cuts.

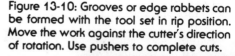

Figure 13-11: This shows how the router may be used with the homemade shaper table. The work, held snugly against the fence, is moved from left to right.

A SPECIAL SETUP. Much controlled work can be done with the router by making and installing the project that is shown in Figure 13-12. This is only a sheet of plywood with a wide slot (or dado) run across its center. The plywood is secured to a strip of wood that fits the table slot ordinarily occupied by the guide fence. The fulcrum pin is included to provide support when the router is used to shape irregular edges. The guides shown in Figure 13-13 are part of the project and serve particular purposes, as we will show.

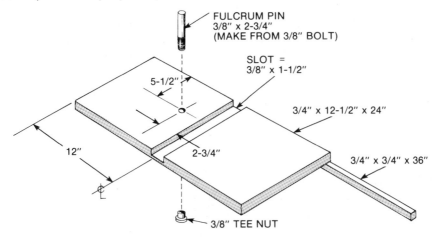

Figure 13-12: This project will make it easy to have complete control over many router operations.

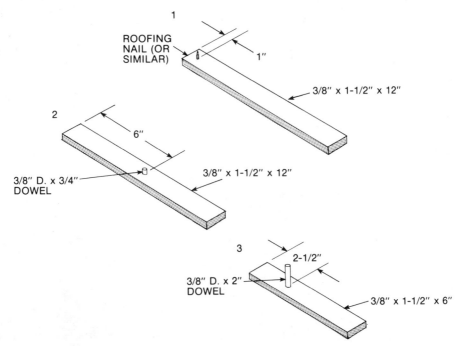

Figure 13-13: These guides are used in the special table that was shown in the previous illustration.

Guide number 1, used as shown in Figure 13-14, establishes a pivot point so work can be rotated for circular cuts. In this case, a circular groove is needed so a straight bit is locked in the router. The distance from the pivot to the cutter is set to suit the work, and then the guide's position is locked with a small brad driven through the guide and into the table.

The center of the work is indented with an awl or similar device, and then the work is placed over the pivot. The cut starts by lowering the router to penetrate the work and then slowly rotating the work against the cutter's direction of rotation (Figure 13-15). Very deep cuts can be done by making repeat passes.

Many workers use this system to form circular parts. Work with the smallest straight bit available. Keep deepening the cut with each pass until the cutter is through the work. Hold the work firmly; make the last pass very slowly. Be sure the cutter is situated over the slot in the table.

The pivot system may also be used to shape circular edges (Figure 13-16). Mount the work on the pivot and hold it firmly while bringing the cutter forward to make contact. Then, with the rip lock tightened, slowly rotate the work to make the cut.

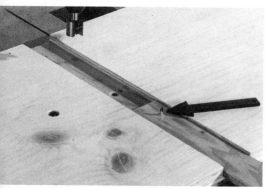

Figure 13-14: The number 1 guide establishes a pivot point so work can be rotated for circular cuts. The arrow indicates the nail that is used as a pivot. Guides are locked in place with small brads.

Figure 13-15: Using the pivot guide to form a circular groove. The work is held flat on the table and rotated in a clockwise direction.

Figure 13-16: Here, the pivot guide is being used to shape circular edges.

IRREGULAR EDGES. There are two ways to shape curved edges. One system, shown in Figure 13-17, uses guide number 2 and the fulcrum pin. This setup makes it possible to work with bits that do not have a pilot. The guide is locked in the table so its dowel pin is exactly centered under the bit. The bit's height is adjusted for the cut. In this case, a large V-grooving bit will be used to form a chamfer.

The pass is started by bracing the work against the fulcrum pin and then slowly advancing it into the cutter until it bears firmly against the dowel pin in the guide (Figure 13-18). At this point the work may be swung free of the fulcrum pin. Move the work slowly. Be sure to keep the work against the dowel pin and flat on the table throughout the pass.

The second method of shaping irregular edges is shown in Figure 13-19. Here, the cutter has an integral pilot which makes it possible to do the work in freehand fashion. Even though it is not shown in the photograph, the fulcrum pin can be used to advantage on this operation even if only to get the cut started.

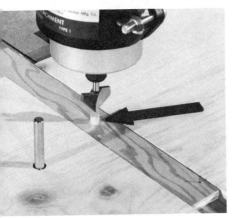

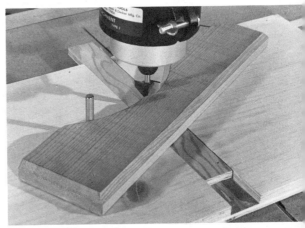

Figure 13-17: The number 2 guide is organized in this way when a pilotless bit is used to cut irregular edges. The guide and the cutter are positioned on the same vertical center line.

Figure 13-18: Start the cut by bracing the work against the fulcrum pin and then slowly advancing it until it makes contact with the cutter and is firmly against the guide's pin.

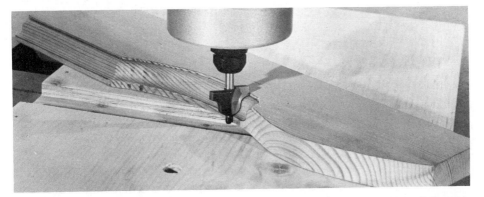

Figure 13-19: Irregular edges can also be shaped with cutters that have integral pilots. In such cases, the work bears against the pilot.

INTERNAL ROUTING. Because the router is adjustable vertically by raising or lowering the radial arm, it is possible to place work and then lower the router so the cutter can work on inside edges (Figure 13-20). The cut can be controlled by using the number 2 guide or by working with a piloted bit.

PATTERN ROUTING. This system can be used when routing is required on many similar pieces. An example application is a set of drawer fronts having the same routed design. The sectional view in Figure 13-21 shows how pattern routing works. The pattern, tack-nailed to the underside of the work, rides the guide pin and thus controls the cut.

Figure 13-20: Internal cuts are done by first placing the work and then lowering the cutter. The cut can be controlled by using the number 2 guide or by working with a piloted bit.

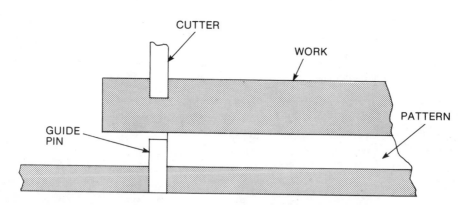

Figure 13-21: This sectional view shows how pattern routing is accomplished.

The number 2 guide is locked in the table so its dowel pin is exactly centered with the router bit. The dowel pin and the router bit must have similar diameters. In this case, each is 1/4" (Figure 13-22).

The pattern, shaped like the cut that is required, is secured to the underside of the work either with small flathead screws or brads (Figure 13-23). Often, the pattern is equipped with several screws that project just enough so the work can be held without slippage.

Start with the cutter elevated above the work and with the pattern bearing against the guide pin. Slowly lower the cutter to the required depth and then move the work to make the cut, being careful to keep the pattern in constant contact with the guide pin (Figure 13-24).

CURVED GROOVES. This method solves the problem of forming grooves that must be parallel to a curved edge. The number 3 guide is locked in the table in the position shown in Figure 13-25. The distance from the guide to the cutter equals the edge-distance of the groove. After the bit is lowered to the required cut-depth, move the work so its edge constantly bears against the guide pin.

As you make the pass, keep the work positioned so a line that is a tangent to the curve at the point of cut will be perpendicular to the guide pin's center line.

Figure 13-22: The number 2 guide is locked in place so its dowel pin is accurately aligned with the cutter. It is all right to work with a cutter that is larger than the pin as long as they have the same vertical center line.

Figure 13-23: The pattern, which is a duplicate of the shape that will be routed, is tack-nailed to the underside of the work.

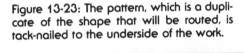

Figure 13-24: Routing is done by lowering the bit to the required depth and then moving the work so there is constant contact between the pattern and the guide pin.

Figure 13-25: Grooves that must be parallel to a curved edge are made this way. The distance between the cutter and the dowel pin equals the edge distance of the groove.

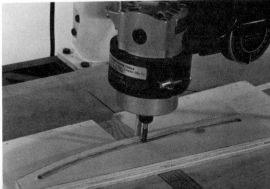

FREEHAND ROUTING. Since a router bit can cut in any direction, it is an ideal tool to use for intricate designs, nameplates, house numbers, and so on.

The design is sketched on the surface of the work; the router's height is adjusted for the desired cut-depth. If, for example, house numbers are being formed and they must be raised, the background is removed as shown in Figure 13-26. If the figures were to be incised, then, of course, cuts would be limited to the number areas.

Since this is a freehand operation with the work having to be moved in many directions, the final appearance of the project will depend on how carefully you work. Use a large bit to remove the bulk of the waste. Then switch to a smaller bit to do the touch-up work close to figures.

FORMING MOLDINGS. The parts that are shown in Figure 13-27 can all be formed with router operations. The final design depends on how the tool is moved—crosscut position, rip position, angular cuts—and the type of router bit that is used. Parts so formed can be used for decorative details on projects or as material for assembling frames.

Figure 13-26: Freehand routing is done to produce projects like nameplates and house numbers. Cuts must be made in all directions so the work must be held firmly and moved slowly.

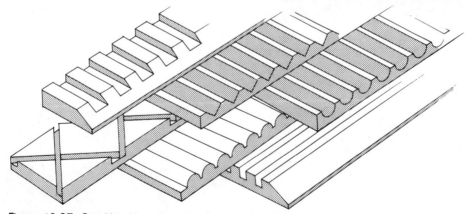

Figure 13-27: Cuts like this can produce various types of molding or components for decorative projects.

Some of the most popular designs call for making cuts across stock that has to be ripped to a useable width. This is a crosscut action, whether the cut is completely across the stock or stopped as shown in Figure 13-28. In this situation, a roller head stop is used to limit the length of the cut.

Cut-spacing can be controlled by making a mark on the guide fence, but this leaves room for error. It is more advisable to use the method shown in Figure 13-29. A nail through the guide fence acts as a mechanical spacer. The work is moved so that each cut, placed against the nail, accurately positions the work for the next cut. In a later chapter we'll show a special guide fence with a series of holes through it so the nail-guide can be positioned for various spacings.

Pieces that are formed using these techniques can be used as is, but they may also be strip-cut to form slim moldings as shown in Figure 13-30.

Figure 13-28: Cuts across the stock are made with the tool in crosscut position. Use a roller head stop when you wish to limit the length of the cuts.

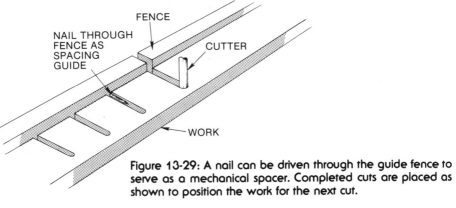

Figure 13-29: A nail can be driven through the guide fence to serve as a mechanical spacer. Completed cuts are placed as shown to position the work for the next cut.

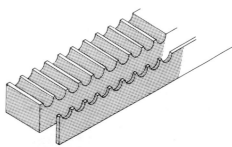

Figure 13-30: Surface-routed work can be strip-cut to produce slim moldings.

SPECIAL TABLES. To this point, all router operations have been done with the tool in vertical position, but it can be used in horizontal position as well. Because of the way the router is mounted, there is a limit to how close a cutting bit can be to the table. Therefore, a higher work surface with its own fence, like the one shown in Figure 13-31, must be installed.

To situate the router when starting from the crosscut position, loosen the yoke lock and rotate the router 90° toward the column. Raise the radial arm as high as possible, then loosen the bevel lock and tilt the router downward 90°. Tighten the bevel lock and move the router as far back as it will go. This puts the router in a horizontal position with the cutter end pointing forward.

Figure 13-31: This auxiliary table, with its own fence, allows the router to be used in horizontal position.

The following procedure suggests a way to position the router so it will have more room behind the fence. Swing the radial arm to the left about 10° or 15° and then rotate the router counterclockwise until its axis is perpendicular to the fence. The opening in the fence can still be positioned correctly in relation to the cutter because the project can be moved longitudinally.

Edges can be shaped by positioning the cutter and the work as shown in Figure 13-32. The pass is made from left to right. The cutter can be elevated to shape top corners but it is advisable to have the cutter under the work whenever possible. One reason for this is that the cutter won't cause gouge marks should you accidentally lift the work during the pass.

Figure 13-32: The work is placed flat on the table and snug against the fence, then moved from left to right for the cut.

Figure 13-33: In this illustration, a V-grooving bit is being used to form chamfers. Whenever possible, organize the setup so the cutter will be under the work.

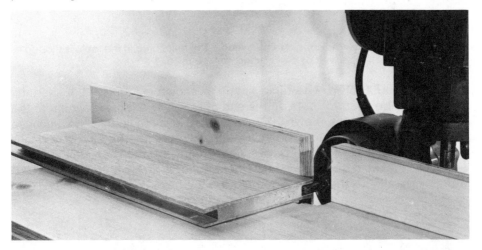

Figure 13-34: The horizontal router setup has practical applications as well as decorative ones. Here, a straight bit is being used to form an edge groove.

As shown in Figure 13-33, a V-grooving bit can be used to chamfer edges. When a similar cut is required on four edges, make the second cut on one surface after turning the stock end for end. Flip the stock so that it rests on the opposite surface and repeat the procedure.

The setup can be used for practical as well as decorative applications as demonstrated by the edge-grooving being done in Figure 13-34. The cutting can be done with a straight bit whose diameter equals the width of the groove. The cutter's height is adjusted so the groove will be centered. Another way is to work with a bit whose diameter is **less** than the groove's width. Set the cutter so its height above the table will equal the edge distance of the groove. Make one pass, then flip the stock so it rests on its opposite surface and make a second pass.

Construction details for the auxiliary routing table are shown in Figure 13-35.

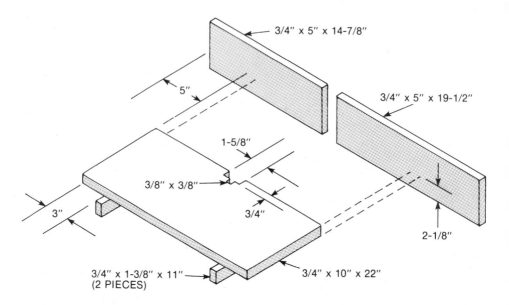

Figure 13-35: This is how the special table is made. The relief area in the table is shaped as shown so that piloted as well as plain cutters can be used.

A SECOND TABLE DESIGN. This table, set up as shown in Figure 13-36, permits the router to be used for cuts on the end of stock. The table is similar to the number 2 table that was shown in Chapter 9, but its dimensions differ because of the router's position and size. To position the router for this kind of horizontal cutting, start with the tool in crosscut position and with the router elevated well above the table. Loosen the bevel lock and rotate the router downward 90° until it is parallel to the table. Then tighten the bevel lock.

Figure 13-36: The second table permits the router to be used in this position.

A typical operation is shown in Figure 13-37, where a straight bit is being used to cut an end groove. The work remains in a stationary position; the router is moved forward to make the cut. It is advisable to clamp the work when repeat passes are required. If the same cut is needed on many pieces, a stop block arrangement should be used to position the work.

Other shapes that can be formed with the router used in this position— among them, round-end mortises and dovetail tongues—will be shown in Chapter 19 on "Wood Connections."

Figure 13-38 shows how the table is made.

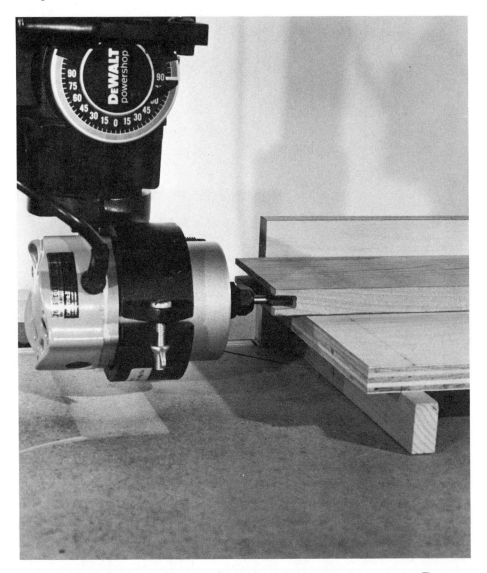

Figure 13-37: The work is held stationary, the router is moved to make the cut. This setup permits many types of cuts that are useful in wood joinery. Some of them will be shown in Chapter 19 on "Wood Connections."

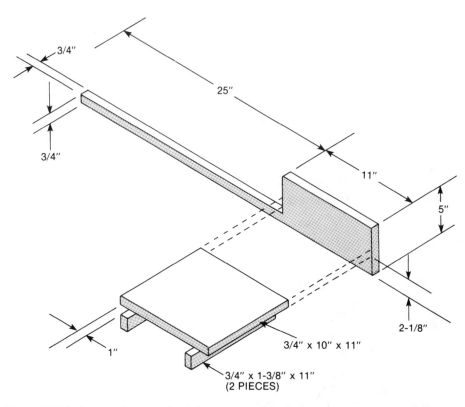

Figure 13-38: Construction details of the second table that is used with the router in horizontal position.

Chapter 14
Using the Radial Arm Saw for Drilling

It may seem strange to think of the radial arm saw as a drilling tool, yet much of the flexibility which makes it so suitable for sawing and other woodworking operations can be utilized for drilling and boring. In some cases, standard drilling chores that are difficult, if possible to do on a conventional drill press, can be done more easily and more accurately on the radial arm saw.

One reason is that drilling is done with the cutting tool in a horizontal position. The action is that of a horizontal boring machine, a tool that is common in industry but rarely found in a small shop. Some of the jobs that are easier to do when the drilling tool can be used in horizontal mode include drilling into the edge of stock when dowels are used to reinforce edge-to-edge joints; drilling holes into the end of stock; drilling into miter cuts; drilling concentric and radial holes. This kind of work can be done regardless of the length of the workpieces.

HOW DRILLING TOOLS ARE MOUNTED. The machine has a threaded auxiliary spindle at the end of the motor opposite the main arbor. The spindle accommodates a three-jaw chuck, which is a vise-like device that grips the drilling tool. Before mounting the chuck, remove everything that might be on the main arbor—cutting tool, collars, lock nut—but remount and secure the saw guard. The guard can remain as a protective device for the main arbor, which will always be turning as drilling jobs are done.

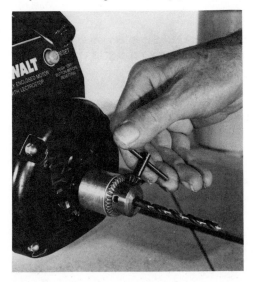

Figure 14-1: A three-jaw chuck mounted on an auxiliary shaft, which is on the motor end opposite the main arbor. A special key is used to secure drilling tools.

Fraction	Letter	No.	Decimal
		80	.0135
		79	.0145
1/64			.0156
		78	.0160
		77	.0180
		76	.0200
		75	.0210
		74	.0225
		73	.0240
		72	.0250
		71	.0260
		70	.0280
		69	.0292
		68	.0310
1/32			.0312
		67	.0320
		66	.0330
		65	.0350
		64	.0360
		63	.0370
		62	.0380
		61	.0390
		60	.0400
		59	.0410
		58	.0420
		57	.0430
		56	.0465
3/64			.0469
		55	.0520
		54	.0550
		53	.0595
1/8			.1250
		30	.1285
		29	.1360
		28	.1405
9/64			.1406
		27	.1440
		26	.1470
		25	.1495
		24	.1520
		23	.1540
5/32			.1562
		22	.1570
		21	.1590
		20	.1610
		19	.1660
		18	.1695
11/64			.1719
		17	.1730
		16	.1770
		15	.1800
		14	.1820
		13	.1850
3/16			.1875
		12	.1890
		11	.1910
		10	.1935
		9	.1960
		8	.1990
		7	.2010
13/64			.2031
		6	.2040
	O		.3160
	P		.3230
21/64			.3281
	Q		.3320
	R		.3390
11/32			.3437
	S		.3480
	T		.3580
23/64			.3594
	U		.3680
3/8			.3750
	V		.3770
	W		.3860
25/64			.3906
	X		.3970
	Y		.4040
13/32			.4062
	Z		.4130
27/64			.4219
7/16			.4375
29/64			.4531
15/32			.4687
31/64			.4844
1/2			.5000
33/64			.5156
17/32			.5312
35/64			.5469
9/16			.5625
37/64			.5781
19/32			.5937
39/64			.6094

Fraction	Letter	No.	Decimal	Fraction	Letter	No.	Decimal	Fraction	Letter	No.	Decimal
1/16			.0625			5	.2055	5/8			.6250
		52	.0635			4	.2090	41/64			.6406
		51	.0670			3	.2130	21/32			.6562
		50	.0700	7/32			.2187	43/64			.6719
		49	.0730			2	.2210	11/16			.6875
		48	.0760			1	.2280	45/64			.7031
5/64			.0781		A		.2340	23/32			.7187
		47	.0785	15/64			.2344	47/64			.7344
		46	.0810		B		.2380	3/4			.7500
		45	.0820		C		.2420	49/64			.7656
		44	.0860		D		.2460	25/32			.7812
		43	.0890	1/4	E		.2500	51/64			.7969
		42	.0935		F		.2570	13/16			.8125
3/32			.0937		G		.2610	53/64			.8281
		41	.0960	17/64			.2656	27/32			.8437
		40	.0980		H		.2660	55/64			.8594
		39	.0995		I		.2720	7/8			.8750
		38	.1015		J		.2770	57/64			.8906
		37	.1040		K		.2810	29/32			.9062
		36	.1065	9/32			.2812	59/64			.9219
7/64			.1094		L		.2900	15/16			.9375
		35	.1100		M		.2950	61/64			.9531
		34	.1110	19/64			.2969	31/32			.9687
		33	.1130		N		.3020	63/64			.9844
		32	.1160	5/16			.3125	1			1.0000
		31	.1200								

Figure 14-2: Twist drills come in letter, number, and fractional sizes. The chart shows what is available in each category and gives the decimal equivalent.

To mount the chuck, insert the Allen wrench in the front end of the main arbor as you would when tightening the lock nut to secure a saw blade. Hold the Allen wrench, which will keep the arbor still, and thread the chuck onto the auxiliary spindle. Hand pressure will be enough to firmly seat the chuck.

The special key provided with the chuck is used as shown in Figure 14-1. Turn the key counterclockwise to spread the jaws of the chuck. Turn the key clockwise after a drill bit is inserted until the jaws of the chuck are tight against the shank of the tool. Then remove the key. The latter caution may seem unnecessary, but at times operators forget to remove it, and it becomes a projectile when the tool is turned on.

DRILLING TOOLS. Because of the chuck's direction of rotation, conventional drill bits may be used. However, because the tool has a single speed, it isn't possible to use all **types** of drilling tools. Expansive bits, hole saws, fly cutters, and other tools that must run at slow speeds should not be used in the radial arm saw.

This doesn't impose too much of a restriction on general drilling in wood since twist drills, for example, are available in a broad size range, as shown in Figure 14-2. Some types of spade bits are designed to cut efficiently at higher-than-average speeds. If the tool you try to use vibrates when you turn on the machine or if it chatters when it penetrates the work, you are probably using a wrong cutter. Drilling should progress smoothly and holes produced should be clean.

GENERAL PRACTICE. The bit must be fed into the work so that it is constantly cutting. Forcing the bit will cause it to choke, but feeding too slowly will do more burnishing than cutting and will also cause premature dulling of cutting edges.

Some drilling tools, like twist drills, have flutes that are designed to carry away waste material. They should be retracted occasionally when drilling so the waste will be ejected and the flutes kept clear.

Many times it is wise to drill pilot holes first. For example, if you need 1/2" holes, drill 1/4" holes first and then open them up to full size. This will help you to be more accurate and will result in cleaner holes.

Whenever a jig, fixture, or guide isn't used to position work, the location of the hole should be indicated by accurate layout. The easiest way is to draw lines that intersect where the center of the hole must be. Work with a square and a sharp, hard pencil. Indent the intersection with an awl or something similar. This will provide a seat for the point of the drill bit.

Dividers or a compass can be used to transfer measurements or to mark a line for spacing between holes.

SURFACE DRILLING. In many cases, holes can be drilled in the surface of work by setting up for the job as shown in Figure 14-3. The tool itself is set up in the out-rip position. This situates the drilling tool so it faces the back of the machine. Note that the work is in the guide-fence slot behind the wide, movable table board so it can be firmly held merely by tightening the table clamp screws.

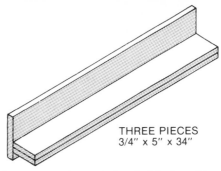

Figure 14-3: Surface drilling can often be done in this way. The work is locked between table boards. Use a backup piece when the hole goes through the work.

Figure 14-4: A simple height block and fence assembly can be used for edge drilling. A piece of 2" stock may be substituted for the two table boards.

THREE PIECES
3/4" x 5" x 34"

Figure 14-5: A more sophisticated unit for edge drilling. Long table and fence provide good work support. A special guide is used to space holes accurately and automatically.

A back-up piece, clamped in place, is used when the hole must be through the work. This will eliminate the splintering that occurs where a drill breaks through. The work receives additional support from a block of wood placed between it and the column.

Edge-distance for holes is established by raising or lowering the radial arm; drilling is done by moving the motor along the arm. Use a roller head stop when the hole must be drilled to a particular depth. In a situation like this, it is advisable to use the stop even when the hole is through. This will prevent any possibility of moving the bit far enough to hit the column.

Holes can be drilled at an angle merely by swinging the radial arm to the right or the left. Be careful on angled holes when making the initial contact, since the point of the bit may tend to wander. Feed very slowly until the drill point has penetrated.

EDGE DRILLING. Because there is a limit to how close to the table a drilling tool can come, stock to be edge-drilled must be elevated to a correct position. This can easily be done by putting together a height-block fence assembly like the one shown in Figure 14-4. However, since the radial arm saw is such a fine horizontal boring machine, it is wise to consider a more sophisticated fixture. The one shown in Figure 14-5 has a substantial table and fence to support long work and is designed with adjustable guides so that spacing between holes can be accurate and automatic. The unit locks in the guide fence slot behind the wide, movable table board.

Figure 14-6 shows how the fixture is put together. Don't neglect to install the tee-nut before the center piece is put in place.

Work to be drilled is placed on the fixture's table as shown in Figure 14-7. The edge distance of the holes is determined by raising or lowering the radial arm. Use a roller head stop if hole depth must be limited. If holes are needed through the stock, be sure to use a piece of scrap wood between the work and the fence.

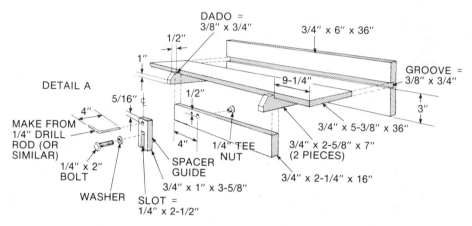

Figure 14-6: Construction details of the special edge-drilling fixture. Detail A shows how the spacer guide is made.

Figure 14-7: Holes are formed by moving the drill bit toward the column. A roller head stop, locked on the arm between the column and the yoke, is used to control hole-depth.

The distance between holes can be gauged with layout marks, but spacing can be more accurate and automatic if the spacing guide is used (Figure 14-8). Drill the first hole, then lock the guide to provide correct spacing and so its pin will engage the hole. Thereafter, the work is moved so each new hole will be engaged by the pin.

When work like this is done for dowels used in edge-to-edge joints, it isn't necessary for the holes to be exactly centered in the edge of the stock. Just be sure to place the same surface of each part down on the table. The same surface of the parts must be on the same plane when the pieces are assembled.

The guide pin works with 1/4" holes. If larger holes are needed, the 1/4" holes can be opened up after the initial operation.

Figure 14-8: The spacer guide can be rotated and is adjustable vertically so it can be used for various stock thicknesses and hole spacings. The lock pin engages a hole already drilled and so positions the work for the next hole.

HOW TO DRILL A MORTISE. The mortise (or cavity) that is required for a mortise-tenon joint can be formed in the following way. Mark the edge of the stock to indicate the center line of the mortise. Place the work on the table and adjust the height of the radial arm so the point of the drill bit, whose diameter equals the width of the mortise, is aligned with the center line mark. Drill two holes that will be the end-points of the mortise and then, between them, drill a series of overlapping holes to clean out the bulk of the waste material (Figure 14-9). Use a roller head stop to control the depth of the holes—actually, the depth of the mortise being formed.

The small amount of stock that remains after the drilling process is cleaned away with a sharp chisel. Mortises formed this way will have round ends. This doesn't reduce the strength of the joint but does require the ends of the tenon to be rounded off to match.

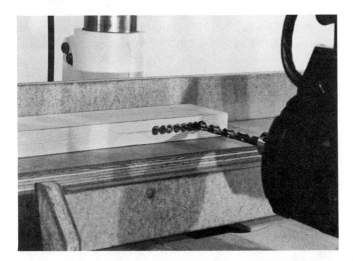

Figure 14-9: A series of overlapping holes drilled on a common center line will remove the bulk of the waste when forming a mortise. Remaining material is cleaned out with a chisel.

RADIAL HOLES IN CYLINDERS. Place a V-block on the table so the V faces the drilling tool. Adjust the height of the radial arm so the point of the drill bit will be exactly on the center line of the V. Pull the drilling tool away, place the work in the V, and drill the holes as shown in Figure 14-10.

This same setup can be used when a hole is needed in the corner of a square piece. An example of application is a square leg whose position will be secured with a screw.

Figure 14-10: A V-block makes it easy to accurately drill radial holes in cylinders. The point of the drill bit must be aligned with the center of the V.

END DRILLING. In general, end drilling on the radial arm saw is done by situating the drilling tool in a horizontal position that is parallel to the guide fence. The work is placed on a height block, which may have its own fence, and is moved into the cutting tool. A more flexible system which permits either the work or the tool to be fed and which allows for other types of drilling operations requires the work table that is shown in Figure 14-11.

The project, which is made as shown in Figure 14-12, includes an adjustable fence which assures that work to be end-drilled will be square to the drilling tool, a sliding pivot guide for drilling radial holes in stock edges, and an optional guide for positioning work for drilling in the end of miter cuts.

To position the tool for use with the table, set it in the in-rip position. This will position drilling tools so they point **away** from the column. The project locks in place behind the tool's main table in the slot ordinarily occupied by the guide fence. Place the project so that a drill bit will be on the center line of the slot in the table.

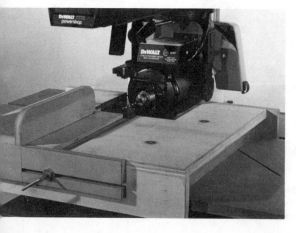

Figure 14-11: This special table for end drilling has its own adjustable fence and may be equipped with guides for other drilling chores.

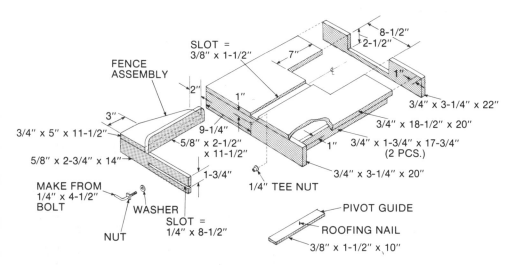

Figure 14-12: Construction details of end-drilling table. Install the tee-nut before parts are assembled. The pivot guide is used to control circular work that needs edge radial holes.

Work to be end-drilled is placed as shown in Figure 14-13. There are several ways to control the depth of a hole. In the illustration (Figure 14-13), the drill bit position is secured by tightening the rip lock on the radial arm. Work is moved along the fence until it is halted by the stop block that is clamped to the table.

A second method calls for holding the work securely on the table while the bit is moved into it by pulling the motor forward. In this case, the depth of the hole is controlled by using a roller head stop.

A third method requires that a "stop" be used right on the drilling tool (Figure 14-14). This practical gadget comes in several sizes, each of which is adjustable to suit drill bits of various diameters. You know the hole will be at the depth you want when the stop hits the edge of the work.

Figure 14-13: End holes can be drilled by locking the bit's position and then moving the work forward to a stop block that controls hole-depth. It is also possible to secure the work and move the bit forward, in which case a roller head stop is used to limit the depth of the hole.

Figure 14-14: This kind of stop is used on the drilling tool. Various sizes are available and each is adjustable for different size bits. The distance the bit is allowed to project from the front of the stop determines the depth of the hole.

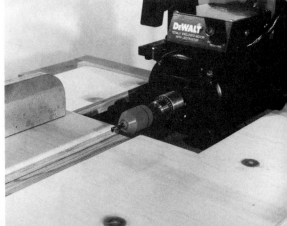

DRILLING IN MITERS. The only difference between simple end-drilling and drilling in miters is that the work must be positioned at a specific angle so the drill bit will be square to the surface of the cut (Figure 14-15). To position the work, make a guide like the one shown in Figure 14-16. This is clamped to the fence and the work is held firmly against it while the drilling is done. The work may be hand-held or, for more security, can be locked in place with a clamp.

Figure 14-15: A special guide is clamped to the fence to position work that has been miter-cut. This assures that the holes will be perpendicular to the surface of the cut.

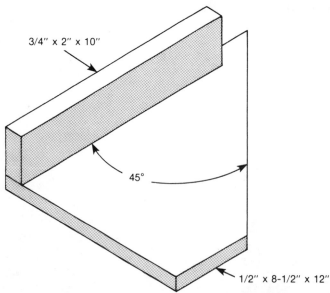

3/4" x 2" x 10"

45°

1/2" x 8-1/2" x 12"

Figure 14-16: Construction details of the miter guide.

CONCENTRIC HOLES. Holes can be drilled in the end of cylinders by working as shown in Figure 14-17. The fence is locked in place so the vertical center lines of the drill bit and the V-block will be similar. The height of the drill bit must be on the horizontal center line of the work. The center of the work can be marked by using a center finder. Commercial units are available, but you can make one along the lines suggested in Figure 14-18.

Place the work in the tool and mark one diameter. Turn the work approximately 90° and mark a second diameter. The intersection of the marks will be the center of the work. Note that you can find the center of square as well as round work.

Figure 14-17: The V-block positions cylinders for concentric drilling. The bit must be centered over the V and its point must be on the work's horizontal center line.

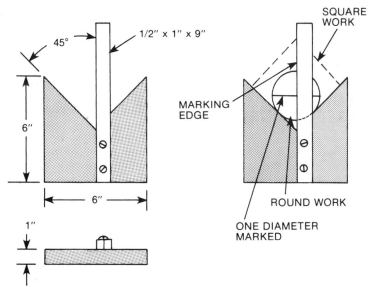

Figure 14-18: This homemade tool is used to locate centers on the end of round or square stock.

RADIAL HOLES IN EDGES. Figure 14-19 shows how the pivot guide (detailed in Figure 14-12) is used to control the position of circular work that requires edge radial holes. The work, marked with diameters to indicate hole positions, is centered over the pivot point in the guide. The work is rotated the required number of degrees, depending on layout, for each hole (Figure 14-20). Since the pivot guide is tack-nailed to the table, the distance from the center of the work to the point of the drill will be constant. Use a roller head stop or a stop on the drill bit to control the depth of the holes.

Figure 14-19: The position of the pivot guide is secured with a small brad driven through it into the table.

Figure 14-20: The work is placed so its center is over the pin in the guide. Then it is rotated the desired number of degrees for each hole required. Control hole-depth with a stop on the bit or by using a roller head stop.

EDGE HOLES. Edge holes are easy to drill by using the fixture that was described early in this chapter, but if the operator wishes, the end drilling table can be equipped for similar operations by adding the fence that is shown in Figure 14-21. The fence, put together as shown in Figure 14-22, is locked to the table with one or two clamps. The work is placed flat on the table and against the fence, thus assuring that its edge will be perpendicular to the drill bit (Figure 14-23).

Drilling is done by pulling the motor forward. Control hole-depth by using a roller head stop.

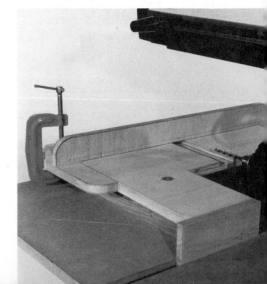

Figure 14-21: The end-drilling table can also be used for edge drilling if it is equipped with its own fence.

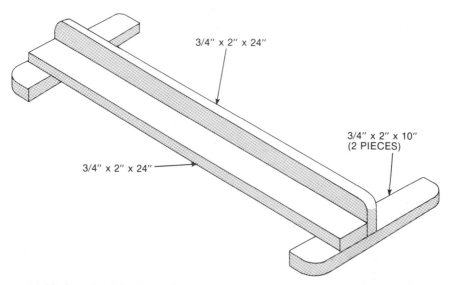

3/4" x 2" x 24"

3/4" x 2" x 10"
(2 PIECES)

3/4" x 2" x 24"

Figure 14-22: Details of the fence that can be made for the end-drilling table.

Figure 14-23: The fence is clamped to the table to position work for edge drilling. With this setup, and also with the edge-drilling fixture that was shown earlier, there is no limit to the length of work that can be handled.

RADIAL HOLES IN SURFACES. This kind of work, like edge radial holes, is also done with a pivot guide, but since the work must be positioned on a vertical plane, a system like the one in Figure 14-24 must be used.

Figure 14-24: This vertical support system makes it possible to accurately drill radial holes in surfaces. The arrow indicates the pivot guide's pin.

The support unit is shown in Figure 14-25. The vertical part locks behind the wide, movable table board in the guide-fence slot. The horizontal part is dimensioned and cut out so it will brace against the column. Thus, drilling pressure will not cause deflection that can spoil accuracy.

The pivot guide is held in place with a small brad. The work, marked for hole locations, is centered over the pivot pin. Holes are drilled by moving the drilling tool toward the column with hole-depth controlled with a roller head stop.

The work can be hand-held, but it is advisable to use a clamp as shown in Figure 14-26. Rotate the work so the tip of the drilling tool is on a layout mark. Secure the work with a clamp and then do the drilling.

The vertical support piece is U-shaped so the radial arm can be moved up or down. This, plus the fact that the pivot guide is adjustable, affords a reasonable amount of flexibility in the placement of work and location of holes.

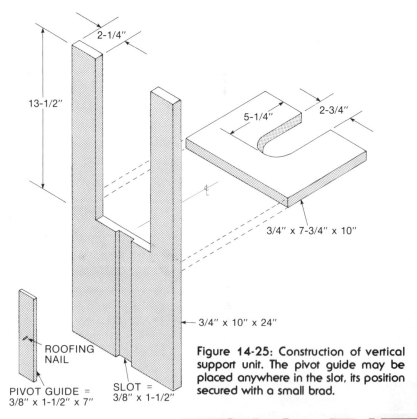

Figure 14-25: Construction of vertical support unit. The pivot guide may be placed anywhere in the slot, its position secured with a small brad.

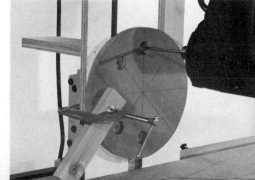

Figure 14-26: The work is centered over the pivot pin and then rotated to position it for each of the holes required. The work can be hand-held, but it is advisable to use a clamp as shown here.

Chapter 15
Curve Cutting—
The Radial Arm
As A Saber Saw

There is more to woodworking than straight cuts. Cornices with scalloped edges, cut-out numbers and letters, ornamental fretwork, silhouettes, and pierced work are examples of common woodworking chores that become possible when a sawing tool can follow a curved line. Ordinarily, this type of work requires a special tool like a band saw or jigsaw, but it is feasible on a radial arm saw if the machine can be equipped with an accessory saber-sawing attachment like the one shown in Figure 15-1.

Figure 15-1: The saber saw attachment slips onto the motor's main arbor and is secured with the same nut that locks other cutting tools. Note that the saw blade can pass through a hole which is already in the table.

Unlike the router setup where an individual self-powered tool is used, the saber saw unit mounts directly on the radial arm saw's motor arbor and so operates with the same power that drives any other accessory. The mounting is firm and assures minimum vibration, so that as long as the rules of good practice are followed, saber sawing can be done on materials as fine as veneers and as heavy as 2" planks.

HOW THE SABER SAW IS MOUNTED. Elevate the radial arm to its maximum height and remove all materials that might be on the motor arbor: cutting tool, saw guard, lock nut, and collars. Slide the saber saw onto the motor arbor until its inboard surface abuts the motor's end bell. The two locating pins that project from the saber saw's housing must mate with the two holes that are in the end bell. This assures vertical alignment of the attachment.

Two L-shaped locking studs with thumb nuts are provided. Tighten the nuts only after the foot of each stud has been rotated to slip into the groove normally occupied by the saw guard. The final step is to place the lock nut on the arbor and to tighten it by using the Allen wrench and the open end wrench as if you were securing a saw blade.

INSTALLING AND POSITIONING A SAW BLADE. Loosen the set screws that are in the saber saw's chuck and insert the blank end of the saw blade about 3/8". The teeth of the blade will point downward. Adjust the right-hand set screw so the blade will be centered in the U-shaped opening of the spring hold-down, and then secure the blade by tightening the left-hand set screw.

Notice that a hole is provided in the machine's table (Figure 15-1) so the saw blade can freely move up and down. To achieve blade alignment with the hole, first lower the radial arm until the end of the saw blade almost touches the table. Move the motor back until the blade is near the hole. Then, by swinging the arm slightly to the left and rotating the motor toward the front of the table, the blade can be positioned so it is directly over the hole. Be sure to lock all controls—in this case, rip, miter, and yoke locks.

Lower the saber saw until the spring hold-down rests with a slight amount of pressure on the work (Figure 15-2). The job of the hold-down is to prevent the saw blade from lifting the work on "up" strokes. Don't allow it to bear too heavily on work surfaces, since this will make it difficult to move the work and can even mar material.

Figure 15-2: Adjust the height of the saber saw on all cuts so the spring hold-down will bear on the work with only enough pressure to keep the work from jiggling. Too much pressure will make it difficult to move the work and can mar the work's surface.

The saber saw can be operated in almost any position depending on how the radial arm, rollerhead, and yoke are positioned. This means, of course, that you must provide a clearance hole for the saw blade whenever you use the saber saw in a special position. It is all right to do this, but be sure the hole is located so that it avoids hitting any metal part of the table's understructure.

Later we'll show a design for a special table that allows the saber saw to be used in various positions without having to blemish the regular table and that provides for particular operations like pivot sawing.

SABER SAW BLADES. Since saber saw blades are gripped only at one end, they must be reasonably rigid in order to cut without twisting and bending. Those that will work best for most operations should be about 3-1/2" long and 1/4" wide. This is not an extreme restriction since many blade styles with those dimensions are available. Figure 15-3 lists typical saber saw blades along with recommendations for their use. The three blades shown in Figure 15-4 are a useful assortment with which to start. Starting at the top and reading clockwise, the number of teeth per inch that the blades have are 20, 7, and 10. Thus, the operator can be immediately organized to do fine through rough cutting with a minimum assortment of blades.

SABER SAW BLADES (TYPICAL)

BLADE NAME (or types)	TEETH PER INCH	CUT FINISH TO EXPECT	CUTTING SPEED	REMARKS
Wood cutting (coarse)	7	Rough	Fast	Use on softwoods 3/4″ and thicker.
Wood cutting (medium)	10	Medium	Medium	Use on softwoods under 3/4″ thick.
Wood cutting (hollow-ground)	7	Smooth	Medium	Good for hardwoods under 3/4″ thick. Also good for softwoods up to 2″ thick when a good cut-finish is required.
	10	Very smooth	Medium	Good for plywood up to 3/4″ thick—may also be used on lumber.
	7	Medium	Fast	Good for plywood up to 1″ thick when fast cutting and a reasonably smooth finish are required.
Double cutting	7	Rough	Fast	Can be used on most wood and fiber materials—blades have teeth on both edges so cutting can be from two directions.
	10	Medium	Medium	
Metal cutting	20	Fine	Slow	Can be used on ferrous metals up to 3/16″ thick—blade should be high speed steel and specially heat treated.
	10	Medium	Medium	Use on nonferrous metals up to 1/4″ thick—blade material should be high speed steel and properly heat treated.
Knife blade	No teeth	Smooth	Fast	May be used on leather, cardboard, rubber, composition tile, and similar materials.

Figure 15-3: The blades listed here are representative of types that are available for radial arm saber saws. Remember that this type of saber saw must use down-cutting teeth. Standard up-cutting blades, such as those used in portable saber saws, can't be used. Don't work with blades that are longer than 3-1/2″.

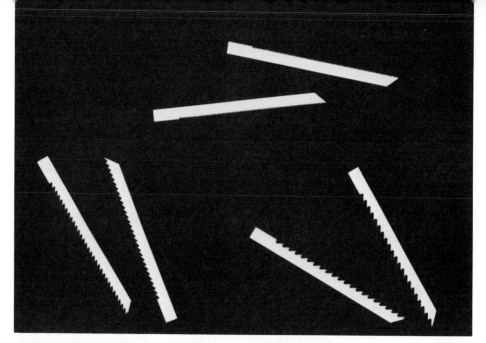

Figure 15-4: The three blades shown here are a useful assortment to start with for general woodcutting. From the top and reading clockwise, they have 20, 7, and 10 teeth per inch.

Generally, it is wise to select a blade with the least number of teeth which will freely cut the material being worked and which will move around the sharpest curve in the pattern without binding. As you will discover, a coarse blade, because it cuts a wider kerf and so provides more room for the blade to maneuver, can often turn a tighter corner than a fine blade.

Blades with many teeth will have less set and so will cut more smoothly, but don't expect them to cut as fast or as freely as blades with few teeth. A multi-tooth blade **should** be selected when cutting thin materials in order to have as many teeth actually working as possible.

Saber saw blades are economical enough so they can be considered disposable. Keep spares on hand so sharp ones will always be available.

GENERAL PRACTICE. Take a stance that will keep you relaxed and comfortable. Many saber-sawing jobs take time so that a strained position will become tiring and will affect work quality. Usually, the left hand works as a guide to move material and keep the blade on line, while the right hand feeds the work (Figure 15-5). However, because of the nature of saber saw work—there often is much twisting and turning involved—no one need abide by one specific rule.

It is not poor practice to use both hands so that each is contributing to guiding **and** feeding. Sometimes the right hand will guide while the left hand feeds. Much depends on the cut-pattern and the line of feed in relation to the saw blade. The whole purpose of the procedure is to keep the blade cutting where it's supposed to. When cutting around a curve, take care to keep the blade tangent to the line.

Never crowd the blade by forcing the cut. On the other hand, being overly cautious won't accomplish much. The teeth on the blade are there to cut, not to burnish. A reasonable feed is one that allows the teeth to constantly cut and produce sawdust.

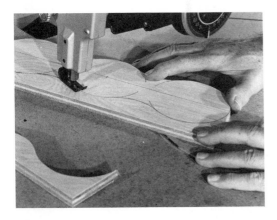

Figure 15-5: Generally, the right hand feeds the work while the left hand moves the work to keep the blade on the cut-line. Changes from the basic procedure are often necessary because of the nature of the work.

Don't force blades around corners too tight for them to negotiate. This can cause the wood to burn, or the blade to break, and probably the cut-line to run off. When you must cut around a corner or a curve the blade can't handle in normal fashion, first make relief cuts as shown in Figure 15-6. The relief cuts allow waste material to fall away as the blade gets to them and so provide more room for the blade to make the turn. Note that the relief cuts can be used for inside or outside turns.

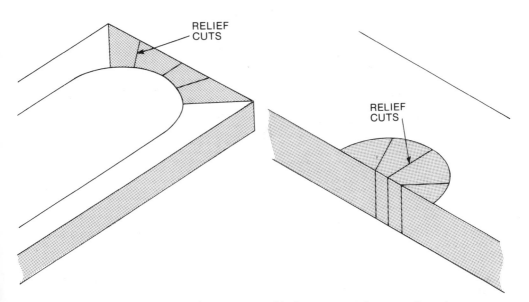

Figure 15-6: Relief cuts can be used to permit a blade to turn a tight corner. Since the waste material falls away as the relief cuts are reached, the blade has more room to maneuver.

Another way to work on outside curves is shown in Figure 15-7. The cut is made to the point where the blade starts to bind and is then run out to the edge of the stock. This is repeated until the cut is complete. How many tangent cuts are required will depend on the radius of the curve and the type of saw blade.

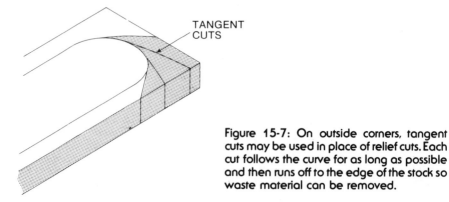

Figure 15-7: On outside corners, tangent cuts may be used in place of relief cuts. Each cut follows the curve for as long as possible and then runs off to the edge of the stock so waste material can be removed.

The cut sequence for producing a narrow slot is shown in Figure 15-8. The first cut is made directly to a corner and then the work is back-tracked so another approach can be made for the second cut. This cut swings off to meet the first one so the bulk of the waste can be removed. The third cut goes to the second corner and the remainder of the waste is removed by "nibbling," which merely means making parallel, overlapping cuts.

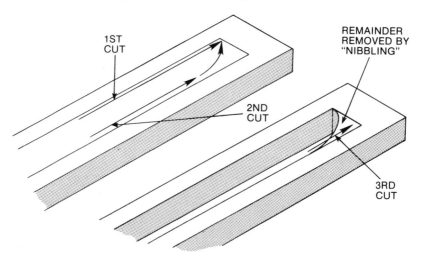

Figure 15-8: This is the cut-sequence to follow when the saber saw is used to form a narrow slot. "Nibbling" means making overlapping, parallel cuts.

When there is room for the blade to maneuver, square, inside corners can be formed as shown in Figure 15-9. Actually, this is a kind of "piercing" work which we will discuss later; but briefly, an insertion hole for the saw blade is drilled through the work and the first cut is made from the hole to a corner. The work is back-tracked until the blade is again in the hole and the second cut is made to meet the first one. This cleans out the corner and allows the blade to make the third cut to another corner. The work is back-tracked a reasonable distance so the approach for the fourth cut can be accomplished. The third and the fourth cuts are then repeated for any remaining corners.

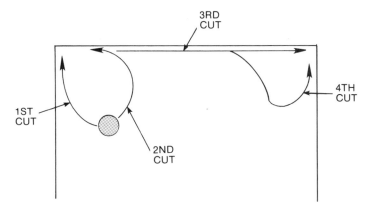

Figure 15-9: Square, internal corners are cut away by following this cut-sequence. The third and fourth cuts are repeated for any remaining corners.

Figure 15-10 shows two examples of internal work involving round corners. In "A," since a sharp corner is involved, the first cut is made from an insertion hole to the corner. The work is then back-tracked until the blade is again in the insertion hole and the second cut is made to meet the first one. In "B," because of generous radii, the cutting can be done in a single pass, starting at the insertion hole and following the arrows.

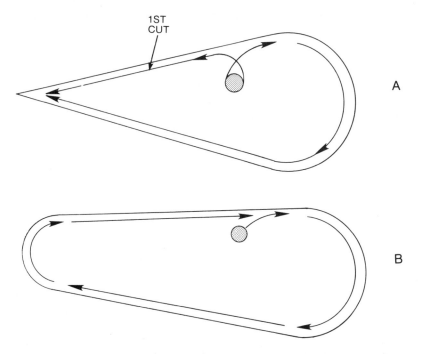

Figure 15-10: In some cases, as in B, some internal cuts can be accomplished with a single-directional pass. "A" illustrates when cut-direction must be judged by the form.

INLAY WORK. The saber saw plays only a part in some types of inlay work, being used to form the piece that will be inlayed (Figure 15-11). Whether to form the recess first and then cut the insert to fit or whether to do the reverse is a matter of personal preference. A safety measure for the first procedure is to cut the insert slightly oversize and then to bring it to an exact fit by sanding.

With the second method, the insert piece is used as a pattern to mark the work for routing. The end result will depend on how carefully the routing is done.

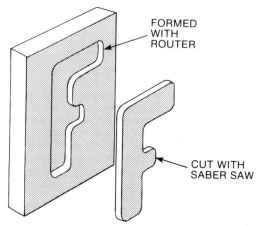

FORMED
WITH
ROUTER

CUT WITH
SABER SAW

Figure 15-11: The saber saw is a partner in inlay work when it is used to shape the piece that will be inserted. The shaped piece can be used as a pattern to mark the work for the routing operation.

DUPLICATE PIECES. It is often possible to produce two similar pieces by making a single cut. The pattern must be something along the lines shown in Figure 15-12; that is, a cut that can be accomplished in a fairly straightforward manner. The technique won't work if, for example, there is a square corner anywhere along the cut-line. Figure 15-13 shows samples of work that can be done by using the one-cut idea.

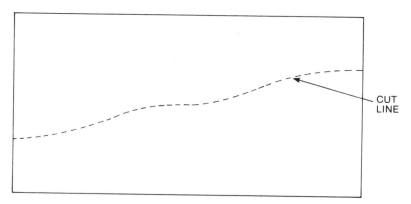

CUT
LINE

Figure 15-12: It is often possible to plan a profile so a single cut will produce two identical pieces. The cut must be fairly straightforward. The technique won't work if there is a square corner anywhere along the cut-line.

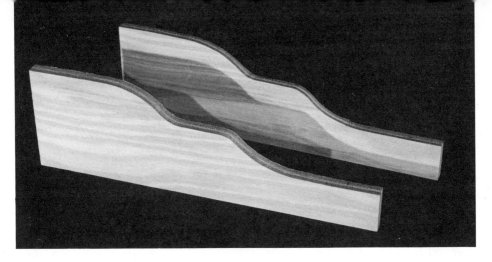

Figure 15-13: An example of identical parts that were produced by making a single cut.

"Pad-sawing" is the method to use when many similar pieces are needed. It involves cutting parts to overall size and then stacking them so they can be cut like a solid piece. The individual pieces are held together with brads or they can be tightly bound with tape. Sawing is done by following the pattern on the top piece so, of course, every piece in the stack will be cut the same way. The saber saw can cut through material 2" thick which means, for example, that eight pieces of 1/4" plywood can be stacked and cut to produce as many duplicate parts.

PATTERNS AND LAYOUT. Since the prime purpose of the saber saw is to cut curves and patterns, it is usually necessary to lay out cut-lines before working. At times, the pattern can be marked directly on the work; at others, especially if the design might prove useful at some future date, it is advisable to work on paper and then to transfer the design to the work by using carbon paper.

If the design is intricate, or difficult to draw on wood, it is still wise to first work on paper even if the pattern will have one-time use. In this case, the paper pattern can be attached to the work by rubber cement. Apply a thin coat of the cement to the back of the pattern. As soon as it is tacky, press the pattern smoothly onto the work.

If a pattern will be used many times, it is advisable to make it of 1/4" plywood or hardboard. It then becomes a permanent part of your shop equipment.

Many workers use magazine illustrations, photographs, and such as patterns. When a ready-made pattern or design is not an acceptable size, it can be enlarged or reduced by using the transferring-by-squares method. This involves marking the original pattern in squares of one size and the work or a sheet of paper in squares of another size (Figure 15-14). Then the pattern is transferred square by square. If the pattern is marked in 1/2" squares and the paper in 1" squares, the transferred design will be twice the size of the original. This technique is reversed when the work must be smaller than the original pattern.

A SPECIAL TABLE. The special table, which is designed specifically for saber saw work, is shown in Figure 15-15. This provides an elevated work surface so the saber saw can be used anywhere along the cut-line and includes a pivot-guide

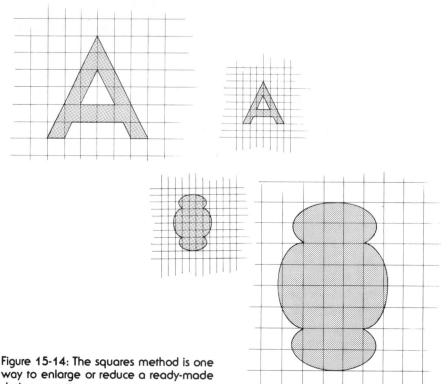

Figure 15-14: The squares method is one way to enlarge or reduce a ready-made design or pattern.

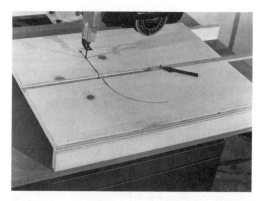

Figure 15-15: The special table permits the saber saw to be used at any point along the cut-line. The arrow indicates the pivot guide's pin over which the work is centered for automatically controlled circular cuts.

system so work can be mechanically guided for part or full-circle cuts. When oversize work must be cut, the saber saw is brought fully forward and then rotated to the out-rip position (Figure 15-16). When the saw is in this position, there is no limit to the length of the work and little restriction on its width.

The table is constructed as shown in Figure 15-17. First cut the platform to size, then form the groove and drill the holes that are called for. The 3/8" hole is the starting hole for the saw blade. The 5/8" hole, which is on the center line of the kerf and centered in the table groove, permits the saw blade to be tilted for bevel cuts. The back strip fits into the slot normally occupied by the guide fence so the table can be locked in place by using the table clamp screws.

Figure 15-16: Locking the saber saw in the out-rip position permits sawing work of any length. Also, there is little restriction on the width of work that can be handled.

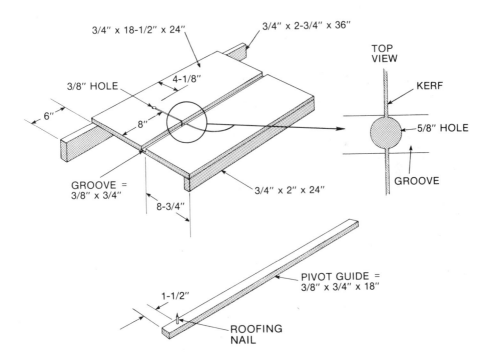

Figure 15-17: Construction details of the special saber-sawing table. The lower detail shows how the pivot guide is made.

Follow this procedure to install the table and to form the cut-line. Leave the saw in crosscut position and raise the radial arm to maximum height. Position the auxiliary table and move the saber saw until the saw blade is centered over the 3/8" hole. Then, lock the table and lower the radial arm until the blade is about halfway through the hole. Turn on the machine and slowly pull the saber saw forward to maximum crosscut position. Loosen the yoke lock and rotate the saber saw forward 90° so the tool clicks into the out-rip position. At this point the saw blade will be parallel to the table's groove. Return the saw to its neutral position—the blade will be in the 3/8" hole.

Working with the special table doesn't change standard cutting procedures. However, since the saber saw can be locked at any position along the table's cut-line, it can be situated for maximum convenience, depending on the particular type of work being done.

PIVOT SAWING. Any arc or circle can be cut freehand, but using the pivot system makes it easier to be accurate and provides a way to guarantee duplication of parts when similar pieces are needed.

Place the pivot guide (shown in Figure 15-17) in the table groove and lock the saber saw in a position that puts the points of the blade's teeth directly on line with the pin in the guide. Use a compass to mark the work; then, without the pivot guide in place, do a freehand cut just to bring the blade to the line of cut. Remove the work and center it over the pin in the guide. Then replace the work and guide, securing the guide's position by driving a small brad through it into the table. The cut is then finished by rotating the work slowly in a clockwise direction as shown in Figure 15-18.

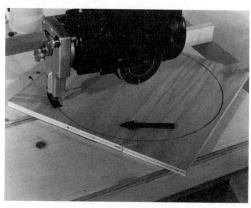

Figure 15-18: A true circle results when the pivot-guide system is used. The text explains two ways in which the cut can be started.

Another possibility is to make freehand cuts to remove the bulk of the waste from the work. Place the saber saw in neutral position and situate the work and the pivot guide on the table. The distance from the pin in the guide to the cut-line in the table will be the radius of the work. Hold the work firmly and pull the saber saw forward as if you were crosscutting until the points of the blade's teeth are in the center of the table's groove. Secure the rip lock and then rotate the work to complete the cut. This system works well because the lead-in cut, made by pulling the saber saw, will be operating on a tangent to the work-circle.

PIERCING. Piercing is done to produce internal cutouts without the need of a lead-in cut from any edge of the stock. The system calls for drilling a blade insertion hole in each area of the stock that will be cut out. Cutting starts with the saw blade in the insertion hole and proceeds in routine fashion (Figure 15-19). Often, because of the height of the special table and the thickness of

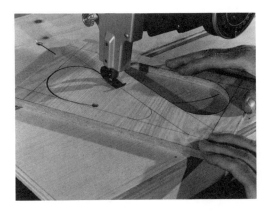

Figure 15-19: Piercing—internal cutouts—is possible because the blade can be positioned in an insertion hole before the cut is started. Each piece to be cut out must have its own insertion hole.

the stock being cut, it isn't possible to slide the work under the blade even when the radial arm is at maximum height. However, it is a simple matter to place the blade in the insertion hole and in the saber-saw chuck after the work has been positioned.

Since the insertion hole does not have to be any special size, it is often possible, design permitting, to do some predrilling that will provide rounded corners; the holes will also serve for blade insertion. An example design that permits using the technique is shown in Figure 15-20.

DOTTED LINES =
CUT LINES

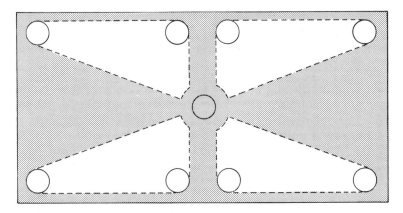

Figure 15-20: It is often possible to locate blade-insertion holes so they become part of the design.

STRAIGHT CUTTING. Straight cuts that are part of a pattern are cut freehand, but there are occasions when working with a guide can be useful. For example, when the tool is organized for saber sawing and parts of the project being made have straight ends or sides, it may be more convenient to make the cuts with the saber saw than to convert to the conventional sawing mode.

The setup to be used for crosscutting is shown in Figure 15-21. The guide (Figure 15-22) is a simple affair that is secured with a clamp to the auxiliary

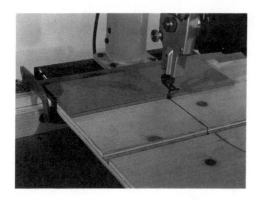

Figure 15-21: This simple guide, which clamps to the auxiliary table's rear support piece, serves as a fence when the saber saw is used for crosscutting operations.

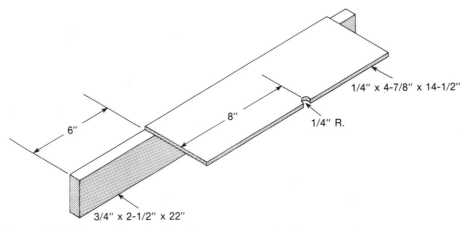

1/4" x 4-7/8" x 14-1/2"

6"

8"

1/4" R.

3/4" x 2-1/2" x 22"

Figure 15-22: Construction details of the crosscut guide. The semicircular opening can be formed with a round file.

table's rear support piece. Position the guide so the saber saw blade will be centered in the semicircular cutout. The cutout can be formed with a round file.

Cutting is basically a crosscut procedure. The work is held against the guide and the saber saw is pulled through to make the cut (Figure 15-23). The cuts will be very acceptable as long as you don't rush. Pull the saber saw slowly, and allow the saw teeth to cut as they should.

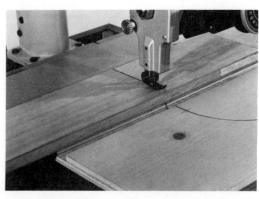

Figure 15-23: Hold the work firmly against the guide and move the saber saw forward as if you were making a crosscut with a circular blade. A slow, steady feed produces the best results.

For a ripping guide, all that is required is a straight piece of stock that can be clamped to the table as shown in Figure 15-24. In this case, the saber saw's position is secured and the work is moved to make the cut.

Several alternatives are possible if the setup that is shown is not convenient for the size of the work. The saber saw can be placed in the out-rip position with a fence-guide clamped parallel to the front of the table, or the saber saw can be rotated while the blade is in the 5/8" hole so work can be fed across the table at an angle. Be sure the clamped-on guide is parallel to the side of the blade.

There may be a tendency when ripping for the work to move away from the guide. To avoid this, feed the work very slowly, be sure the guide is parallel to the side of the blade, and be sure the saw blade is sharp.

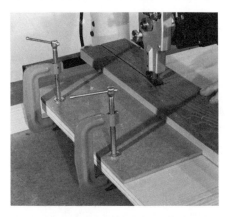

Figure 15-24: A piece of wood or hardboard with a straight edge is the only guide needed for ripping operations. The text explains how the saber saw can be organized for ripping operations on oversize work.

CUTTING CYLINDERS. When the diameter of the work is large enough, the groove in the table can be used like a V-block to keep the work secure while the blade is pulled through for the cut (Figure 15-25). Be sure the hold-down spring is positioned to keep the work firm. Feed the blade very slowly.

This setup also allows cutting grooves on the circumference of the work. After the work is placed, pull the saber saw forward to whatever depth-of-cut is desired. Tighten the rip lock and then slowly rotate the work to complete the groove. The cut will be more accurate if you butt the end of the work against a stop block clamped to the table.

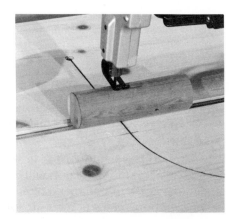

Figure 15-25: The saber saw can be used to crosscut cylindrical work. The groove in the table can be used like a V-block when the work has sufficient diameter.

SPIRALING DOWEL. Many craftspeople use conventional dowel rods to reinforce edge-to-edge joints and similar wood connections. This is all right, but the lengths of dowel will do a better job if, like dowels made for the purpose, they have spiral grooves so glue can travel and so excess glue can escape from the hole. This spiraling can be done with the saber saw by providing a V-block jig like the one shown in Figure 15-26.

Figure 15-26: This V-block jig is especially useful for spiral-cutting conventional dowel rods that will be cut to specific lengths for use in various wood joints.

The saber saw, with its blade in the 5/8″ hole in the table, is rotated counterclockwise to an angle of about 15° and its position secured by tightening the yoke and the rip locks. The blade's position is set to cut to a depth of about 1/16″. The dowel, with its end close to the saw blade, is nestled in the V and then slowly rotated to make the cut, as shown in Figure 15-27. Because the blade is at an angle, the work will automatically feed forward as it is rotated. The results are best when the work is rotated at a slow steady pace.

Figure 15-27: The V-jig is clamped to the table and the saber saw is locked in a position that will produce the needed depth of cut. The dowel will automatically feed past the blade as it is rotated.

The angle at which the blade is set is not critical, but the greater the angle, the further apart the spiral cuts will be. Often, this technique is used to establish guide lines for hand-shaped spiral columns.

Construction details of the V-jig for spiral cutting are shown in Figure 15-28.

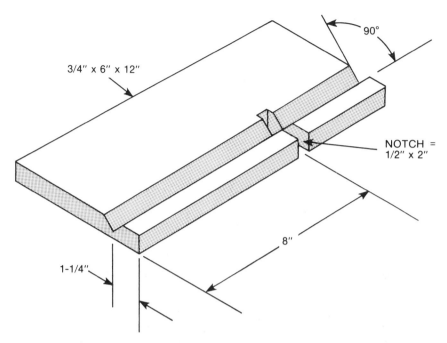

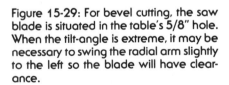

Figure 15-28: This is how the V-block jig is made.

BEVEL CUTTING. The saber saw can be used to form parts with beveled edges when the blade is situated in the 5/8" table hole and the motor is tilted as shown in Figure 15-29. The degree of blade tilt will, of course, depend on the bevel angle that is required.

Figure 15-29: For bevel cutting, the saw blade is situated in the table's 5/8" hole. When the tilt-angle is extreme, it may be necessary to swing the radial arm slightly to the left so the blade will have clearance.

A unique application of bevel cutting combined with internal cutting, or piercing, can create some pleasing results. The technique can be understood by studying the illustrations in Figure 15-30. If an internal circular cut is made with the blade perpendicular to the work as in "A," the center section will simply fall through the part from which it was cut. If, however, the same cut is made with the blade tilted as in "B," the beveled disc will fall only part way through the beveled opening. The disc will jam in place like the bung in a barrel.

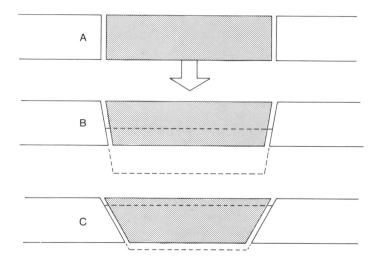

Figure 15-30: When an internal disc is cut with the blade in perpendicular position (A), the cutout will fall through the part from which it was cut. When the blade is tilted, the disc will jam in place (B). The greater the tilt of the blade, the less projection the disc will have (C).

As shown in "C," the greater the blade tilt, the less the cut-out disc will project. An experimental cut will help you determine just how much the blade can be tilted. Much depends on the thickness of the stock and the blade that is used, which, of course, determines the width of the kerf. To start, experiment with blade tilts of 5° to 15°.

When you cut, be sure to **always** keep the inside piece (the part that will project) on the same side of the blade. If you veer from this, the direction of the bevel will change and the parts will not mesh as they should.

Figure 15-31 shows a cross-sectional view of a project made by using the bevel-cutting technique—in this case, a tray with a raised lip.

To assemble bevel-cut pieces, coat the mating areas with glue and, after jamming the parts together, allow them to rest until the glue is dry.

The insertion hole on the cut-line that allows the saw blade to get started can be filled with a wood dough after the pieces have been assembled.

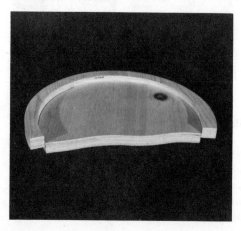

Figure 15-31: This cross-sectional view of what will be a tray with a raised lip is an example of what can be done by bevel cutting. Square or rectangular projects can be accomplished the same way. It is critical for the inside piece (the part that will project) to be on the same side of the blade throughout the cutting procedure.

Chapter 16
Special Techniques
Increase Work Scope

The phrase "special techniques" isn't meant to suggest an area of complicated procedures but rather an assortment of particular methods that round out the scope of work in a way not possible with only basic cutting. Most of the work can be done without much fuss and with standard cutting tools like saw blades and dadoing tools. In some situations, the special technique is an unusual way of using the cutter or feeding the work. Other times, a specially designed jig or fixture is needed.

It isn't necessary to rush through this chapter in order to acquire these techniques. It's better to browse through it and then return to a particular section when the technique will be useful on a project.

TAPER CUTS. Taper cuts are straight cuts that are not parallel to the edge of the stock. Taper cuts can be used, for example, to form square table legs that have a smaller cross section at one end. The legs of the plywood stand that was shown in Chapter 4 were taper-cut.

The radial arm saw can be used to cut tapers in several ways, and each of them calls for an arrangement that will position the work to gauge the amount of taper required.

Tapers can be cut in crosscut position as long as the machine is capable of making the length of cut required. A notch, which is shaped to equal the required taper, is cut in the edge of a board and the board is clamped in place as shown in Figure 16-1. Position the guide so its notched edge will be flush against the saw blade, and clamp it securely. Note that a stop block on the fence secures the guide at one end while a C-clamp holds it at the opposite end.

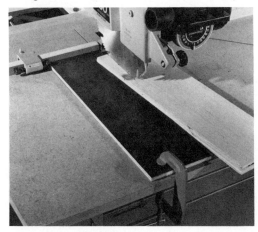

Figure 16-1: Notched jigs can serve two purposes. They can position work that must be taper-cut or they can serve as a guide for cutting wedge-shaped pieces. Be sure the jig is secured as shown.

With the saw in neutral position, place the work firmly in the notch and then pull the blade through as you would for any crosscut. If the taper is required on both edges of the stock, flip the work and make a second pass as shown in Figure 16-2. This system may be used whether you are forming tapers or have a need for some small wedge-shaped pieces.

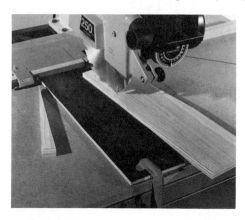

Figure 16-2: If the taper cut is required on both edges of the stock, the second cut is made by flipping the stock so the uncut side can be positioned in the notch.

A STEP JIG. A step jig, like the one shown in Figure 16-3, becomes a useful production tool when many similar pieces are needed. Cut-settings, which are determined by the steps in the jig, are fixed so that all pieces will be duplicates no matter how many are cut. Because the jig has several steps, it can be used to position work that requires the same taper on opposite edges.

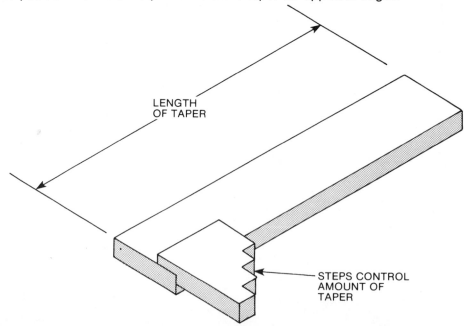

LENGTH
OF TAPER

STEPS CONTROL
AMOUNT OF
TAPER

Figure 16-3: How to make a step jig. Only two steps are required even if the work is square and must be taper-cut on four sides. Having extra steps makes the jig useable for various sizes of tapers.

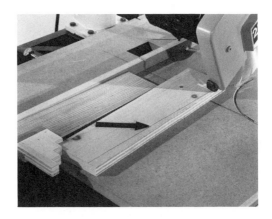

Figure 16-4: For the first cut, the work is placed in the jig as shown. The arrow points to the line along which the saw blade will cut.

The tapering is done in much the same way as a rip cut except that the jig rides against the guide fence (Figure 16-4). Position the saw blade (in this case in out-rip position) so the distance from it to the guide fence will equal the width of the jig plus the width of the work where the taper starts.

The blade, of course, cuts straight, but since the jig holds the work at an angle, the work is tapered (Figure 16-5). When the taper is needed on both edges of the stock, flip the stock and place it in the second step of the jig. Then make another pass (Figure 16-6). When constructing a step jig, it is advisable to make the jig's leg wide enough so hands can be positioned well away from the saw blade.

Figure 16-5: The cut is made by moving the jig and work into the saw blade. Place hands so they are well away from the saw blade. Here, the saw is in the out-rip position so the pass is from left to right.

Figure 16-6: When a similar taper is required on the other edge of the stock, the stock is flipped and then situated so it will be positioned by the second step in the jig.

A VARIABLE TAPER JIG. A variable taper jig, made like the one in Figure 16-7, can be set for any taper-cut within its capacity. It provides a straight leg that rides the guide fence and an adjustable leg that is set for the amount of taper required. Keep the legs of the jig clamped together when you attach the hinge that permits adjustments. The crosspiece that is used to lock settings can be made of thin hardwood, a strip of sheet metal, as well as hardboard.

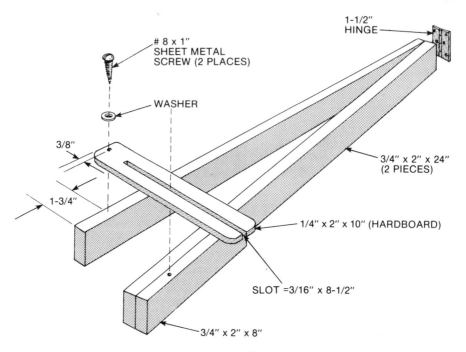

Figure 16-7: Construction details of a variable taper jig. Keep the legs of the jig clamped together when you attach the hinge.

After the jig is made, hold it in closed position and make a mark across each leg 12" from the hinged end (Figure 16-8). By measuring between these two marks as you open the jig, you can determine the amount of taper per foot. For example, a 1" spacing will set the jig to cut 1" of taper per foot.

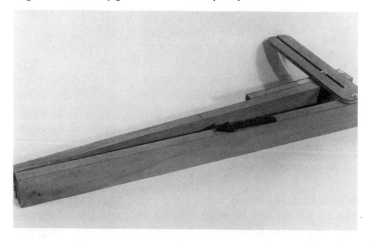

Figure 16-8: Mark the legs 12" away from the hinged end. The distance between these marks will indicate the amount of taper per foot.

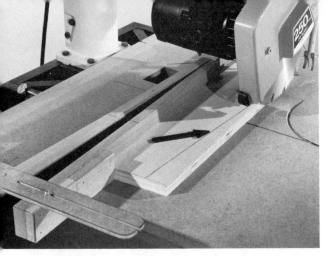

Figure 16-9: The straight leg of the jig rides against the guide fence. The work is placed against the slanted leg and butted against the jig's stop block. The arrow shows the cut-line.

The jig is used with the saw organized for ripping. Place the straight leg of the jig against the guide fence and the work against the angled leg (Figure 16-9). Be sure the work butts against the jig's stop block. The saw blade's distance from the guide fence should equal the width of the jig plus the width of the work where the taper is to start. Make the pass as you would any rip cut (Figure 16-10). The stop block is long enough so the cut can be completed with ample clearance between the blade and the jig's crosspiece.

Figure 16-10: Jig and work are moved into the saw blade. Because of the length of the stop block, the cut will be complete before the saw guard comes near the jig's crosspiece. If the same taper is required on both edges of the stock, make the second cut after opening the jig to twice the original setting.

If the same taper is required on opposite edges of the stock, open the jig to twice the original setting before repositioning the work and making the second pass. If a part requires tapers on all four faces—for example, a square table-leg—make a cut on one face and, without changing the jig's setting, make a cut on the adjacent face. Then, double the jig's setting and make the two remaining cuts (Figure 16-11).

A taper cut, or any angular cut on a project component that can't be handled with a jig, can be accomplished as shown in Figures 16-12 and 16-13. A straight piece of wood, positioned so it will be parallel to the line of cut, is clamped or tack-nailed to the underside of the work. The work is moved with the guide strip riding the front edge of the table. In the photograph, since the tool is set up for out-ripping, the work-feed direction is from left to right.

This table edge-guide system can also be used to make rip cuts on stock that does not have an edge straight enough to ride the guide fence.

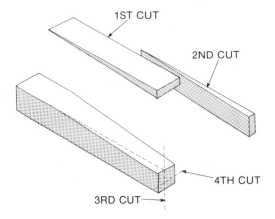

Figure 16-11: This is the sequence of passes to follow when work must be tapered on four surfaces. The jig is at one setting for the first two cuts. Then the setting is doubled for the third and fourth cuts.

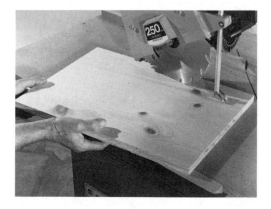

Figure 16-12: Any taper or angular cut can be accomplished on oversize work by using this technique. The work is guided by the strip that is tack-nailed or clamped to the work.

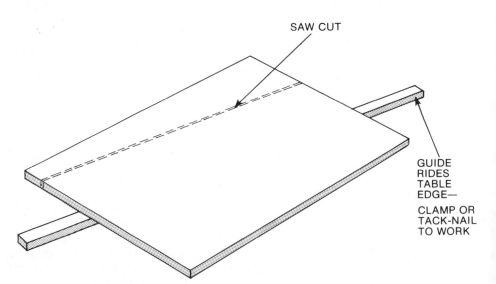

Figure 16-13: How the guide-strip method is organized. The strip, which is parallel to the line-of-cut, rides against the front edge of the table.

PATTERN SAWING. Pattern sawing is a production method of cutting any number of similar odd-shaped pieces; that is, parts that would be a nuisance to shape by making conventional crosscuts and rip cuts. The system, which is shown in Figure 16-14, sets up a mechanical means of gauging cuts. Since the size and shape of the work are determined by a pattern, all parts will be exact duplicates.

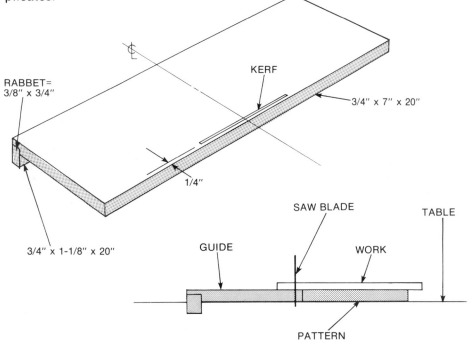

Figure 16-14: This is how to make the guide for pattern sawing. The text explains how to go about forming the kerf.

The guide is set up as shown in Figure 16-15. First elevate the saw blade so that it is a few inches above the table. Center the guide under the saw blade and secure its position by placing its back strip in the slot normally occupied by the guide fence. Lower the blade until it almost touches the guide, and then

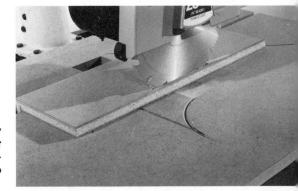

Figure 16-15: The kerf in which the saw blade moves should be 1/4" from the front edge of the guide. The dimension is not critical but, whatever it is, should be taken into account when the pattern is made.

lock its position so it will cut 1/4" in from the guide's front edge. Lower the blade slowly until it forms the kerf in the guide.

The pattern, a duplicate of the work but 1/4" smaller on all edges, is tack-nailed to the underside of the work as shown in Figure 16-16. The original shape of the work is not important since the guide will assure that the ultimate form will be correct.

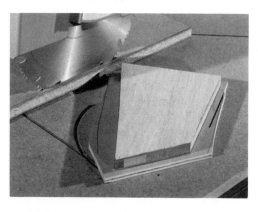

Figure 16-16: The pattern is a duplicate of the work but smaller on all sides by the distance between the front edge of the guide and the saw blade.

The cut is started by placing the pattern flat on the table and against the infeed end of the guide. In Figure 16-17, since the saw is set up for out-ripping, the infeed end of the guide is at the left. Work-feed direction is toward the right. Be sure to keep the pattern snug against the guide as you make the cuts. Although the photograph doesn't show it, the saw guard and the antikickback assembly should be correctly organized as for any ripping operation.

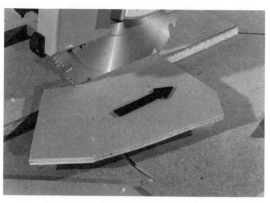

Figure 16-17: The pass is made so the pattern rides against the guide. This is a ripping operation, so the saw guard and the antikickback assembly should be correctly installed even though the photograph doesn't show them so.

WOOD BENDING BY KERFING. Commercial woodworking plants make wood pliable enough for bending by using steam and special jigs. It's a tried and true method but impractical in many shops because of the equipment that is required. A solution, enjoyed by many woodworkers, is to use "kerf curving" so wood can be bent as shown in Figure 16-18.

The trick is to make a number of deep, parallel cuts in the face of the stock that will be the inside of the bend. This turns the opposite face into a flexible veneer at each of the kerfs. The kerfs are confined to a particular area when the wood must bend at one point (Figure 16-19).

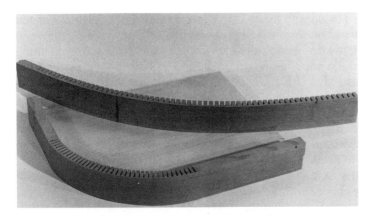

Figure 16-18: Wood is not difficult to bend after it has been kerfed like the pieces shown here.

CLOSE SPACING
AND DEEP KERFS
MAKE BENDING
EASIER

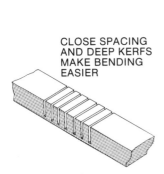

CONFINE
KERFS TO
BEND AREA

Figure 16-19: Confine the kerfs to the area of the wood that requires bending. The closer the kerfs are spaced and the deeper they are, the sharper the bend can be.

The closer the kerfs are spaced, and the deeper they are, the more sharply you can bend the wood. But overdoing the kerfing will be a waste of time and can weaken the stock needlessly. A simple way to gauge how far apart and how deep the kerfs should be for any given radius is shown in Figure 16-20.

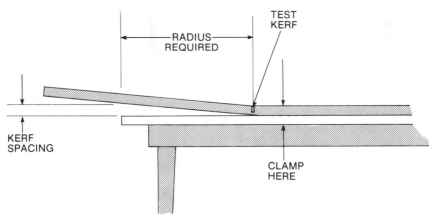

Figure 16-20: This system can be used as a guide in determining how far apart the kerfs should be for a particular bend radius. Be sure the test piece is the same type of wood that you wish to bend.

Make a sample kerf in a scrap of wood that is the same type and thickness as the piece that requires bending. Clamp the work to a flat surface as shown in the drawing, then lift the free end of the work until the kerf closes. The distance between the flat surface and the underside of the work will be the correct kerf spacing. This will also give you a place to start. You may find, when bending the wood, that some extra kerfs will be needed. Kerf-bent areas will always be stronger when you use the least number of kerfs and minimum depth-of-cut.

Since there will be many kerfs to cut and they should be equally spaced, the work will be more accurate and will proceed faster if you make a special fence like the one shown in Figure 16-21. Lock the fence in place and pull the blade through it to form the fence kerf. Then remove the fence and drill a series of equally spaced holes on a common center line. Size the holes to suit a 5d or 6d nail (the nail diameter must not be more than 1/8"), and space the holes about 3/16" or 1/4".

Figure 16-21: If you make a special fence like this one, you can use a nail as a guide for gauging kerf-spacing. Size the holes so you can use a nail with a diameter that is less than 1/8".

The nail acts as a guide for positioning the work for each kerf. Each cut made is placed over the nail, so spacing for the next cut is automatically determined (Figure 16-22).

Figure 16-22: Each kerf that is cut is placed over the nail so the work will be accurately positioned for the following cut.

After kerfing, bring the wood to shape slowly—don't force it. Wetting the unkerfed side will make stubborn pieces easier to bend. When necessary, the kerfs can be hidden with thin strips of veneer. Another way is to fill the kerfs with a thick mixture of wood dough. If the work will be used outdoors, coat the kerfs with waterproof glue before making the bend.

Another way that wood can be bent without steaming is shown in Figure 16-23. The wood in the bend area is thinned out by making repeat passes with a dadoing tool. The thickness of the material that is left will depend on the sharpness of the bend. The sharper the bend, the thinner the material must be. The thinned out area should be reinforced with glue blocks after the bend has been made.

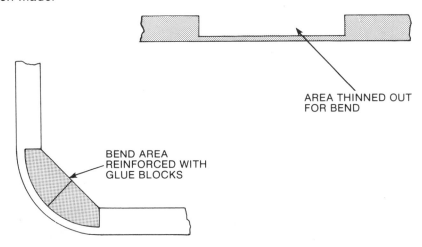

AREA THINNED OUT
FOR BEND

BEND AREA
REINFORCED WITH
GLUE BLOCKS

Figure 16-23: Wood can also be bent by thinning out the stock in the bend area. Glue blocks, placed after the bend is made, will provide strength.

DOUBLE-BLADE CUTTING. There are several advantages to being able to mount two saw blades on the arbor. One example is shown in Figure 16-24 where two kerfs are cut in one pass, thereby reducing production time by 50%. The idea works because the arbor is long enough to permit mounting two saw blades with spacers between them. If you use large washers as spacers (Figure 16-25), you will have considerable control over the spacing between blades.

Be aware of certain limitations. Be sure to leave enough exposed arbor so the lock nut can be firmly tightened. Don't mount anything that will prevent the use of the saw guard. Be sure the spacers you use have flat surfaces.

Figure 16-24: Kerfing with two blades. This technique will considerably reduce the time it takes to form, for example, kerfs for bending stock.

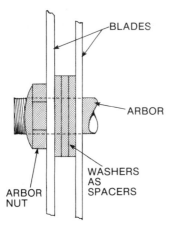

Figure 16-25: How two spaced blades can be mounted on the arbor. Always be sure there is enough threaded arbor exposed so the lock nut can be securely tightened.

Double-blade work can be done to speed up decorative cutting, as shown in Figures 16-26 and 16-27. When doing work like this, provide sufficient spacing between the blades so that small areas between cuts won't chip out.

Figure 16-26: You can form decorative kerfs faster and more accurately when you work with two saw blades.

Figure 16-27: Combining angular cuts with simple crosscuts can produce interesting patterns. Don't space the blades so closely that small parts of the pattern will be chipped out.

Double-blade cutting can be used to speed up the production of thin strips. The work, as shown in Figure 16-28, is done like a rip cut; each pass will produce two pieces. A word of caution—the saw blades will tend to throw back the strip that is captured between them, so be sure to work with a pusher and to organize the saw guard and antikickback assembly correctly. Another safety factor is to work so that you are not directly in the line of cut.

It is also possible to work with saw blades of different diameters or to combine a saw blade with a dado assembly. As shown in Figure 16-29, the diameters of the cutting tools must be suitable for the work being done.

One use for this technique is to make a cutoff and a shoulder cut for a rabbet at the same time (Figure 16-30). This is useful when you need, for example, a number of similar drawer fronts. How deep the rabbet shoulder-cut can be

Figure 16-28: Speeding up the job of strip-cutting by working with two saw blades. The blades will tend to throw back the strip that is between them. Be aware of this and be sure to use the antikickback assembly even if the photograph doesn't show it.

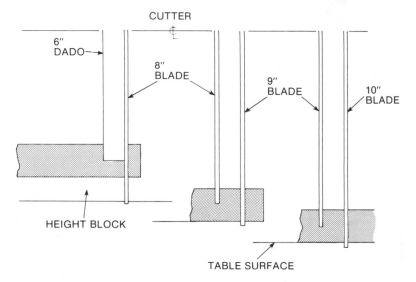

CUTTER

6" DADO

8" BLADE

9" BLADE

10" BLADE

HEIGHT BLOCK

TABLE SURFACE

Figure 16-29: You can combine blades of different diameters—even a dado assembly with a saw blade. Tool diameters must be suitable for the work that will be done.

Figure 16-30: An example of work that can be done with blades of different diameters. One pass does a cut-off and forms the shoulder for a rabbet.

will depend on the size of the blade. If you wish a deeper cut than you can get by working as shown in the photograph, use a height block under the work. Don't let the outside blade cut any deeper than it should into the tool's table.

This operation can be carried a little further by mounting a dado assembly with the saw blade. Now, as shown in Figure 16-31, a full rabbet cut and a cutoff can be accomplished in one pass. When necessary, the work can be raised on a height block (Figure 16-32) so the dadoing tool can be set to cut as deep a rabbet as you need.

Be sure, when you use a height block, that there will be enough guide-fence area above the block for the work to bear against. Work with a higher guide fence when necessary. Hold the work firmly; make the pass slowly. The dado-blade combination will be removing a considerable amount of material, so you must give the cutters enough time to work correctly.

Figure 16-31: By combining a saw blade with a dado assembly, you can cut off and form a complete rabbet in a single pass. Keep the work firm—make the pass very slowly.

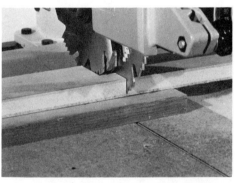

Figure 16-32: To avoid having the saw blade cut into the table, thin work can be raised with a height block. Be sure there is enough fence above the height block for the work to bear against. Make a special fence when necessary.

COVING. Coving is a unique procedure that can be used to produce shapes like those shown in Figure 16-33. Cove cuts are frequently seen on furniture projects with components that have internal or exterior round corners. A wooden rain gutter, small troughs in a pencil tray, or the chalk groove on a blackboard can be formed by cove cutting.

Often, coving is done as a supplementary step to produce a shape like the one shown in Figure 16-34C. In this case, the work is a split lathe-turning that is shaped as a uniform cylinder but with end areas left square to provide a solid footing when the work is coved.

Projects that require a concentric opening, whether they are turned in a lathe or not, are accomplished in similar fashion. If initial work on the piece is done in a lathe, the work is mounted as a split turning. After lathe-shaping, the pieces are separated and the coving is done on each piece. After coving,

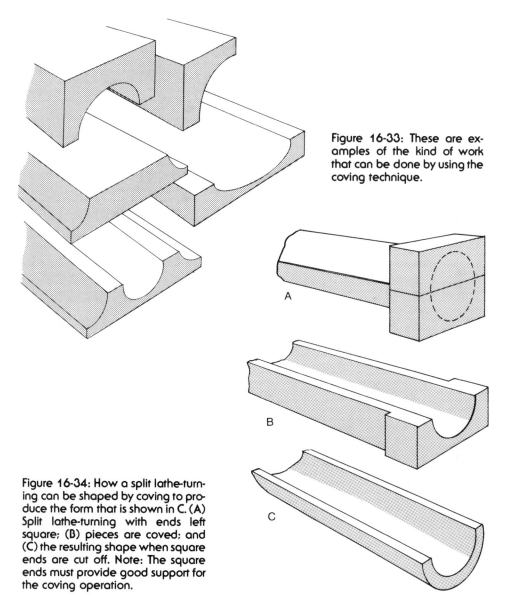

Figure 16-33: These are examples of the kind of work that can be done by using the coving technique.

A

B

C

Figure 16-34: How a split lathe-turning can be shaped by coving to produce the form that is shown in C. (A) Split lathe-turning with ends left square; (B) pieces are coved; and (C) the resulting shape when square ends are cut off. Note: The square ends must provide good support for the coving operation.

the two pieces are permanently assembled. The shape of the opening (Figure 16-35) will depend on how the coving was done.

Coving is a unique operation in that a saw blade (or a dadoing tool) made for straight cutting is used to produce a semicircular shape. It works because the cutting tool is set obliquely to the line of cut and the action is a scraping one rather than a true sawing action. Most jobs are done by feeding the work as if you were making a rip cut but with the saw blade swung and tilted as it would be for a compound angle cut. The cove is shaped by making repeat passes with the blade adjusted after each pass to cut (or scrape) no deeper than 1/16" to 1/8".

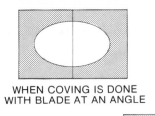

WHEN COVING IS DONE
WITH BLADE AT AN ANGLE

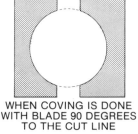

WHEN COVING IS DONE
WITH BLADE 90 DEGREES
TO THE CUT LINE

Figure 16-35: Parts that require concentric openings can be made by coving similar pieces and then assembling them as shown here.

The width of the cove, its depth, and its shape can be controlled by the angle of the blade, how much it is tilted, and by the number of passes that are made (Figure 16-36). The more passes you make, the wider and deeper the cove will be. The shape of the cove is controlled mainly by the angle of the saw blade. Truest arcs occur when the surface of the blade is at right angles to the direction of feed.

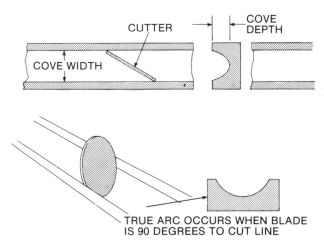

Figure 16-36: The shape and width of the cove are affected by the angle of the blade; the depth of the cove by the blade's height above the table.

Examples of Cove Cuts. Figure 16-37 shows how an edge cove is made. Raise the radial arm so the saw blade will be several inches above the table. Rotate the blade toward the back of the machine until it is at about a 45° angle, and then tilt the blade about 15°. Lock both of the settings, and then position the work and adjust the height of the blade so the blade's teeth just touch a corner of the work. Tighten the rip lock and make the first pass. Be sure to use a push stick to get the work past the saw blade. Continue to make passes, lowering the blade 1/16" to 1/8" for each pass until the cove has the width and depth you need. The final pass should be made with the blade barely touching the work. This will produce the smoothest finish.

Figure 16-37: Doing an edge cove with the blade tilted about 15° and swung toward the column about 45°. These settings produce a particular cove shape. Variations are infinite.

Figure 16-38 shows how a full cove is formed. Here, the blade tilt is at zero and the blade has been rotated about 80° toward the back of the machine. Repeat passes, each made after a very slight depth-of-cut adjustment, result in the cove shape.

Figure 16-38: A center cove done with the blade tilt at zero setting and the blade swung about 80°. Notice how the shape of this cove differs from the edge cove in the previous photograph.

The setup that is shown in Figure 16-39 will produce a true arc with a radius equal to that of the saw blade. Start with the blade in normal crosscut position, then tilt it down toward the table about 10° or 15°. This puts the blade's cut-line at right angles to the work-feed line. If you did this down the center of a piece of stock and made enough passes to get to full-blade capacity, you would have a cove about 9" wide and about 3" deep.

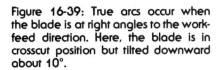

Figure 16-39: True arcs occur when the blade is at right angles to the work-feed direction. Here, the blade is in crosscut position but tilted downward about 10°.

These are just examples of how coving is done, but they don't offer control over cove dimensions. You can expect the cove to get wider and deeper with each pass. The parallel rule that is shown in Figure 16-40 will help predetermine the size of a cove. Pivot the rule so the distance between the long arms equals the width of the cove. Rotate the blade until its angle is such that the "front" teeth touch one arm and the "back" teeth touch the other arm. This sets the width of the cove, but the adjustment must be done with the blade set for the cove depth. This is just a question of placing the stock on the table and lowering the saw blade the correct distance from **the top of the work**. The center line of the cove should be on the center line of the saw blade.

Figure 16-41 shows an example of a decorative panel that was formed by doing cove cuts.

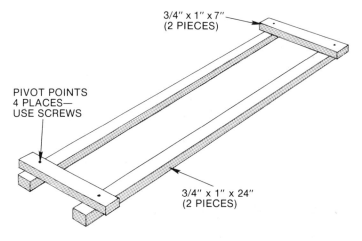

3/4" x 1" x 7"
(2 PIECES)

PIVOT POINTS
4 PLACES—
USE SCREWS

3/4" x 1" x 24"
(2 PIECES)

Figure 16-40: This parallel rule will help to predetermine the width of the cove. The text explains how it is used.

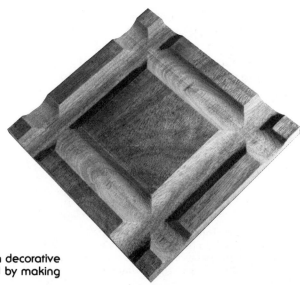

Figure 16-41: An example of a decorative panel that was surface-shaped by making cove cuts.

SAUCER CUTS. Saucer-like forms are shaped by following a procedure that is related to coving in that the blade is used in a scraping action rather than a cutting one. A typical setup is shown in Figure 16-42. Start with the blade in crosscut position and raised well above the table. Tilt the blade downward until it clicks into the 45° setting. Tighten the rip lock and clamp the work in position so it is centered under the saw blade. Lower the saw blade until it barely touches the surface of the work and then return it to vertical position. Now, with the motor on, swing the blade through its full tilt range. Continue the procedure, lowering the blade about 1/16" for each pass, until the cut is the correct depth. Back up the work with a scrap piece when the saucer cut must be through the stock.

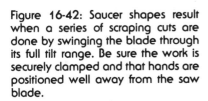
Figure 16-42: Saucer shapes result when a series of scraping cuts are done by swinging the blade through its full tilt range. Be sure the work is securely clamped and that hands are positioned well away from the saw blade.

Be sure to keep your hands in a safe position. The feed hand can be kept on top of the saw guard while the other keeps the bevel lock in released position. Some workers prefer to use the rod of the antikickback assembly as a lever for moving the blade through the tilt range. No matter how you work, it is critical, as always, to keep your hands well away from cutting areas.

Saucer cuts can be used to create, for example, round picture frames. Often, they can be treated further like the example in Figure 16-43 to make unique project components.

Figure 16-43: Saucer-cut pieces can be treated further to make interesting project components. Here, a wide dado forms a rectangular opening.

CIRCLE CUTTING. You can cut circles with an ordinary saw blade if you do the job as shown in Figure 16-44. Lock the saw in out-rip position with the blade elevated enough to clear the work. Drive a small nail through the center of the work and into the table. The nail must be on the blade's center line and positioned so the distance from it to the blade will equal the radius of the work. Lower the saw blade until it is cutting about 1/16″ deep, and then rotate the work in a clockwise direction. Make repeat passes, lowering the blade for each, until the cut is complete.

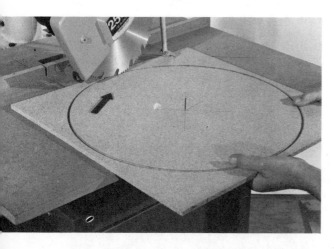

Figure 16-44: Circular pieces can be cut with a regular saw blade when this pivot method is used. The arrow shows the direction in which the work must be turned. Make repeat passes to achieve full depth-of-cut.

If you follow the same procedure but situate the pivot point so it is not in line with the blade's center, you will be forming a circular cove (Figure 16-45).

When the work is so large that the pivot point can't be established on the saw table, set up a sawhorse or a stand so the pivot point can be set up off the table.

Figure 16-45: You can form a circular cove by setting the pivot point off the center line of the saw blade.

CUTTING "DIAMONDS." Strips of beveled lumber can be cut in a particular fashion to form individual "diamond" shapes that can be used as is or assembled as many-pointed star shapes like the one in Figure 16-46.

Figure 16-46: Diamond-shaped pieces can be assembled to form multipointed stars. The text explains how the number of points can be controlled by the method of cutting.

Many variations are possible, but the true diamond shape results when the cross section of the beveled material is an isosceles triangle (Figure 16-47A). Once the stock is formed, a series of compound-angle cuts are made to produce the individual pieces. Swing the radial arm to 45° and tilt the blade to the same angle used to form the bevels. This setting will produce pieces that can be assembled as an eight-point star. For a specific number of points, divide the number required into 360° and set the radial arm at this figure.

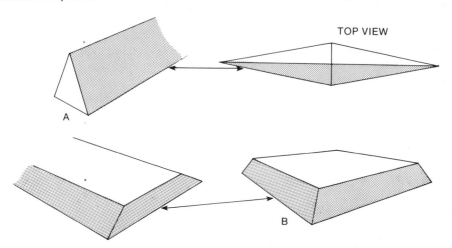

Figure 16-47: The strips can first be cut so a cross section will be an isosceles triangle as in A or they can be cut as in B. The degree of the bevel is variable and this permits cutting an infinite number of shapes.

Place the stock against the guide fence and make the first cut, as shown in Figure 16-48. The first cutoff is scrap. The second cut is made by turning the stock end for end and by placing it on the **right** side of the blade, as shown in Figure 16-49. This cutoff will be the first useable piece. The third cut is made

Figure 16-48: To produce pieces that can be assembled as an eight-point star, set the arm at 45° and tilt the blade to the same angle used to cut the bevels. The first cut is made this way, with the cut-off pieces discarded as scrap.

Figure 16-49: The second cut is made with the work turned end for end and then situated this way. This cutoff will be the first useable part. The text explains how succeeding cuts should be made.

after the stock has been turned end for end and placed on the **left** side of the blade. The piece that is cut off when the work is on the left side of the blade is scrap. Continue the procedure until you have the required number of diamond shapes.

The shapes that are shown in Figure 16-50 result when the lumber is bevel-cut like the form that is shown in Figure 16-47B. Those that are shown in Figure 16-51 are a variation of the basic idea.

Be very accurate when you position the work for each of the cuts. Use a hollow-ground blade for all operations.

Figure 16-50: The parts being cut in the two preceding illustrations can be assembled to form this type of eight-point star.

Figure 16-51: This is just one of the many variations that are possible by following the basic procedures but working with different cut-angles.

ROTARY PLANING. The primary function of a rotary planer is to surface rough stock and to reduce stock thicknesses. But because the radial arm saw allows the tool to be used in various ways, its usefulness extends to the kind of work shown in Figure 16-52.

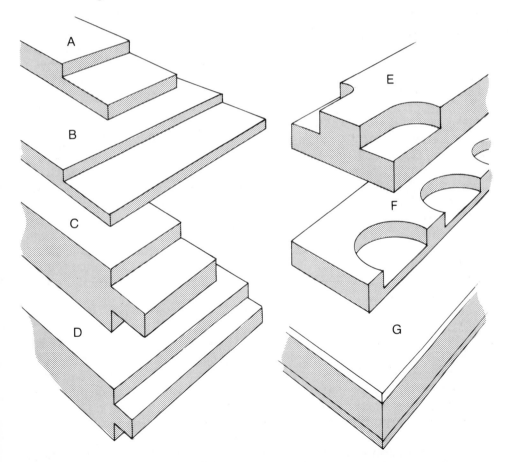

Figure 16-52: The rotary planer is a fine tool for surfacing stock but can also be used to form shapes like these: (A) End rabbet; (B) edge rabbet; (C) tenon; (D) tongue; (E) decorative cuts; (F) scallops; and (G) panel raising.

The rotary planer consists of two knives mounted on the motor's main arbor (Figure 16-53). The two knives should be installed before the planer is mounted, but their ultimate position should not be adjusted at this time. Put the knives in place, but just finger-tighten the retaining cap screws that secure them.

Figure 16-53: The planer mounts on the motor's main arbor. Be sure to adjust the projection of the knives by following the procedure outlined in the text.

Remove all items from the arbor—collars, cutting tool, lock nut—and thread the planer onto the arbor until it butts against the shoulder of the shaft. Place the large Allen wrench in the opening at the end of the arbor; then, gripping the planer by its outer rim, turn it counterclockwise with enough pressure to seat it securely. Be careful to place hands so they can't slip across the knives. The knives are sharp.

Raise the radial arm until the planer can be tilted 90° downward so its cutting plane will be parallel to the table. Swing the radial arm so the planer will be over a flat area of the table (away from the rip-trough), and lower the arm until the disc-like projection on the planer-head touches the table top. Raise the radial arm just a bit to get no more than about 1/64" between the planer and the table. Loosen the knife-holding cap screws and allow the knives to drop down until they rest on the table. Then tighten the screws securely with the Allen wrench that is provided. Remember that the sharp point of the cutting bevel on the knives should point forward. They should lead into the planer's direction of rotation which, when the tool is in vertical position, will be counterclockwise.

This is the correct setting for the knives and allows a 1/8" depth-of-cut. THE TOOL GUARD THAT WAS SHOWN FOR SHAPING OPERATIONS IN CHAPTER 12 SHOULD BE USED WITH THE ROTARY PLANER EVEN THOUGH IT IS NOT SHOWN MOUNTED IN THE PHOTOGRAPHS.

SURFACE PLANING. Set the planer in vertical position and raise it above the table so it can clear the surface of the stock. Put the work under the planer and lower the radial arm until the planer's knives just touch the work. Situate the planer for the cut; then lower it so it will make a cut about 1/16" deep. Tighten the rip lock, and then very slowly move the work along the guide fence as shown in Figure 16-54.

When the stock is wider than the cut-path of the planer, all you have to do is make repeat passes, locking the planer in a more forward position for each. Notice that the fence shown in the photograph has a cut-out area so the planer can be brought close to the table.

Figure 16-54: Work is surfaced by using the planer in vertical position. Keep the depth-of-cut to about 1/16" and make the pass so the knives will be cutting with the grain of the wood. Always use the safety guard even though it is not shown in the photographs.

Surface planing will be most successful when the stock is moved so the knives cut **with** the grain of the wood and when the depth-of-cut is held to a minimum. When a shallow cut doesn't do the job, lower the planer slightly and make a second pass.

PANEL RAISING. The work is done as shown in Figure 16-55. Tilt the cutter to about 10° or 15° and lock it in position (with the rip lock) for the cut-width required. Adjust for depth-of-cut by lowering the radial arm. The latter adjustment should be just enough to leave a slight shoulder on the work.

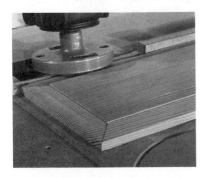

Figure 16-55: To do panel raising, use the planer in vertical position but tilted 10° to 15°. Move the work from right to left as if you were doing surface planing. Plan depth-of-cut so a slight shoulder will remain on the stock.

As with all work that is shaped on four edges, do the crossgrain cuts first. Don't try to hand-hold work that is narrow. Use a substantial back-up block to feed the work past the cutter. Results will be best when you get to the final shape by combining slight cuts with repeat passes.

RABBETS AND TENONS. Although there are limitations here simply because the rotary planer has a limited depth of cut, there are situations in woodworking where a shallow rabbet can be useful. The advantage of the planer is that it can cut a very wide rabbet, as shown in Figure 16-56. Here, the work is held securely against the guide fence and the planer is pulled forward to make the cut. Use a clamp to secure the work if it tends to move while you are cutting.

To form a tenon, just cut opposing rabbets as shown in Figure 16-57. The depth-of-cut limitations of the planer are not so critical here since the mortise can be sized to suit the tenon.

Figure 16-56: Rabbets are cut by pulling the planer across the work. Depth-of-cut is limited, but the rabbet can be as wide as you wish. Hold the work very firmly, or clamp it.

Figure 16-57: A tenon is formed by making two opposing rabbet cuts. Be sure to correctly position the work for the second cut, either by lining it up with a mark on the fence or by working with a stop block.

DECORATIVE CUTS. The planer is not a "decorating" tool, but in some situations it can be used to surface-cut a panel that will serve as an interesting detail on a project. The cuts being made on the part in Figure 16-58 represent the type of work that can be done. These are just stopped cuts. The length of the cuts can be controlled by feeding to marks on the work or by using a stop block on the guide fence. Be sure to keep the work flat on the table when you move it away from the cutter at the end of each pass.

Figure 16-58: This type of decorative work is done by making stopped cuts. You can make passes to marks on the work or control them by using a stop block. Be sure to keep the work flat on the table when you pull it away from the cutter.

HOW TO DO DADO TURNING. The radial arm saw can be used to do a certain amount of work that is ordinarily done on a wood-turning lathe. The technique is possible because of specially designed jigs that allow work to be mounted between centers just as it would be in a lathe. The work is then turned against a dadoing tool which does the cutting. **Warning: Extreme caution should be taken when making turnings on a radial saw since the dado cutters are exposed.**

The jig shown in Figure 16-59 locks in place in the slot normally occupied by the guide fence. It is adjustable to accommodate various lengths of work and has locking centers that are easily made from ordinary bolts. Carefully study the construction details in Figure 16-60 before starting to make the project. The fence component is made of several pieces so the T-slot in which the carriage slides move can be formed without a special cutting procedure. Be sure to assemble parts so the slides can move while you are holding the carriages securely. The detail in the drawing shows how the centers are made. The points can be shaped by working on a grinder or with a hand file.

Figure 16-59: This adjustable jig lets you do turning jobs by working with a dado assembly. Cuts can be limited to a specific area or they can be lengthened by repositioning the jig. SINCE THE DADO CUTTERS ARE EXPOSED, USE EXTREME CAUTION WHEN TURNING ON A RADIAL ARM SAW.

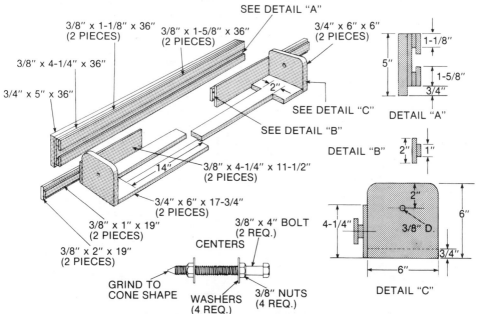

Figure 16-60: Construction details of the turning jig. Make it carefully so the carriages can easily slide but without wiggling. The centers are made from ordinary bolts.

To mount work, situate the carriages so the distance between them will be about 2″ more than the length of the work. Secure the carriages to the fence by using two C-clamps, and then secure one center by turning its lock nuts in opposite directions. Remember that one nut is on the **outside** of the carriage-upright and the second nut is on the **inside**. Put the work in position and adjust the second center. It should bear against the work with enough pressure to keep the work secure (Figure 16-61).

Figure 16-61: The nuts keep the centers firm because they bear against opposite surfaces of the carriage. Note the C-clamp that secures the carriage. Use a C-clamp on each carriage.

Turning is done with the dado assembly in crosscut position as shown in Figure 16-62. The height of the dado and its forward position are both controls for depth of cut. The cut is made by slowly rotating the work against the direction of rotation of the cutter (Figure 16-62). Grip the work firmly with your hand well away from the cutting tool. Don't try to take deep bites. A slow work rotation combined with a conservative depth of cut will produce best results.

The carriages are repositioned when the cut must be wider than that which the dado can produce in a single pass. It is also possible to leave the carriages in a fixed position and to resituate the dado for successive cuts by swinging the radial arm and rotating the dado. Be sure that all locks are tightened before doing any cutting.

Figure 16-62: Rotate the work so cutting is done against the direction of rotation of the dado assembly. A slow rotation with a conservative depth-of-cut will produce best results. Keep hands away from the cutter.

Many woodworkers who lack lathe equipment get by with ready-made spindles. When a spindle lacks a tenon for assembly, it can easily be formed by working as shown in Figure 16-63. The setup is organized so the dado is at the end of the work. Cutting is done in routine fashion—rotating the work against the cutter's direction of rotation and lowering the dado as successive passes are made until the tenon's diameter is correct. In some situations, the size of the work can be a hindrance. A solution is to drill more holes for the centers so they can be placed in a lower position when necessary.

Tenons are usually located concentrically, but when a job calls for an unusual location, the tenons can be formed off-center as shown in Figure 16-64.

Figure 16-63: Workers who make use of ready-made spindles can mount them in the jig and form tenons in this fashion. Note that "turning" work can be done on square as well as round stock.

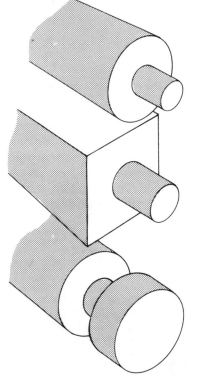

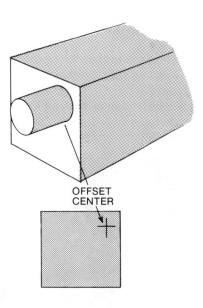

OFFSET
CENTER

Figure 16-64: Tenons can be formed so they are "on" or "off" center.

A SECOND DADO-TURNING JIG. The second jig design is shown in Figure 16-65. This also works with adjustable carriages, but here, they are guided by a groove that is cut in the platform and their position is secured by tightening the sheet metal screws. The centers that were shown for the first jig are also used with this one.

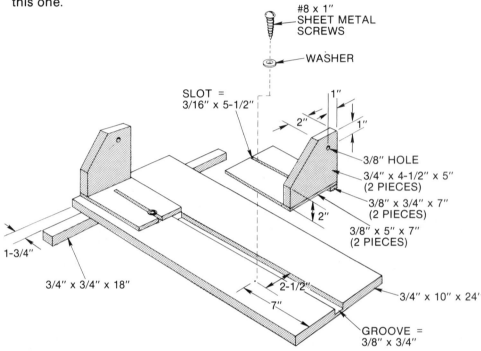

Figure 16-65: Construction details of the second jig. The centers that are used with the first jig are also used with this one.

The jig is locked to the table as shown in Figure 16-66. An advantage is that the jig can stay in a fixed position while the cutter is located by moving it along the radial arm. In the photograph, the jig is locked in the normal guide-fence slot, but it can be moved farther back when necessary and locked behind the wide table board. Since the jig also has longitudinal freedom, there is much flexibility in terms of work size and how the cutter can be positioned.

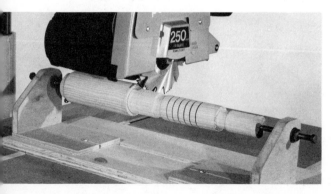

Figure 16-66: The jig locks in place in the slot normally occupied by the guide fence. Here, the dado assembly is in out-rip position. It is also possible to lock the jig on the right side of the table so the dado assembly can be used in the in-rip position.

Work procedure is much the same as with the first jig. Grip the work firmly, well away from the cutter, and rotate it slowly against the cutter's direction of rotation. When the work is so large that it can't fit under the motor, it's a simple matter to move the jig away and to rotate the dado toward the back of the machine. Cutting will not be affected when the dado is at an angle to the center line of the work.

This setup can be used to form tapers as well as straight cylinders. The job is done by mounting the work on one true center and one off-center as shown in Figure 16-67. As the work is turned, the cutter will be removing more stock from one "side" of the work.

Figure 16-68 shows how a saw blade can be used to form grooves. It is advisable to work with an 8" hollow-ground blade. Don't ever make grooves so deep that the stock will be weakened. Always check to be sure, with both jigs, that the centers are holding the stock firmly.

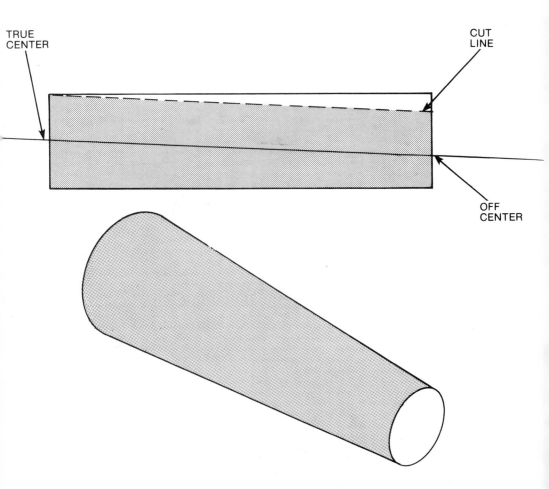

Figure 16-67: Tapered cylinders can be formed by mounting work on a true center at one end and an "off" center at the other end.

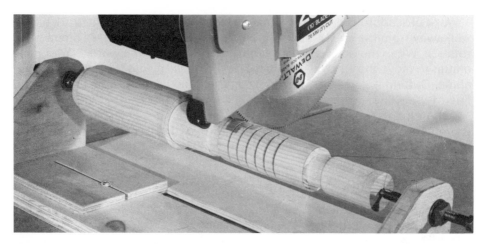

Figure 16-68: Grooves on a circumference can be formed with a saw blade. Work with an 8" hollow-ground blade. Don't make grooves so deep that they weaken the stock. Start with the blade above the work. Then slowly lower it to make contact.

Work that is made round by cutting with a dadoing tool will not be as smooth as you might wish. A way to do a sanding job while the work is still mounted in the jig is shown in Figure 16-69. Here, a sanding drum (which we will discuss later) is mounted on the motor's arbor and is pulled back and forth while the work is slowly rotated. The slower you turn the work and the more passes you make with the drum, the less chance there will be of creating flat areas. When the sanding drum is used, it doesn't matter which way the work is rotated.

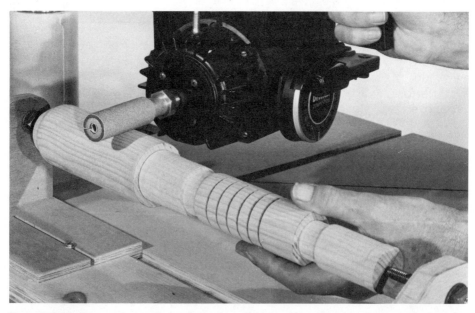

Figure 16-69: You can smooth a cylinder by working with a drum sander mounted on the arbor. Move the drum back and forth as you rotate the work. There will be more on drum sanding in the following chapter.

FORMING FLUTES OR REEDS. To do this kind of work, the shaper head is mounted on the arbor as it would be for routine shaping operations. The work is placed between the jig's centers and located so the work and the cutting portion of the shaping knives will have a common vertical center line (Figure 16-70). Raise the radial arm until the shaping knives barely scrape the surface of the work. Then lower the arm so the knives will cut 1/16" to 1/8" deep, and very slowly pull the cutter forward.

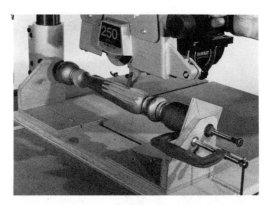

Figure 16-70: How to do reeding or fluting. Be sure the jig and the work are securely locked. Pull the cutter forward very slowly. Don't try to make deep cuts in a single pass. The shaper knife is a combination bead-and-quarter round. Only the bead portion of the knife's profile is cutting.

With this technique, the work is mounted between centers in such a way that it can be firmly locked in position for each pass made with the cutter. How this is done is shown in Figure 16-71. The guide plate, attached to the work with nails, allows the work to be rotated but provides a means of locking the piece's position against the carriage by means of a C-clamp. The guide plate can be round as well as square. If it is marked with radial lines, it can be used as a gauge to turn the work the desired number of degrees for successive cuts. The marks on the guide plate can be aligned with a mark made on the carriage.

Be sure that all is secure before making cuts. If the cuts are deep, form them by making repeat passes. The technique can be handy as long as the size of the work permits the shaper head to be used in such fashion. There is a limit to how far above the table the shaper head can be situated.

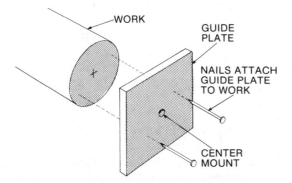

Figure 16-71: A guide plate must be attached to the work when doing any reeding or fluting job. When the guide plate is clamped to the carriage, the work will be securely held for the cut. The text explains how the plate is used to gauge cut-spacing.

KERFED MOLDINGS. Strips of wood can be kerf-cut along any of the lines shown in Figure 16-72. All of the cuts that are shown are made with the saw in crosscut or miter position. The depth of the cuts is not important, except that they should not be deep enough to weaken the strips. The spacing of the cuts and the pattern that is created are a matter of personal choice.

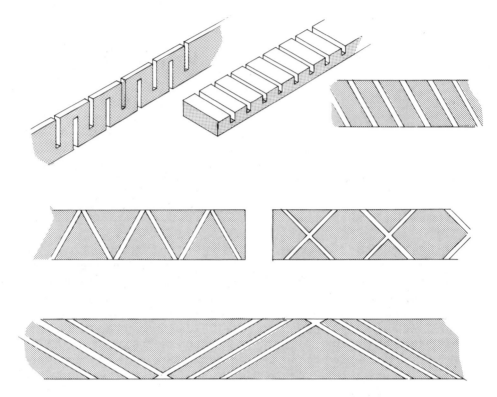

Figure 16-72: Many types of moldings can be formed by kerf-cutting.

Kerf-cut strips can be used as is or they can be mounted in one of the ways shown in Figure 16-73.

Some interesting pierced panels can be created when the work is cut and then assembled as shown in Figure 16-74. Kerfs of uniform spacing are cut in opposite surfaces of the stock. The stock is then strip-cut into pieces about 1/4" thick and assembled as shown. Glue or contact cement can be used to hold the pieces together.

DRILLED MOLDINGS. Examples are shown in Figure 16-75. The basic technique is to drill into the edge of stock as if you were forming holes for dowels. Then the stock is strip-cut into as many pieces as are needed. Variations depend on how the drilling is done. An example is two pieces of wood, clamped firmly together, that are edge-drilled on the joint line. When the pieces are separated, each will have a semicircular groove. After the pieces are strip-cut, they can be assembled in some of the ways shown in the photograph.

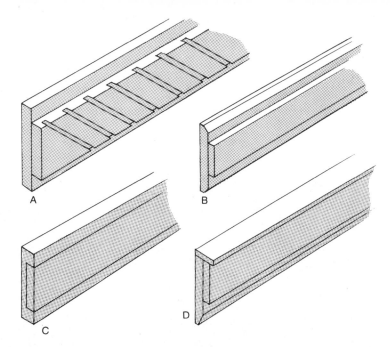

Figure 16-73: Kerf-cut moldings can be used as is or they can be mounted in one of the ways shown here: (A) Molding mounted on plain backing; (B) the backing strip can be chamfered or beveled; (C) molding inlayed; and (D) backing with one chamfered edge and a cap strip.

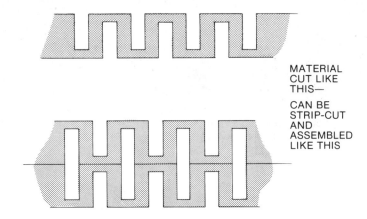

MATERIAL CUT LIKE THIS—

CAN BE STRIP-CUT AND ASSEMBLED LIKE THIS

Figure 16-74: Wide pieces of material that are kerfed as shown in the top sketch can then be strip-cut and assembled as shown in the bottom sketch. Join the pieces with glue or with contact cement.

Figure 16-75: Examples of drilled moldings. The basic procedure is to edge-drill stock as if you were forming holes for dowels. The stock is then strip-cut into slim pieces. Many variations are possible depending on how the drilling is done.

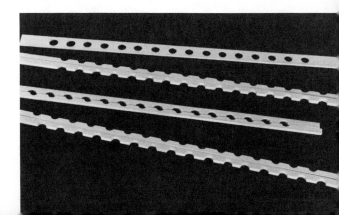

CURVED MOLDINGS. Slim, curved moldings, like those shown in Figure 16-76, are made by doing the shaping work on a piece of stock that is large enough to be safely handled. Shaping of the curved edge is done by following the techniques that were described in Chapters 12 and 13 on shaping and routing, respectively. The molded edge is then cut off by working with the saber saw.

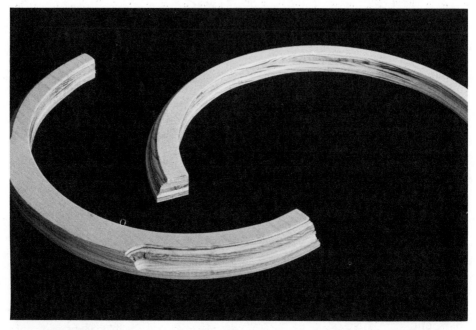

Figure 16-76: Curved moldings are formed by doing the shaping on stock that is large enough to handle and then sawing off the part that is needed. It is very poor practice to precut parts like this before shaping.

Chapter 17
Sanding—
The Finishing Touch

The radial arm saw offers two major methods of doing sanding chores—disc sanding and drum sanding. The two tools can't cover every sanding procedure. They are not useable, for example, for sanding an oversize plywood panel, a job done best with a portable sanding machine. But, they can cover about 90% of the sanding jobs encountered in a woodworking shop.

The advantage of using a disc or a drum on the radial arm saw lies in the tool's flexibility. Both items attach directly to the motor's main arbor, therefore they can be positioned in various ways, like other accessories, to suit the job on hand. Because this is so, it is often possible to create a setup that can't be duplicated even by an individual disc or drum-sanding machine.

ABRASIVES. There are three factors to consider when choosing an abrasive—the **type,** the **grit size,** and the method of **coating.**

The grit number of an abrasive is actually a **mesh number** which indicates a particular size screen that was used to filter the abrasive particles during the manufacturing process. Particles that pass through a number 12 screen would measure 12 to the inch if they were placed in a line. When screening becomes impractical because of the size of the particles, a complex flotation system is used to arrive at the same results. Grit sizes range from No. 12 (the coarsest) to No. 600 (the finest).

Originally, grit sizes were referred to by number or symbol. Today, many manufacturers are using words like "fine," "medium," or "coarse," sometimes together with a number, to identify the size of the grit. Each of the word categories, as shown in Figure 17-1, can cover a number of different grits.

The type of abrasive has to do with the material that does the sanding. Garnet, a natural mineral, and aluminum oxide, a manufactured material, are both considered excellent for power sanding. Silicon carbide is another synthetic material and is probably one of the hardest abrasives manufactured. It does a good job on metals and can be used to smooth down undercoats and primers.

Flint, a natural quartz mineral, is the least expensive but also the least durable of all the abrasives. It is actually the oldest of modern abrasives, but today it is usually relegated to chores like removing paint and old finishes and other jobs that quickly clog the paper. Figure 17-2 lists abrasives and suggests various grit sizes that can be used for different applications.

Coatings are referred to as "closed coat" or "open coat." Closed coat refers to particles that are densely packed. The result is a durable, fast-cutting abrasive surface, but one that can easily clog under particular conditions. Open coat products have abrasive particles spaced so that only about 50% to 70% of

COMPARATIVE GRADES
OF ABRASIVE PAPERS

COMMON NAME	GRIT	EQUIV. "0" # or symbol
	600	
	500	
	400	10/0
Very	360	
fine	320	9/0
	280	8/0
	240	7/0
	220	6/0
	180	5/0
Fine	150	4/0
	120	3/0
	100	2/0
Medium	80	1/0
	60	1/2
	50	1
Coarse	40	1-1/2
	36	2
	30	2-1/2
Very	24	3
Coarse	20	3-1/2
	16	4
	12	4-1/2

Figure 17-1: Abrasive papers are graded by name, number, or symbol. This chart shows the relationship between the various categories.

the backing is covered. This type doesn't cut as fast as closed-coat designs simply because it has fewer abrasive particles. On the other hand, it won't clog as quickly.

Open coat abrasives are a good choice when working on gummy wood, soft metals, and plastics—situations where the waste will quickly clog the disc or the drum.

SUGGESTIONS FOR TYPE OF ABRASIVE AND GRIT TO USE ON VARIOUS MATERIALS

ABRASIVE	DESCRIPTION	WHEN USED ON	GRIT SUGGESTED FOR		
			ROUGH	FINISHING	
			WORK	MEDIUM	FINE
Aluminum oxide	Manufactured, brown color, bauxite base, good general-use paper.	Hardwood	2-1/2—1-1/2	1/2—1/0	2/0—3/0
		Aluminum	40	60—80	100
		Copper	40—50	80—100	100—120
		Steel	24—30	60—80	100
		Ivory	60—80	100—120	120—280
		Plastic	50—80	120—180	240
Garnet	Natural mineral, red color, hard and sharp, excellent for general woodworking.	Hardwood	2-1/2—1-1/2	1/2—1/0	2/0—3/0
		Softwood	1-1/2—1	1/0	2/0
		Composition board	1-1/2—1	1/2	1/0
		Plastic	50—80	120—180	240
		Horn	1-1/2	1/2—1/0	2/0—3/0
Silicon Carbide	Manufactured, fast cutting, very hard.	Glass	50—60	100—120	120—320
		Cast iron	24—30	60—80	100
Flint	Natural form of quartz, low cost but not as durable as others.	Removing paint, old finishes, other jobs that quickly clog the paper.	3—1-1/2	1/2—1/0	

Figure 17-2: Here are suggestions for the grit and the type of abrasive to use for various operations.

GENERAL PRACTICE. The common procedure is to work through progressively finer grits of paper until the work is as smooth as necessary. But the critical factor is choosing the proper grit to begin your work. There is little point in starting with a coarse grit if the wood was purchased in sanded state. Always work with the finest paper that will produce desired results.

Whenever possible, work so the abrasive particles will cut **with** the grain of the wood. Don't force the work. Remember that sanding is done to **finish,** not to **shape.**

Abrasives are cutting tools. Use your hands so they can't slip into the disc or drum. Obey all the safety rules. Wear safety goggles and a respirator.

Don't be too quick to discard used abrasive papers. Often, a worn "coarse" paper can do the job of a "medium" paper. Abrasives will last longer if you keep them from clogging by frequently cleaning them with a brush. Don't do the cleaning when the disc or the drum is turning.

THE DISC SANDER. The disc sander is a flat, metal plate, 8″ in diameter, with a threaded hub that allows it to be mounted on the motor's main arbor. The one shown in Figure 17-3 has a slight bevel on its circumference that makes it easier to do certain chores more accurately. The abrasive sheets used with the disc are shown in the same illustration. These are pressure sensitive. All you have to do to mount them is peel off the backing—which exposes the adhesive— center them over the disc, and then press them firmly in place. Removing worn sandpaper is just as easy; simply peel it off.

Mounting the Disc. Follow the procedure given below to mount the disc on the disc sander.

1. Place the two arbor collars on the shaft against the spacer. Then, thread the arbor nut completely onto the shaft. Securely tighten it against the two arbor collars using the standard wrenches included with your machine.

2. Thread the sanding disc onto the shaft (sandpaper side out) until the hub of the disc touches the arbor nut.

3. Place the open end wrench on the arbor nut with one end of the wrench resting against the table top. Grasp the 8″ disc with both hands and turn it counterclockwise to tighten the disc securely against the arbor nut. Remove the open end wrench. A mounted sanding disc is shown in Figure 17-4.

Figure 17-3: The sanding disc used on the radial arm saw has an 8″ diameter. The abrasive discs are available in various grits and are pressure sensitive. Applying them to the sanding disc is just a matter of peeling off the protective backing paper.

Figure 17-4: The sanding disc mounts on the motor's main arbor. The text tells how to mount the disc so it will function without becoming loose.

HOW TO MAKE A DISC SANDER TABLE. The most efficient way to use a disc sander is to equip it with a table like the one shown in Figure 17-5. This one is made so the horizontal center line of the disc can be level with or slightly above the table's surface. The table is constructed as shown in Figure 17-6. The long leg of the table sits in the guide-fence slot so the table's position can be secured by using the table clamp screws. The groove in the table is for various accessories (Figure 17-7) that are used to position work for particular kinds of disc sanding. Lock the table in place so there is a gap of 1/16" to 1/8" between the edge of the table and the disc's surface. Be sure to tighten the rip lock before working.

Figure 17-5: This special table allows the disc sander to be used like any individual disc-sanding machine. The arrow indicates the direction in which the disc will turn.

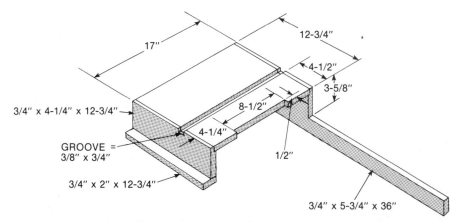

Figure 17-6: Construction details of the special disc sander table. The long leg of the accessory fits in the slot normally occupied by the guide fence.

253

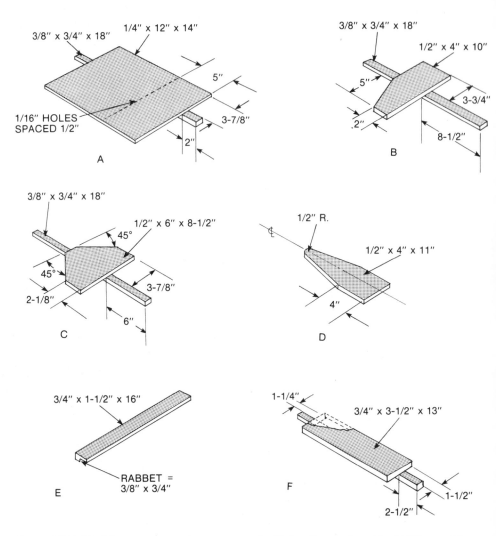

Figure 17-7: All of these accessory items are used with the disc sander table: (A) Pivot guide; (B) right angle guide (miter gauge); (C) 45° miter guide; (D) parallel curves guide; (E) fence; and (F) guide for sanding to width (typical). The purpose of each one is described in various sections of the chapter.

DIRECTION OF ROTATION. The disc turns in a clockwise direction; therefore, whenever possible, place the work on the right side of the tablo so the "down" side of the disc is used. When the "up" side of the disc is used (Figure 17-8), the disc's rotation will tend to lift the work off the table and waste material will be thrown upward. Even so, it is sometimes necessary to use the "up" side, as when edge-sanding a long piece, by sweeping it across the entire diameter of the disc. When such work is done, keep a firm grip on the work and maintain a gentle contact with the disc throughout the pass.

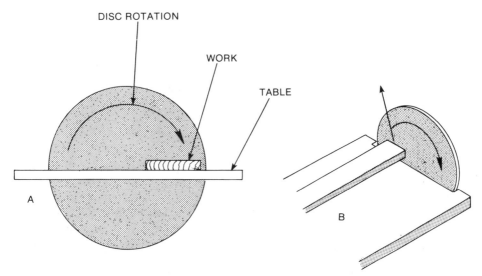

Figure 17-8: The disc rotates in a clockwise direction; therefore, whenever possible, place work on the right side of the table (A). Work placed on the left side of the table will tend to lift (B). Also, waste will be thrown upward.

To some extent, you can choose the abrasive-surface speed at which you work. This is not **revolutions per minute,** but relates to the fact that the center area of the disc turns fewer **inches per minute** than the outer edge. Also, if you held a piece of work directly against the center of the disc, you would get circular marks on the work but do very little sanding.

END SANDING. To smooth the end of a piece, hold the work flat on the table so it is at right angles to the disc. Then, move it forward to make contact with the abrasive. It is advisable to move the work across the radius of the disc as the sanding is done.

This kind of work can be done freehand but will be more accurate if you use the right-angle guide that is shown in Figures 17-9 and 17-7. With the guide in place (Figure 17-10), you will be sure that the sanded end will be square to adjacent edges. Hold the work firmly against the guide before moving it forward to make contact. Lock the guide in place with a clamp when you must sand many similar pieces.

Figure 17-9: The right-angle guide (miter gauge) rides in the table's groove. Generally, it should be positioned so the work will bear against the radius of the disc on the "down" side.

Figure 17-10: Work to be end-sanded is placed against the miter gauge and then moved directly forward against the disc. It is all right to move the work across the "down" side of the disc.

EDGE SANDING. You can do a respectable job of sanding edges with the disc if you work as shown in Figure 17-11. Hold the work firmly and sweep it across the disc so the "down" side of the disc is doing the work. This means that you hold the work at a slight angle rather than parallel to the disc. Use light pressure and don't hesitate during the pass. Stopping at any point will cause the disc to remove more material in one area than in others.

SURFACE SANDING. It is better to do surface sanding by following a system we will show a little later; but when the work is narrow, it's possible to do a reasonable job by making the pass as shown in Figure 17-12. Hold the work and sweep it across the disc in the manner described for edge sanding. Work with a coarse or medium paper if you are surfacing rough stock. Use a fine paper if you are finishing a surface. Any arc marks on the work can be removed by hand-sanding in line with the grain of the wood.

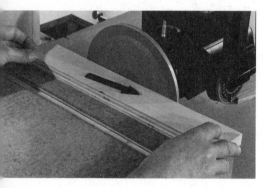

Figure 17-11: Edge-sand work by sweeping it across the disc. Apply more light pressure against the "down" side of the disc than against the "up" side.

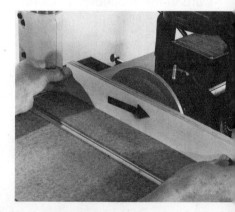

Figure 17-12: Surface sanding, within the limits of the disc, can be done, but arc marks will result regardless of how fine the abrasive is. However, the marks can be removed by hand-sanding in line with the grain of the wood.

SANDING CURVES. Round corners are sanded smooth after the stock has been cut to approximate shape. Place the work flat on the table so the straight side is parallel to the disc. Move the work forward to make very gentle contact, then smoothly rotate it until the corner is turned (Figure 17-13). Use the left hand to apply light pressure and the right hand to rotate the work.

A corner can be prepared for rounding by making straight saw cuts (miter cuts) to remove the bulk of the waste. Sanding will remove whatever waste is left. The system works best if coarse paper is used for the first sanding and fine paper is used for the last touch.

Long, outside curves are handled as shown in Figure 17-14. The pass is made as though the edge were straight, but the disc must constantly be tangent to the curve. This means that the work must be gently rotated as it is moved forward. Any hesitation will cause the disc to form a flat area.

You can do a good job of sanding inside curves as long as the radius of the curve is not very small. On such work, only the outer edge of the disc is used (Figure 17-15). The bevel on the disc makes this kind of work more feasible than it would be if the disc had a square edge. Use very little pressure; move the work without hesitation.

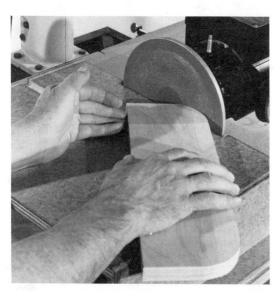

Figure 17-13: To round off corners, start with a straight side of the work parallel to the disc, then slowly rotate the work until the arc is complete. Use the left hand to apply light pressure while the right hand turns the work.

Figure 17-14: Outside curves are handled just like straight edges except that the surface of the disc must be tangent to the curve throughout the pass. Any hesitation will cause the disc to form a flat.

Figure 17-15: To sand inside curves, work so only the outer edge of the disc will be sanding. This is a more feasible operation because the disc has a beveled edge.

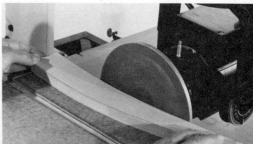

SANDING CIRCLES. Circular pieces can be sanded freehand, but the work will be more accurate if you use a pivot-guide system. This calls for the table accessory that is shown in Figures 17-16 and 17-7A. There are two ways to organize the work. One, leave the disc in normal position and place the accessory on the table with the pivot nail placed so the distance from it to the disc equals the radius of the work. Swing the disc away from the table slightly. After the work has been placed over the pivot nail, bring the disc back (while it is turning) to make contact.

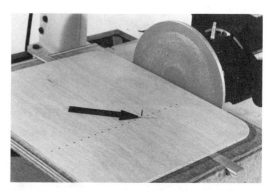

Figure 17-16: The pivot-guide jig is a sheet of plywood with a line of holes so the small nail which acts as the pivot point can be placed at various distances from the sanding disc.

The second method is to follow the first procedure to the point where the pivot nail is correctly situated. Then, move the table away from the disc, mount the work, and move the table back to its original position. At this point, the work will be in contact with the disc. Lock the table in place and start the sanding.

Sanding is done by slowly rotating the disc, preferably in a clockwise direction (Figure 17-17). This system can be used to bevel circular pieces. The only difference is that the disc is tilted to the degree of bevel required.

The pivot jig can also be used to sand rounded ends (Figure 17-18). Be sure the work is placed so the pivot nail will be on the work's center line.

Figure 17-17: After the work has been placed over the pivot pin and contact is made with the disc, turn the work slowly and steadily. A clockwise rotation is better even though the work may be turned either way.

Figure 17-18: The pivot guide may also be used to round off stock-ends. Be sure the pivot point is on the center line of the work.

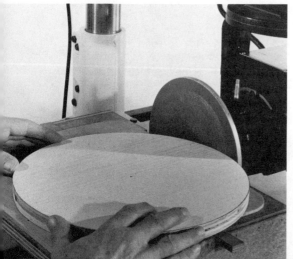

SANDING MITERS. The only difference between sanding a miter cut and a square edge is the angle at which the work must be placed. Because the miter angle is critical in relation to how parts go together at assembly time, it is wise to work with a guide like the one shown in Figures 17-19 and 17-7. The reason the guide has two angular edges is as follows. When the miter cut piece has flat surfaces, each end of the work can be sanded by using one edge of the guide. The second end is sanded merely by flipping the stock and turning it end-for-end. If the work has a contoured surface—a molding—it can't be flipped. The second end is sanded by positioning the work at an angle that opposes the original one. The guide makes this possible because it can be used to position work as shown in Figure 17-20.

Cross-miters can be sanded as shown in Figure 17-21 as long as the width of the stock is within the capability of the sanding disc. Another way to sand cross-miters is shown in Figure 17-22. It is just a matter of tilting the disc to the angle that is required. In this situation, the work is "captured" between the disc and the table, so be gentle when feeding the work forward. Be sure to tighten the bevel and rip locks.

Figure 17-19: Work with the miter guide to be sure that miter cuts will be accurately sanded. The guide can stay in one position if the work has flat surfaces so it can be flipped and turned end-for-end for sanding the opposite end. If the work is shaped, like this piece, the guide position is changed as shown in the next illustration.

Figure 17-20: Turn the guide around so the work can be positioned this way for sanding the second end.

Figure 17-21: When the width of the work allows it, cross-miters (or bevels) can be sanded this way.

Figure 17-22: This is another way to sand cross-miters. Tilt the disc to whatever angle is needed, then move the work directly forward. Don't force the work against the disc. Light pressure does the job.

SANDING TO WIDTH. The sanding disc can be used to sand an edge and, at the same time, bring the work to uniform width. The setup required is shown in Figure 17-23. The guide, made along the lines shown in Figure 17-7F, allows the pass to be made so the work contacts the disc only on the "down" side. The final width of the work is then determined by the distance between the guide and the disc. It is important that the angle of the guide be such that the work will not contact the disc on the "up" side. The clearance in the offset area doesn't have to be more than about 1/16" or 1/8". Actually, it isn't necessary to make a special guide. Any straight piece of wood, clamped to the table at the correct angle, will serve the same purpose.

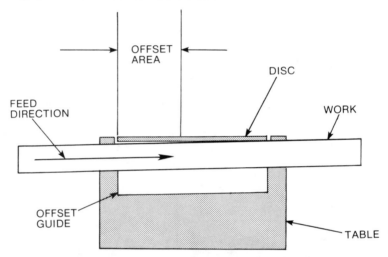

Figure 17-23: Work can be sanded to a precise width when this arrangement is used.

The pass is started by positioning the work snugly against the guide, then moving it past the disc while maintaining contact with the guide (Figure 17-24). The clearance dimension is not critical, but keeping it to a minimum will allow more of the "down" side of the disc to work.

Curved pieces can be sanded to a specific width by using the guide that is shown in Figures 17-25 and 17-7D. The guide is clamped to the table so the distance from its point to the disc equals the width of the work. Pass the work between the guide and the disc, turning the work as the pass is made to maintain the point of tangency.

It is assumed that the stock has been saber-sawed so a minimum of material must be removed by sanding. Also, the inside edge (the one that bears against the guide) must be sanded smooth before the outside edge is done.

PATTERN SANDING. This is a good technique to use when many similar pieces must be sanded. Figure 17-26 is a cross-sectional view that shows how the technique works. The pattern is a duplicate of the work but is cut undersize to compensate for the thickness of the guide and the amount of clearance between the disc and the guide. The guide, which can be a small block of wood, is nailed to the table as shown in Figure 17-27. The work, cut slightly oversize, is tack-nailed to the pattern.

Figure 17-24: Pass the work between the offset guide and the disc. The arrow points to the necessary slight gap between the work and the "up" side of the disc.

Figure 17-25: Curved pieces that have a uniform width can be sanded this way. Be sure the disc is on a tangent to the curve through the pass. The inside edge, which rides on the point of the guide, must be smooth to begin.

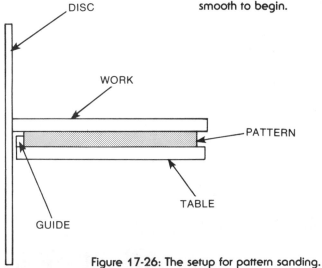

DISC

WORK

PATTERN

TABLE

GUIDE

Figure 17-26: The setup for pattern sanding.

Figure 17-27: The guide is a small block of wood that is nailed at the front edge of the table. The pattern is tack-nailed to the rough-cut work.

261

As you move the pattern/work assembly while keeping the pattern in contact with the guide (Figure 17-28), the work is sanded to match the shape of the pattern.

A simple way to secure work to the pattern without having to tack-nail it is to drive nails through the pattern so the points project on the top side. Then the work is simply pressed down on the points. Use at least two nails so the work can't swivel when being sanded.

POINTING DOWEL OR OTHER ROUND STOCK. This can be done freehand, but the results will be more uniform if you work with the miter guide as shown in Figure 17-29. Hold the work against the guide and rotate it slowly as you feed it forward. The amount of sanding you do will determine whether the dowel will be pointed or chamfered. To get a flat surface—a bevel—move the work directly forward without rotating it at all.

Figure 17-28: Work so that the pattern constantly bears against the guide. The pattern, of course, must be carefully made. The work won't be correct if the pattern has rough edges.

Figure 17-29: Use the miter guide to position dowel or other round work that needs to be pointed or chamfered. Turn the work very slowly while maintaining light contact with the disc.

SANDING BY PULLING THE DISC. In some situations, especially on wide work, it may be preferable to sand miter cuts by working as shown in Figure 17-30. Swing the arm and lock it in position at the required angle. Situate the work on the table so the edge to be sanded will butt against the disc. Move the disc back to neutral position; then, turn on the motor and slowly pull the disc forward so it will sand the work's edge. Be sure the work is securely clamped. Move the disc back to neutral position and turn off the machine before removing the work.

Figure 17-30: You can sand angular crosscuts by moving the disc across the work. Be sure the work is secure. Take a light bite; move the disc very slowly.

SURFACE SANDING. Remove the special disc sander table and then elevate the radial arm until the disc can be tilted downward so its surface will be parallel to the tool table. Raise the disc enough to clear the surface of the work. Then, situate it (by moving the yoke along the arm) so it will be over the path the material will be moved. Tighten the rip lock, then lower the disc until it bears lightly against the surface of the work. Remove the work, turn on the motor, and feed the work from right to left as shown in Figure 17-31. Keep the work snug against the fence and flat on the table throughout the pass.

If the initial sanding doesn't satisfactorily surface the stock, make a second pass after lowering the disc just a fraction. When the stock is wider than the disc's diameter, make additional passes after the disc has been repositioned to cover unsanded areas.

When the disc is used for applications of this nature, it should be covered by using the guard that was shown in Chapter 12 (Figure 17-32).

Figure 17-31: Boards can be surface-sanded by using the disc in this fashion. Use coarse sandpaper when surfacing rough stock, fine sandpaper for finishing. A light cut and a slow feed produce the best results.

Figure 17-32: Always use the guard when the disc is in horizontal position.

DRUM SANDING. The drum sander is the ideal tool to use for sanding uniform or irregular curved edges, but its scope can be greatly increased by following special procedures. The sanding drums that can be mounted on the radial arm saw are shown in Figure 17-33. Both drums are 3" long, but the diameters are 1" and 2-1/2". Having different size drums on hand makes it possible to work on a wide variety of inside and outside radii.

How to Mount the Drum Sander. The procedure is similar to the one outlined for mounting the disc sander. Remove the saw guard and anything that is on the motor's main arbor (Figure 17-34).

1. Place the two arbor collars on the shaft against the spacer. Then, thread the arbor nut completely onto the shaft and tighten it securely against the two arbor collars using the standard wrenches included with your machine.

2. Thread the drum sander onto the shaft until the hub touches the arbor nut.

3. Place the open end wrench on the arbor nut with one end of the wrench resting against the tabletop. Grasp the drum sander with both hands and turn it counterclockwise to securely tighten it against the arbor nut. Remove the open end wrench.

Figure 17-33: Drum sanders that can be used on the radial arm saw. Both are 3" long. One has a 1" diameter, the other's diameter is 2-1/2".

Figure 17-34: The sanding drums mount on the motor's main arbor. Follow the directions detailed in the text.

REPLACING THE SANDPAPER. Following the procedure shown in Figure 17-35, you can make replacement strips by cutting strips of standard sandpaper sheets that are generally available.

1. Cut the sheet into strips 3" wide.

2. Use a board as a gauge for bending each end of the strip. The board for the 2-1/2" drum should measure 3" x 7-3/4"; 3" x 3-1/8" for the 1" drum.

3. Wrap the sleeve around the drum so the bends can slip into the slot that is in the drum.

4. Squeeze and roll the drum slightly so the abrasive strip will fit tightly and the bent ends will be fully in the slot.

5. Hold the strip in position and insert the tube that comes with the drum. Then, with an ordinary screwdriver, turn the tube so it bears against the ends of the sandpaper to hold the strip in position.

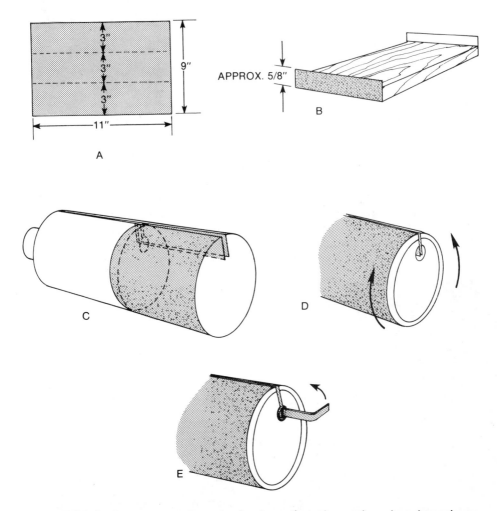

Figure 17-35: Replacement sanding strips (or sleeves) can be purchased ready-made, or you can make your own from standard sheets of sandpaper. The text explains the procedure.

POSITIONING THE DRUM. Elevate the radial arm to its maximum height, and tilt the motor 90° downward so the sanding drum will be in vertical position. Move the motor back until the drum is centered over the opening in the wide table board. Then, lower the drum until its free end is below the table's surface (Figure 17-36). Tighten the rip lock. Some vertical adjustment of the drum is possible; however, never lower it so far that it contacts the table's metal understructure.

Figure 17-36: The tool is positioned so the sanding drum can be set in the cutout that is in the wide table board. Don't lower the drum enough to contact the table's metal understructure.

SANDING CURVES. Inside or outside curves are drum-sanded by moving the work against the drum's direction of rotation (Figure 17-37). Use light pressure, making the pass smoothly and in one steady motion. When the work is so long that you must stop to reposition your hands, pull the work away from the drum and start a new pass at a point where it will overlap the end of the first one. Any hesitation during a pass will cause the drum to indent the work.

During prolonged periods of sanding, it is advisable to frequently change the height of the drum so that more of its abrasive surface can be used. The drum can be raised just so high before its free end clears the table, but its upper area can still be used if you raise the work with a height block.

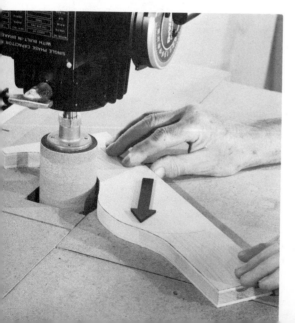

Figure 17-37: The drums are ideal tools for sanding uniform or irregular curves. Because you can work this way, you know that sanded edges will be square to adjacent surfaces.

INTERNAL SANDING. The technique of smoothing inside edges of pierced work doesn't differ from routine sanding except that the work must be situated as shown in Figure 17-38. Elevate the radial arm until the drum is at maximum height, or until the work can be slipped under it, and then lower the drum to working position. If the stock is too thick to permit this, tilt the motor enough to provide clearance. Return the drum to vertical position after the stock has been placed.

Both the "back" and the "front" of the drum can be used, but remember to move the work against the drum's rotation.

A SPECIAL DRUM-SANDER JIG. A simple jig, which is no more than a platform, will allow more of the drum's abrasive surface to be used. The jig (Figure 17-39) is installed as shown in Figure 17-40. The lock-strip, which sits in the guide-fence slot, should be two pieces or relieved in the area of the 3" hole so it won't interfere with the drum.

Figure 17-38: It's easy to sand inside edges of pierced work because the drum can be situated this way. Be sure to move the work against the drum's direction of rotation.

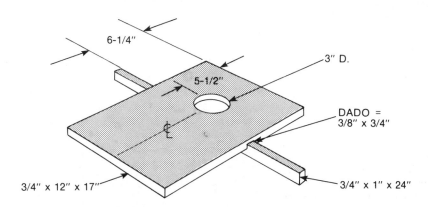

Figure 17-39: Construction details of the special drum-sander jigs.

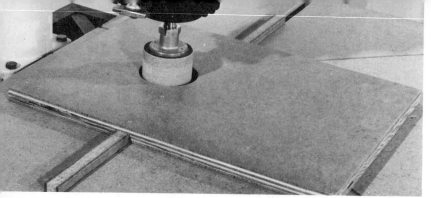

Figure 17-40: The jig is positioned this way. It allows more of the drum's abrasive surface to be used and is also suitable for some special procedures.

STRAIGHT SANDING. Drum sanders are primarily for smoothing curved edges, but if the tool is set up and you need to sand a straight edge, you can avoid having to change to a different sanding tool by using one of the following methods.

For end-sanding, work with the miter gauge that has been shown in various places in the book. Place the work so it just touches the drum. Then, holding the work firmly against the miter gauge, move it smoothly from right to left (Figure 17-41). Light, repeat passes will produce better results than a single heavy one.

Edge-sanding can successfully be done freehand if you use a light touch and move the work across the drum without hesitation (Figure 17-42).

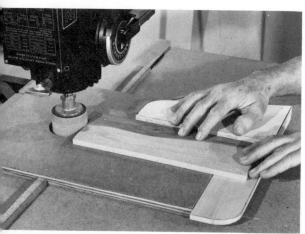

Figure 17-41: End-sanding can be accurately accomplished if you control the work by using the homemade miter gauge. Keep the work firmly against the miter gauge while making a slow pass.

Figure 17-42: Edges can be sanded freehand if you sweep the work smoothly across the drum and do not attempt to remove a lot of material in one pass. Any hesitation will cause the drum to indent the wood.

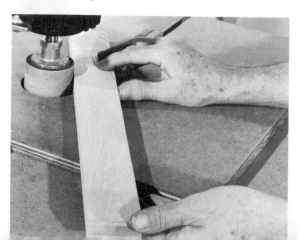

268

Another way to do edge-sanding is shown in Figure 17-43. This system is especially useful when you wish to sand the edge of stock that must be held to a uniform width. Move the drum to the back of the hole in the jig, and then place the work so the guide strip can be tack-nailed in place. Remove the work and bring the drum forward just a fraction. Tighten the rip lock. Then, pass the work between the drum and the guide strip. If the first pass doesn't do the job, make a second one without changing the drum's position. If more material must be removed, make an additional pass after bringing the drum forward a fractional distance.

PIVOT SANDING. After the work has been cut to approximate size on the saber saw, drive a slim nail through its center and place it in position on the jig as shown in Figure 17-44. Make light contact with the drum and rotate the work in the direction indicated by the arrow. The amount of room there is for the drum in the jig's hole allows enough adjustment of the drum so repeat passes can be made. In this situation, the location of the pivot point is not critical as long as the distance from the pin to the drum equals the radius of the work.

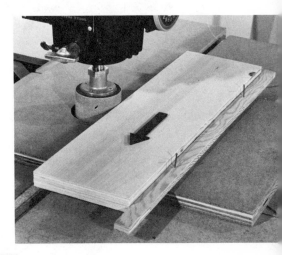

Figure 17-43: Another way to sand edges. This is more accurate than freehand work and assures that the work will have a uniform width. The guide does not have to be parallel to the front edge of the jig.

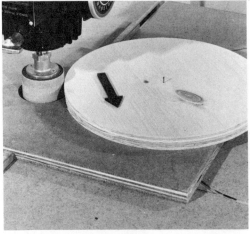

Figure 17-44: Sand circular work by using this simple pivot-guide method. The small nail through the center of the work penetrates the jig just enough to keep the work secure. The pivot point can be anywhere on the jig.

USING THE DRUM IN HORIZONTAL POSITION. This system, as shown in Figure 17-45, is another good way to do edge-sanding. The drum's working position is reached by starting with the drum in crosscut position and then rotating it 90° toward the front of the table. Set the height of the drum by raising or lowering the radial arm. Note that the work is braced between the jig and a straight piece of wood clamped to the table. This is to keep the work vertical while the pass is made. Position the drum so it just touches the work and then make the pass from left to right. Repeat the pass without changing the drum's position. To remove more material, make an additional pass after lowering the drum just a fraction.

The same setup can be used to sand beveled edges (Figure 17-46). The sanding procedure is the same as for a flat edge. The difference is that the drum is tilted to the necessary angle.

Figure 17-45: Edges can be sanded by using the drum in horizontal position. Passing the work between the jig and a straight piece of wood that is clamped to the table makes it easy to keep the work upright while making the pass.

Figure 17-46: Use the same system to sand beveled edges. It's the same as sanding a flat edge except that the drum is tilted to the necessary angle. In situations like this, work-feed direction is from left to right.

A DRUM SANDER TABLE WITH ITS OWN FENCE. This second jig, made as shown in Figure 17-47, makes it possible to do particular sanding jobs by passing work between the drum and the fence. The jig is locked in place and the drum is situated as shown in Figure 17-48. The relief area in the platform allows adjustment between the drum and the fence.

As shown in Figure 17-49, the jig allows surface-sanding of pieces that are not wider than 3". Start the procedure by putting the work in position and then moving the drum forward to make light contact. Tighten the rip lock, remove the work, and then make the pass from left to right. When work-size permits, edges can be sanded by following the same procedure (Figure 17-50). The difference is the work is flat on the table rather than on edge. The relief area in the jig doesn't have to be the size shown in the drawing. Make it longer if you wish to use the technique for sanding wider pieces.

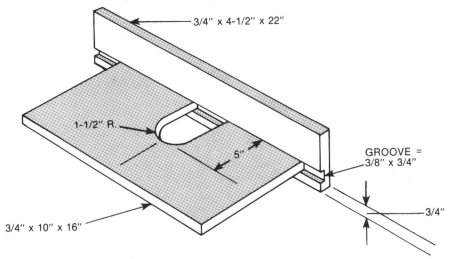

Figure 17-47: This drum sander jig has its own fence. The relief area in the table can be longer than the drawing shows.

Figure 17-48: The jig is positioned this way. The bottom edge of the fence is in the guide-fence slot so the jig is secured by tightening the table clamp screws.

Figure 17-49: Pieces up to 3" wide can be surface-sanded by passing them between the drum and the fence. Take a light cut—make the pass smoothly from left to right.

Figure 17-50: Edges can be sanded by using the same system. A longer relief slot will make it possible to edge-sand wider material.

HOW TO SAND STRIPS. Strip-cut pieces can be surface-sanded by following the procedure shown in Figure 17-51. It is very important to make the pass without hesitation. Any pause will cause the drum to indent the work.

A second method is shown in Figure 17-52. Here, the drum, set in crosscut position, is used with the disc sander table. Set the height of the drum by bringing it to bear lightly against the surface of the work. The direction of the pass is from the back to the front of the machine.

PATTERN SANDING. In order to do pattern sanding, it is necessary to form a disc with a diameter that equals or is slightly longer than the drum's diameter. The disc is placed so it and the drum will have a common, vertical center line. The disc can be attached to the regular table with a couple of brads, but it is better to make a special setup, like the one shown in Figure 17-53, that can be a permanent part of shop equipment.

Figure 17-51: The jig is ideal for surface-sanding very thin material. Strip-cut pieces can be brought to perfect smoothness when they are treated this way.

Figure 17-52: Another way to surface-sand thin material is to situate the drum over the disc sander table so the stock can be treated as shown. In this case, the pass is made from back to front.

Figure 17-53: The drum sander can be used for pattern sanding when it is aligned with a disc that acts as a guide for the pattern.

Figure 17-54 shows how the jig is put together. The rabbeted strip at the front edge is optional. However, it does provide security without having to mar the table. Without it, the front edge of the jig's table would have to be clamped— which can interfere with the work—or secured with small nails.

The pattern is tack-nailed to the workpiece which has been cut to approximate size. The work and pattern are moved into the drum as shown in Figure 17-55. If the disc's diameter equals the drum's, the pattern should be an exact duplicate of the work (A). If the guide-disc is larger than the drum, then the pattern must be smaller by the difference between disc and drum diameters(B).

Move the work so the pattern will be constantly in contact with the guide disc.

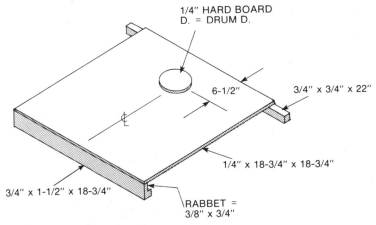

Figure 17-54: The guide-disc can be nailed directly to the regular table, but a special carrier is a better way to go. The text explains why the rabbeted front strip is optional.

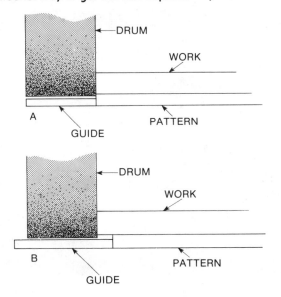

Figure 17-55: The pattern must be an exact duplicate of the work (A) if the guide-disc's diameter is the same as the drum's. If the disc is larger (B), then the pattern must be appropriately smaller.

SANDING RABBETS. Rabbet cuts usually are not sanded. But, at times, when the rabbet-cutting procedure has left too rough a surface or a bit of material must be removed so the joint will be more precise, the drum sander can be used to bring the cut to standard.

Sand edge-rabbets by using the setup shown in Figure 17-56. Use the jig that has a fence; set the position of the drum by rotating it from crosscut position 90° toward the back of the machine. Since there is a limit to how close the drum can come to the table, it may be necessary to elevate the work, either by using strips of wood under the jig's table or by placing a height block under the work.

End-rabbets are sanded as shown in Figure 17-57. The setup is the same as the one described for surface-sanding strip-cut pieces. Here, however, the work is positioned with the miter gauge and is firmly held while the drum is pulled forward to do the sanding.

On all rabbet-sanding operations, the abrasive strip on the drum should be situated so it projects about 1/32" beyond the bottom of the drum in order for the inside corner of the rabbet to be cleanly sanded.

Figure 17-56: Sand edge-rabbets this way. Note that the jig is now secured behind the wide table board. When the drum can't be lowered enough to accommodate the work, raise the jig with strips of wood or use a height block under the work.

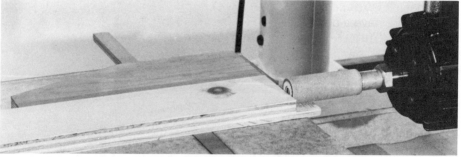

Figure 17-57: End-rabbets are sanded this way. Here, the work is positioned by the right-angle guide and is held steady while the drum is pulled across the cut. When sanding rabbets, adjust the abrasive sleeve so it projects about 1/32" beyond the end of the drum.

Figure 17-58: To form concave shapes, move the work directly into the drum sander. The size of the cove will determine whether to work with the small or large drum. Be sure the work and the drum have a common horizontal center line.

Figure 17-59: Surface sanding can be done this way. Set the tool in in-rip position. Use a fence to guide the work as you make the pass from right to left. Use a pusher to complete the pass.

CONCAVE SANDING. This procedure provides a solution for the problem that occurs when a part with a square end must mate with a round surface. An example is a rail that must connect with a round leg on a chair or table.

The concave shape can be sanded by following the procedure shown in Figure 17-58. Here, the work is placed on the disc sander table and is guided by a straight piece of wood that is clamped to the table, or it can be guided by a fence that is made like the one shown in Figure 17-7E. The drum, situated so it and the work have a common horizontal center line, is secured in position by tightening the rip lock. The shape is obtained by moving the work directly into the drum.

It is advisable to occasionally retract the work to give waste a chance to clear. Use light feed-pressure so the abrasive particles will have a chance to work. The work can be done with either the large or the small drum so there is some flexibility when determining the size of the concave shape.

SURFACE SANDING. Surface sanding can be done in simple fashion if you use the setup shown in Figure 17-59. With the drum sander in crosscut position, rotate it 90° toward the back of the machine, then lower it so it just touches the surface of the work. Make the pass by moving the work along the guide fence from right to left.

Work that is not wider than twice the width of the abrasive strips can be surface-sanded as shown in Figure 17-60. The drum is situated to cover the outboard half of the work. After the first pass is made, the work is turned end-for-end and again moved past the drum. The same illustration shows the use of a height block which may be needed when surface-sanding thin stock, since there is a limit to how close to the table the drum sander can be situated.

Figure 17-60: Work up to 6" wide can be surface-sanded this way. Make one pass, then turn the stock end-for-end and make a second pass. When the drum can't be brought close enough to the table, raise the work by using a height block.

Chapter 18
Still More Uses
for the Radial Arm Saw

The power unit of the radial arm saw is basically a motor that turns an arbor. As we have already discovered, it is possible to mount tools other than saw blades on the arbor. In this chapter, we will discuss the use of grinding wheels, wire brushes, and buffing and polishing accessories. Not all of the processes are essential in power woodworking, but they serve to extend workshop scope by allowing operations to be done that range from sharpening tools to polishing shoes.

GRINDING. Grinding wheels are composed of grains of abrasive material that are bonded together by special means. Each grain is a cutting tool. As it dulls, it exposes a new, sharp grain that takes over the cutting chore. The manufacture of a wheel involves five factors—the abrasive, the grain, the grade, the structure, and the bond.

The **abrasive** is the material that does the work. The most common wheels are of aluminum oxide, an abrasive that is good for grinding high tensile strength materials like high-speed and carbon steels. A silicon carbide wheel is good for low tensile strength materials like bronze, brass, gray iron, aluminum, and copper.

Grain refers to the grit size of the abrasive, and there are as many categories as you find in common sandpaper. "Coarse" grits run from No. 12 to No. 24, "medium" grits from No. 30 to No. 60, and "fine" grits from No. 70 to No. 120. Grits in the "very fine" to "flour size" category can run from No. 150 to No. 600. The grits that are best for general use in a woodworking shop are "medium" and "fine."

Wheel **grade** has to do with the bond, which can run from "very soft" to "very hard." The abrasive grains in a hard wheel will hold together even under extreme pressure, while those in a soft wheel will easily loosen. Generally, hard wheels are used for grinding soft materials, while the soft wheels are used on hard materials. A medium-hard grade is a good choice for general work.

Basically, **structure** refers to how the abrasive grains are spaced. Wheels with abrasive grains that are closely spaced do a good job on hard, brittle materials. Wheels with widely spaced grains do better with soft materials that tend to clog the abrasive.

Bond refers to the material that is used to hold the abrasive grains together. For our purposes, we are concerned with a vitrified bond which consists of special clays and other ceramic materials. The bond material and the abrasive grains are fused at high temperatures to produce a high-strength, porous wheel with a cool cutting action. The vitrified bond is a good choice for general-purpose grinding.

MOUNTING A WHEEL. Remove the saw guard and whatever is on the arbor. Then, mount the inside collar, the grinding wheel, and the outside collar. Tighten the lock nut only enough to secure the wheel. Excessive pressure can put unnecessary strain on the wheel. Do not use wheels that are so thick they don't leave enough arbor for the lock nut to seat correctly. Also, be sure the saw guard can be installed in correct position.

A way to obtain more room on the arbor is to substitute steel flanges for the regular saw-blade collars. The steel flanges work like the collars, but they are flatter and so take up less space on the arbor. The flanges are standard items that can be purchased at a tool-supply center. **Don't improvise**—for example, don't use washers in place of flanges that are designed for the purpose.

SAFETY AND CARE OF WHEELS. The maximum speed at which a grinding wheel can be run will be printed on the paper flanges that are attached to the wheel. Be sure the wheel you select can safely operate at the speed of the radial arm saw. Excessive speed can generate destructive heat and may subject the wheel to centrifugal forces it can't withstand. Both conditions can result in wheel breakage.

Test a wheel for cracks before mounting it. First visually check for chipped edges and cracks. Then, mount the wheel on a rod and tap the wheel gently on its side with a piece of wood. The wheel will produce a clear ringing sound if it is in good condition. A dull thud may indicate a crack that you can't see. If it happens, discard the wheel. Don't take chances! If you doubt the results of your own test, have the wheel checked by a professional craftsperson or return the wheel to the place of purchase.

Grinding wheels have paper washers (or flanges) on each side of the wheel. Their purpose is to equalize the pressure on the sides of the wheel. The paper washers must always be in place and they must have a diameter that is greater than the diameter of the steel flanges or collars.

Common grinding wheels are not made for side-grinding. That is, work should be applied to the front of the wheel, not its sides. There is some tolerance for very light-duty side-grinding, such as touching up the flat surfaces of a screwdriver; but heavy work, like renewing the edge of a cold chisel, mattock, or axe, should never be done on the side of the wheel.

Stand to one side when you turn on the machine and let the grinding wheel run free for a minute or so before you start working. Always wear safety goggles no matter how small a job you are doing.

All grinding operations throw off sparks which can act like firebrands. Be sure the work area is clean—free of sawdust and any other material that can be ignited.

GENERAL PRACTICE. Grinding operations should not be done freehand. Therefore, it is necessary to establish an arrangement like the one shown in Figure 18-1. Note that the saw guard, with its dust nozzle pointing toward the back of the machine, is correctly mounted and that the safety shield that was shown in Chapter 1 is mounted in place of the antikickback assembly. The guard and the shield should be situated so only enough of the wheel is exposed to do the work. The photographs were taken with the guard higher than it has to be and without the shield in place only for purposes of clarity.

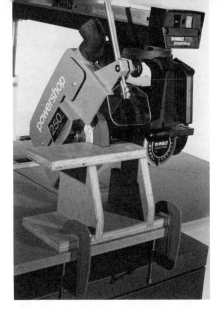

Figure 18-1: The radial arm saw can be used for many grinding operations, but it must be organized as shown in this photograph. Use clamps to secure the stand. Position the saw guard and the safety shield so only the working part of the wheel will be exposed.

Make the special unit by following the construction details in Figure 18-2. With the machine in normal crosscut position, bring the grinding wheel forward so it fits into the notch that is in the platform (or "tool rest") of the unit. Adjust the height of the wheel so its horizontal center line will be on or a fraction above the surface of the tool rest. Keep the gap between the tool rest and the wheel to a minimum—not more than 1/8". Tighten the rip lock and secure the unit's position with clamps.

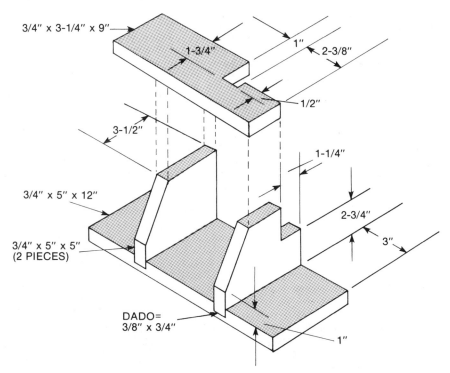

Figure 18-2: Construction details of the special stand for grinding operations.

KEEPING COOL. Tools are carefully heat treated and tempered for the jobs they are designed to do. Overzealous grinding can destroy those characteristics. Discoloration of the edge being ground, caused mainly by overheating, is a warning sign. To avoid it, use a very light touch and don't allow the tool to maintain contact with the wheel for long periods of time. Keep a container of water nearby so you can frequently immerse the tool as you are grinding.

REFIT A SCREWDRIVER. Place the screwdriver directly in line with the wheel and hold it securely on the tool rest (Figure 18-3). Then move it directly forward to make contact. All you want to do here is renew the flat on the edge of the screwdriver so it can fit snugly in the screw's head-slot. If the sides of the screwdriver need some attention, touch them very lightly to the side of the wheel while allowing the slant of the tool to guide the way you hold it.

Often, the sides of a screwdriver can be renewed merely by working them on a sheet of fine sandpaper. Place the screwdriver so its side is flat on the paper and then move the screwdriver in a circle.

SHARPENING TWIST DRILLS. Twist drills can be sharpened freehand, but it is an intricate job that requires some practice to master. Hold the drill as shown in Figure 18-4, so its center line is at the required angle with the face of the wheel. This angle can be judged by placing the cutting edge of the drill flush against the face of the wheel.

Figure 18-3: Screwdrivers are not "sharpened," but their edges must be flat and square so they will fit snugly in screwhead slots.

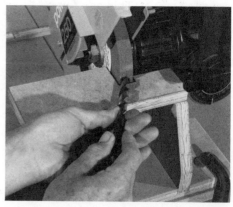

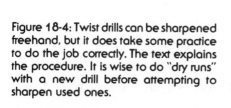

Figure 18-4: Twist drills can be sharpened freehand, but it does take some practice to do the job correctly. The text explains the procedure. It is wise to do "dry runs" with a new drill before attempting to sharpen used ones.

Using a combination action, slowly raise the shank end of the drill while rotating it in a counterclockwise direction until the grinding approaches the cutting-lip. Use very light pressure and don't attempt to work too fast. A good way to practice is to work with a new drill and to keep the grinding wheel still. Do the pseudo grinding while allowing the angle and shape of the drill-point to guide your hands.

There are special holders on the market that make drill sharpening a fairly easy chore. Figure 18-5 identifies the parts of a twist drill and suggests the correct cutting angle for wood or metal working.

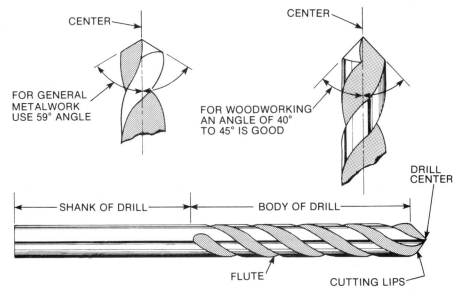

Figure 18-5: The nomenclature of a twist drill. Woodworking requires a sharper cutting angle than metal working.

SHARPENING WOOD CHISELS. Wood chisels work best when they are square across the cutting edge and have a hollow-ground bevel. Squaring the edge, which may be necessary after the chisel has seen considerable use, is done by placing the chisel flat on the tool rest and moving it parallel to the face of the grinding wheel. This can be done freehand, but the results will be more accurate if you use a guide like the one shown in Figures 18-6 and 18-7A. The chisel will be supported by both the guide and the tool rest. Hold the chisel firmly in place and then move the guide slowly from left to right. Remember to keep the cut very light. Make a second pass if more material must be removed.

To do the bevel, make a special guide block that will hold the chisel at the proper angle (Figures 18-8 and 18-7B). If the chisel is narrow enough, it can be moved directly forward against the face of the wheel. If this isn't feasible, then the chisel must be moved across the face of the wheel. Generally, the length of the bevel should be about twice the thickness of the chisel.

Usually, there is some amount of burr left on the cutting edge, so honing by hand on a flat stone should follow the grinding operation (Figure 18-9). Start by holding the chisel on its bevel with a little extra tilt to get some clearance between the heel of the cutting edge and the stone. Make a few circular motions, then turn the chisel over so it rests on its flat side, and repeat the circular motions. Alternate between the two actions until the burrs are gone and the chisel has a keen cutting edge.

When chisels are carefully used, the honing can be repeated a few times before it becomes necessary to repeat the grinding sequence.

Figure 18-6: Work this way to square off the cutting-edge of wood chisels and similar tools. The guide assures that the edge will be parallel to the face of the wheel throughout the pass.

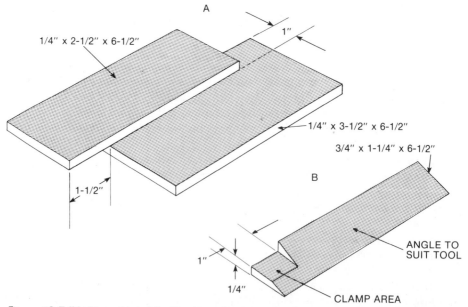

Figure 18-7: Working with guides like this will help to assure that grinding cuts will be accurate.

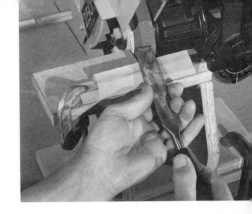

Figure 18-8: The guide holds the chisel at the correct angle. By working in this way, the cutting edge of the chisel will be hollow-ground.

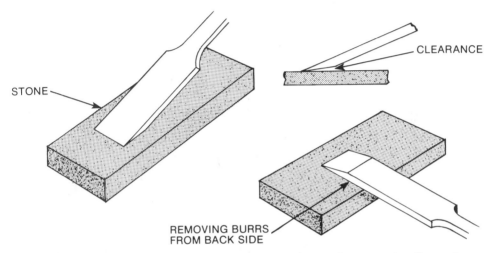

STONE

CLEARANCE

REMOVING BURRS FROM BACK SIDE

Figure 18-9: How to remove the burrs that remain after the grinding operation. First work on the bevel, then with the chisel placed on its flat side. This operation can be done several times before the chisel needs regrinding.

LATHE CHISELS. Gouges and round-nose chisels can be done freehand by working as shown in Figure 18-10. Hold the chisel flat on the tool rest at an angle that puts the chisel's beveled edge flush against the face of the wheel. Then, slowly rotate the chisel while maintaining the correct contact.

Figure 18-10: How to sharpen a gouge. The procedure applies to gouges in sets of hand carving tools as well as to lathe chisels. Rotate the tool against the wheel while you maintain the original bevel angle.

Other lathe chisels (Figure 18-11), since they have flat cutting edges, can be situated by using a guidance system like the systems described for wood chisels.

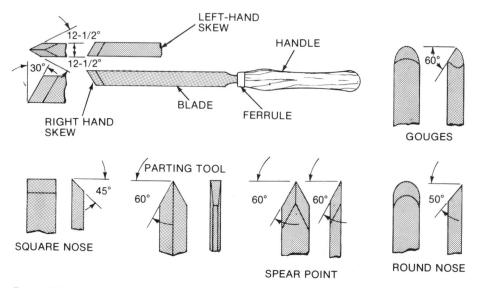

Figure 18-11: Typical lathe chisels and how their cutting edges should be shaped.

SHAPER KNIVES. To renew the cutting edge on a shaper knife, place it flat on an oil stone, cutting edge down, and then move it with a circular motion. Each knife in the set should be rotated the same number of times. If this treatment doesn't produce a satisfactory cutting edge, it probably means that the profile of the knife requires attention—a job that can only be done by professionals with special equipment.

WIRE BRUSHING. Wire brushes are wheels that are made by securing strands of wire in a central hub. Generally, they are available in "fine" and "coarse" grades, which indicates the gauge and stiffness of the wires that are used. Fine grades can be used to produce an attractive brushed effect on soft metals. Coarse grades will remove dirt, grease, and oxide from materials being prepared for soldering or brazing. These are just typical applications; each grade can serve in other ways.

The brushes are mounted on the motor's main arbor as if they were saw blades (Figure 18-12). With all materials removed from the arbor, mount the brush between collars and then secure with the lock nut. It is not advisable to use the saw guard since the wires spread when being used and can damage the guard. A better way is to make a special guard like the one shown in Figure 18-13. The guard, which is secured with the same fastener that locks the saw guard, is made as shown in Figure 18-14. To secure the aluminum strip—which can also be a piece of flashing material—start nailing at one end and continue to add nails as you wrap the metal around the semicircular piece. Adding the insulation and folding back the ends of the metal will cover sharp edges.

Figure 18-12: Wire brushes mounted on the motor's main arbor as if they were saw blades. Generally, tools like this are available in either "fine" or "coarse" grades.

Figure 18-13: The guard that should be used with wire brushes locks in place with the same fastener that is used to secure the saw guard.

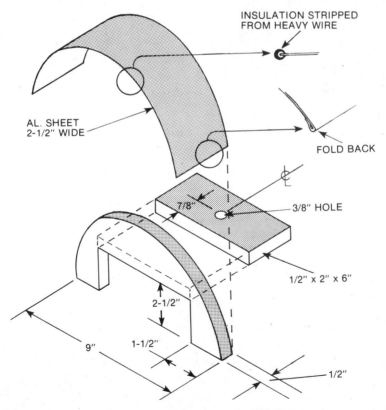

INSULATION STRIPPED
FROM HEAVY WIRE

FOLD BACK

AL. SHEET
2-1/2" WIDE

7/8"

3/8" HOLE

1/2" x 2" x 6"

2-1/2"

9"

1-1/2"

1/2"

Figure 18-14: How to make the guard that is used with wire brushes.

Before working, let the wheel run free for a few minutes, while you stand to one side. Do this so that loose wires, if any, will be thrown off without damage. Don't forget the safety goggles!

Whenever possible, position the wire brush so you can use the saw's table as a platform for your hands (Figures 18-15 and 18-16). Grip the work so your hands are not in line with the brush. Apply light pressure, and hold the work very firmly. You must operate, especially when using a coarse brush, as if the brush were trying to pull the work from your hands. Be especially careful if the work has holes, undercuts, or notches in which the wire brush can snag.

Figure 18-17 shows an unusual but effective application for a wire brush. The texture caused by wire-brushing can't be produced in any other way. Work as if you were doing a crosscutting operation. Set the height of the brush so it just scrapes the surface of the wood. The treatment is most effective on softwoods and species like fir that have areas of soft and hard grain.

Figure 18-15: Generally, the coarse wire brush is used when surfaces must be renewed. It also does a good job of removing scale and rust, cleaning welds, and so on.

Figure 18-16: Use the fine wire brush to refinish surfaces. Here, the fine brush is giving new life to an abused hammer-head. Always work on the "down" side of the wheel. Whenever possible, work so hands can rest on the saw's table.

Figure 18-17: You can give wood an interesting texture by passing the wire wheel across the stock as if you were doing kerfing operations. The texture will be affected by whether you work with a coarse wheel or a fine wheel.

BUFFING AND POLISHING. Buffing wheels will effectively restore the gleam to metal objects that have acquired an unattractive patina. Even materials like bone, ivory, plastics, and so on can be smoothed and polished by applying them to a buffing wheel.

The buffing wheels mount on the motor's main arbor much like saw blades, set between collars and secured with the lock nut (Figure 18-18). The guard that was designed for use with wire brushes may also be used with buffing wheels.

The buffing wheel is no more than a flexible carrier for compounds like white or red rouge, emery, or tripoli. Each of the compounds, as shown in Figure 18-19, works best on particular materials.

To apply the compound to the wheel, which is called "charging," follow this procedure. Turn on the machine and hold a piece of wood against the buffing wheel to remove loose threads. Any threads that do not separate from the wheel can be cut with scissors while the wheel is still.

Hold the compound against the turning wheel until the working edge of the wheel is completely coated. Don't force the compound. Don't forget to wear safety goggles.

Figure 18-18: Buffing wheels are mounted like wire wheels—that is, between collars and secured with the lock nut. Buffing compounds, in stick form, can be purchased in sets that include the most essential varieties.

SUGGESTIONS FOR BUFFING

TYPE OF COMPOUND	ACTION	TYPICAL MATERIALS
White rouge	Buffing Polishing	Aluminum, stainless steel. Chromium, cast brass.
Red rouge	Buffing Polishing	Glass. Gold, silver, other precious metals.
Emery	Clean-up work	Various materials—for removing rust, scale, tarnish. Sharp cutting—use carefully.
Tripoli	Buffing Polishing	Aluminum, brass, pewter, copper, plastics. Also useable on painted work.

Figure 18-19: The compounds to use when buffing or polishing various materials.

Hold the work firmly, but apply it gently to the wheel while moving the work so the wheel can bear against various surfaces (Figure 18-20). Set the wheel in a position best suited for the work. In the photograph, the radial arm is in left-miter position with the motor rotated so the buffing wheel extends beyond the left edge of the table. Whatever position you choose, be sure all locks are tightened securely.

HOW TO MAKE A GRINDER-BUFFER WHEEL. On some metal refinishing jobs, the surface of the material requires grinding before buffing can be effective. A conventional grinder can be used but not when the work has a contour. In such cases, a regular buffing wheel can be converted to grinding operations in the following way.

Spread a quantity of liquid glue on a sheet of wax paper and roll the buffing wheel in the glue until the wheel's edge is completely coated. Spread the glue uniformly with a small stick, then put the wheel aside until the glue is dry.

Mount the wheel on the motor's arbor. While the wheel is turning, sand the glued edge lightly with medium-grit sandpaper until the edge is smooth. Before removing the wheel from the arbor, mark its surface with an arrow that will indicate the direction of rotation. The wheel must always be put back on the shaft so it will rotate in the same direction.

Prepare two sheets of wax paper—one with glue and the other with an abrasive, which is usually powdered emery. Roll the wheel in the glue and then in the abrasive, allowing the weight of the wheel to bear down on the abrasive. Put the wheel aside for an hour or two and then repeat the last operation. The idea is to coat the rim of the wheel with a uniform layer of abrasive material.

Set the wheel aside until the glue has thoroughly dried (about 24 hours). Then, scrape the sides of the wheel to remove any loose particles. Next, the wheel is "cracked." Flex the rim of the wheel with your fingers or press against it with a piece of wood. The end result should be a wheel-rim that is coated with abrasive and covered with small cracks.

Mount the wheel on the arbor, being sure it will turn in the direction indicated by the arrow. Then, "break it in" by lightly grinding a piece of scrap metal. The wheel cuts rapidly, so be sure to use a light touch when applying the work.

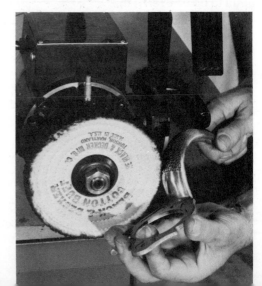

Figure 18-20: Situate the buffing wheel for most convenient work position. Apply the work with minimum pressure. The "dirt" that remains on the work can be wiped off with a soft cloth. Use the guard—wear safety goggles!

Chapter 19
More on
Wood Connections

Joints make the project, but the fanciest joint you can make is not always the wisest choice. It is advisable, when more than one joint design is applicable, to choose the one that is easiest to do. There is little point in going through the process of shaping dovetails if a rabbet, a dado, or a pegged joint will do the job.

Of course, you can shape intricate joints just for the fun of doing them and for the craftsmanship they indicate. But in the practical sense, the simpler joint, reinforced when necessary and joined with a modern adhesive, will provide a sound connection and will save much time.

Joint selection should be made on the basis of strength and appearance. A miter joint puts pieces together so there will be no visible end grain—an important consideration on furniture projects, picture frames, and the like. But it isn't a prime factor if the project is, for example, a rustic outdoor bench.

A bookcase is stronger if the vertical pieces are dadoed to receive the ends of the shelves. But the dado, when viewed from the front, is not a pretty joint because the U-shaped cut is visible. Solutions include covering front edges with molding or flat facing-pieces and doing stopped dadoes which provide strength without being visible.

Consider the stresses on a joint. The weight of items on a shelf tends to bend the shelf away from the vertical part to which it is attached. That's why a dado will do a better job than a simple butt joint.

The contents of a drawer bear down on the drawer's bottom and resist the effort that is applied when the drawer is pulled out. Much of the strain is on the joint between the front and sides of the drawer. That's why dovetails are so frequently used there. The interlocking feature resists the strain and will continue to do so even if the glue in the joint should fail. But the dovetail is not the only joint that does this. The pegged joint, even the combination rabbet-dado, has similar characteristics, is easier to do, and can be done with basic radial arm saw equipment.

Another consideration is the amount of glue area in a joint. Miter joints, cross-bevels, and rip-bevels have little more glue area than a butt joint. That is why they are often reinforced with splines, feathers, or dowels. A rabbet joint has almost twice as much glue area as a butt or miter joint. The finger lap joint, which is often used on exposed areas as a sign of dedicated craftsmanship, provides a maximum amount of glue area.

What stresses will be on the joint? Will it tend to separate, twist, bend? This can be judged before construction starts by studying how the project will be used.

This chapter supplements the joint information that has been presented throughout the book. It also includes new information on such joints as the finger lap and some thoughts on assembly procedures.

Whatever joint you choose—whether it is complex or simple—remember it will only do its job as efficiently as you do yours. A sloppy complex joint is **not** better than a well-executed simple one. Even a simple butt joint will not look as good as it might or hold as it should if the mating surfaces are not square and do not make maximum contact.

JOINTS AND TYPICAL APPLICATIONS. Figures 19-1 and 19-2 show the various types of joints and describe their applications.

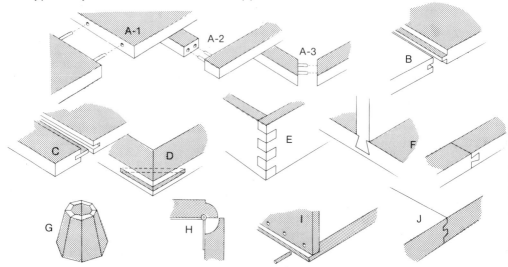

KEY	NAME	TYPICAL APPLICATIONS
A-1	Dowel	Edge to edge joints.
A-2		Butt-joint corners and similar
A-3		mitered corners.
B	Tongue and groove	Edge to edge joints.
C	Splined	Edge to edge joints.
D	Feathered	Miter joints.
E	Finger lap	Box and case corners—drawers.
F	Single dovetails	Splice work—shelves—some types of case work.
G	Compound angle	Picture frames—hoppers—tubs—structures with sloping sides.
H	Drop leaf	Table leaves and similar
I	Pegged	drawer fronts—butt joint reinforcement.
J	Shaped	Edge to edge joints—also used on drawer fronts.

Figure 19-1: The various types of joints and their applications.

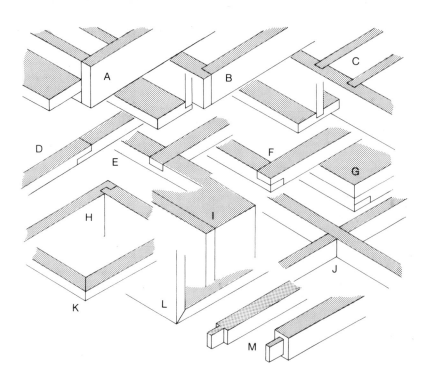

KEY	NAME	TYPICAL APPLICATIONS
A	Butt	Simple constructions, but can look good and be quite strong when reinforced with nails, screws, or dowels.
B	Rabbets	Corners of case work—inserting cabinet backs.
C	Dadoes & grooves	Shelves in bookcases and cabinets—sliding doors.
D	Half-lap splice	Lengthening materials.
E	Middle lap	Frame work.
F	End lap	Frame work.
G	Mitered end lap	Frame work.
H	Combination dado-rabbet	Drawer constructions—case corners.
I	Cross miter	Case—box corners.
J	Cross lap	Table and chair rails or stretchers.
K	Simple miter	Picture frames—cabinet facings.
L	Rip miter	Case work—segment work.
M	Tenons	Chair and table constructions—also frames and general case work.

Figure 19-2: More joints and their applications.

THE FINGER LAP JOINT. The finger lap joint (Figure 19-3) has structural appeal because of the unusual amount of glue area, and it has visual appeal because of the way the shapes come together. It is often called a "box joint" and can be found on many classic pieces—sometimes exposed to indicate craftsmanship, other times in hidden areas simply because it has much strength.

Figure 19-3: The finger lap joint has both structural and visual appeal.

Often, the joint is designed so the width of the fingers and notches equals the thickness of the stock (Figure 19-4). This method works but doesn't always produce the most attractive results. Reducing the width of the fingers and notches to one-half the stock's thickness or even less often contributes to a better looking project. Also, narrow fingers add to the total glue area and make the project stronger.

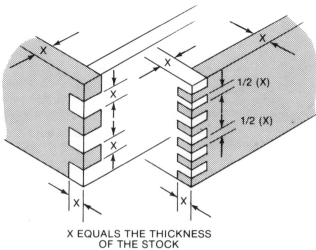

X EQUALS THE THICKNESS
OF THE STOCK

Figure 19-4: The joint can be designed with the finger and notch thickness equal to the stock thickness. However, a more appealing project can be made if the fingers and notches are one-half or less than the stock thickness.

The finger lap joint may also be used to join parts that have different thicknesses (Figure 19-5). The result will be more appealing if the width of the fingers matches the thickness of the thinner part.

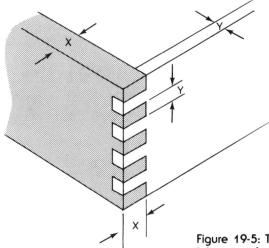

Figure 19-5: The finger lap joint may be used to join parts of varying thicknesses.

Mating parts of the joint can be cut simultaneously if you work with the auxiliary table and use the saw in horizontal position, as shown in Figure 19-6. Here, the width of the notches and thickness of the fingers equal the width of the saw-kerf. For each cut, the blade must be moved a distance that is **twice** the kerf-width. The depth of the notches is controlled by the position in which the workpieces are clamped to the table's fence. Wider cuts are possible when the work is done with a dadoing tool.

Figure 19-6: Using the saw in horizontal position, you can simultaneously cut mating parts of the joint employing an auxiliary table.

In order for the parts to be even when they are assembled, they must be positioned for cutting with one part higher than the other by the width of a groove. This is done by using a height block under one of the pieces (Figure 19-7).

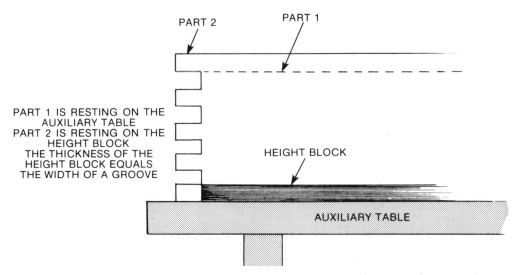

PART 2

PART 1

PART 1 IS RESTING ON THE
AUXILIARY TABLE
PART 2 IS RESTING ON THE
HEIGHT BLOCK
THE THICKNESS OF THE
HEIGHT BLOCK EQUALS
THE WIDTH OF A GROOVE

HEIGHT BLOCK

AUXILIARY TABLE

Figure 19-7: A height block is used under one of the pieces to assure the parts are even when they are assembled. The parts must be positioned for cutting with one part higher than the other by the width of a groove.

Figure 19-8: Dovetail joints can be made on the radial arm saw by using the router and a dovetail bit.

SOME DOVETAIL WORK. Joints like this (Figure 19-8) can be accomplished on the radial arm saw by working with the router and a dovetail bit.

When the cut is required in the surface of stock, use the router in vertical position (Figure 19-9), and pull the cutter through the work by using a crosscut action. Cuts like this can't be deepened by making repeat passes. Thus, set the cutter for full depth-of-cut, hold the work securely or clamp it, and pull the cutter very, very slowly.

End dovetails can be formed by working with the auxiliary table and by using the router in horizontal position as shown in Figure 19-10. The center line of the bit must be exactly on the horizontal center line of the work. Hold or clamp the work firmly. Use a very conservative feed-speed.

Dovetail "fingers," whether required for a surface or end dovetail can be cut this way. Use the same dovetail bit (Figure 19-11). Make one pass, then flip the stock and make a second pass. To be sure the cutter height is correct, first make the cut on a scrap piece that you can check for fit in the dovetail slot.

Figure 19-9: The router is used in vertical position and is pulled through the work using a crosscut action when the cut is required in the surface of the stock.

Figure 19-10: End dovetails are formed by using the router in horizontal position and employing an auxiliary table.

Figure 19-11: Dovetail fingers can be accomplished by making one pass, flipping the stock, and making a second pass. This procedure holds true whether you are cutting the fingers for a surface or end dovetail.

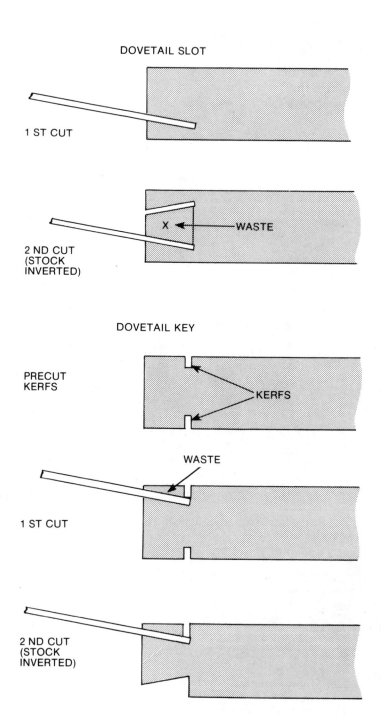

Figure 19-12: The cutting sequence for dovetail slots and keys.

Although it takes considerably more time, dovetails can be formed by work-ing this way with a saw blade. Except for the initial kerfs required for the dovetail key (or finger), all the cuts are made with the work on the auxiliary table and with the saw blade, tilted to the correct angle, in horizontal position (Figure 19-12). The waste that remains after the outline cuts for the dovetail slot are formed is cleaned away with the blade tilted back to normal position. It prob-ably won't be possible to clean out all the waste with saw cuts, but what remains can be removed with a narrow chisel.

Dovetail-shaped keys (Figure 19-13) are often used when sliding compo-nents are needed or when reinforcement pieces are needed across slabs or parts that will be joined edge-to-edge. The dovetail-shaped groove is made with the saw in crosscut position—or rip position if the length of the cut is be-yond crosscut capacity. Make the first two cuts (A) with the blade tilted to the correct angle. Clean out the waste by making repeat passes with the blade in vertical position. Whatever waste remains can be removed with a chisel. Shape the dovetail key by making rip-bevel cuts with the blade set at the same angle used for the groove(B).

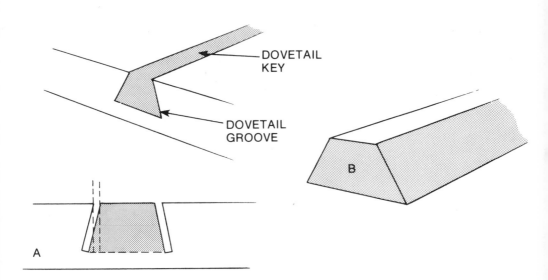

Figure 19-13: (A) The initial cuts of a dovetail groove; (B) the dovetail key.

SHAPED EDGE-TO-EDGE JOINTS. Good edge-to-edge joints can be formed by working with the shaper head and the set of glue-joint knives. The work can be done with the regular or the improvised shaper fence and with the shaper head in horizontal position (Figure 19-14). It is critical for the work to be exactly centered with the cutter. The same knife-shape is used for both parts of the joint; but the second cut, made on a mating edge, is done after the stock has been inverted and turned end-for-end. To be sure of alignment, make some test cuts on scrap stock.

Figure 19-14: Edge-to-edge joints are formed by using the shaper head and the set of glue-joint knives. The shaper head is in horizontal position and the work can be done using a regular or improvised shaper fence.

DOWELS AS REINFORCEMENT. These are general rules for dowel placement when they are used to reinforce edge-to-edge joints (Figure 19-15). Some workers will not include a dowel near the end of parts and will increase spacing to as much as 18″ or 20″. This approach utilizes the dowels for parts alignment more than for strength. Conversely, some workers broadcast closely-spaced dowels over the entire project. The latter approach may be all right for heavy-duty projects subjected to considerable abuse, but it isn't necessary for components like desks or tabletops.

Dowels are often used to reinforce miter joints, as shown in Figure 19-16. The holes are drilled as explained in Chapter 14. It is important for the holes to be drilled perpendicularly to the miter-cut edge. Locate the holes so their position will favor the inside of the frame.

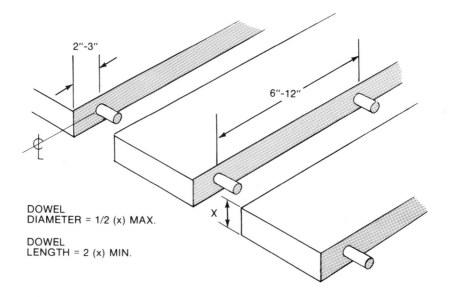

2″-3″

6″-12″

DOWEL
DIAMETER = 1/2 (x) MAX.

DOWEL
LENGTH = 2 (x) MIN.

x

Figure 19-15: The recommended placement of dowels when used to reinforce edge-to-edge joints.

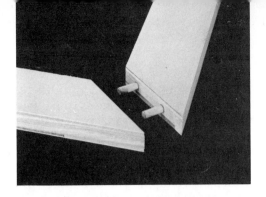

Figure 19-16: When dowels are used to reinforce miter joints, the holes should be drilled perpendicular to the miter-cut edge.

THE COMBINATION DADO-RABBET JOINT. These are the steps to take when forming the dado-rabbet joint on 3/4" stock. The first cut in part A (Figure 19-17) can be made with a dadoing tool in horizontal position. The second cut is made with a saw blade in crosscut position. The cut in part B is made with a dadoing tool used in crosscut position. Accuracy is critical if the parts are to mesh snugly. Note that part A can extend beyond the side piece. This is often done when A is the front part of a drawer.

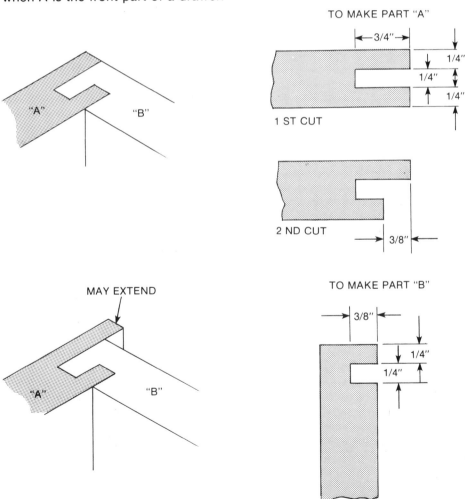

Figure 19-17: The steps in making a dado-rabbet joint on 3/4" stock.

MORTISES. Nomenclature of the mortise-tenon joint is shown in Figure 19-18. The tenon can be cut in various ways, among them, repeat passes with a saw blade or a dadoing tool. It is a good idea to first shape the mortise and then cut the tenon to fit.

The steps to take when drilling a mortise are as follows. Establish a center line; then, using a bit whose diameter equals the width of the mortise, drill the two end-holes (Figure 19-19A). Drill a series of overlapping holes between the two end-holes (B). Whatever waste remains can be cleaned out with a small chisel (C). Mortises formed in this way will have round ends, so the tenon must be shaped accordingly (D).

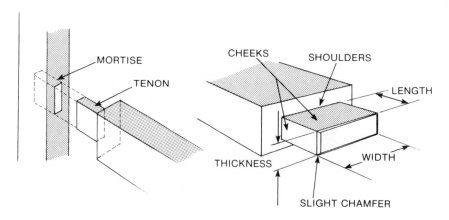

Figure 19-18: Nomenclature of the mortise-tenon joint.

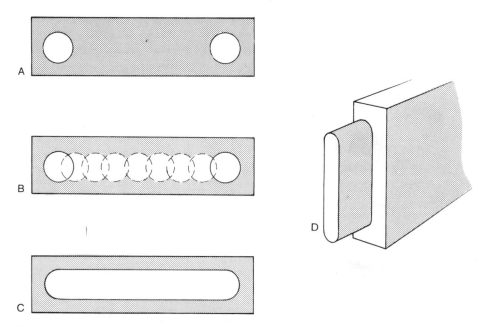

Figure 19-19: The steps to take when drilling a mortise.

Mortises can also be formed by working with the router and a straight-shank bit. Here, the router, used with its auxiliary table, is set in horizontal position (Figure 19-20). The work is braced against a stop block, swung into the cutter, and then moved until the mortise is the correct length. Using two stop blocks, one to start the cut and one to end it, will guarantee accurate work. Adjust the cutter's height so its center will be on the horizontal center line of the work. When necessary, make repeat passes to deepen the cut.

When mortises in stock-ends are required, they can be formed with the router in horizontal position and with the work supported on the auxiliary table (Figure 19-21). Here, the work remains stationary while the router is moved to make the cut. Start the cut by moving the work into the router bit just as if you were drilling a hole. Then, secure the work and finish the cut by moving the router. Feed slowly, make repeat passes to achieve full depth-of-cut.

Figure 19-20: The mortise is formed by using a router and straight shank bit. The router is set in horizontal position and an auxiliary table is employed.

Figure 19-21: To cut a mortise in a stock end, place the router in horizontal position and support the work on an auxiliary table. The work will remain stationary while the router is moved to make the cut.

FEATHER REINFORCEMENTS. Feathers are triangular pieces that are used to reinforce this type of miter joint. Feathers that are cut from solid stock should be cut so the grain runs in the direction indicated in Figure 19-22. Feathers can also be cut from thin plywood or hardboard. Don't preshape the pieces. Form them as rectangles. After they have been inserted and the glue is dry, the excess material can be cut off and the joint can be smoothly sanded.

Grooves for feathers can be cut with the saw in horizontal position and with the work supported by the auxiliary table, as shown in Figure 19-23. Position the work by using the miter-guide. Make the mark for placement on the table so the groove-depth will be the same in each piece. Be sure the height of the blade is such that the groove will be centered in the stock. A 1/8" kerf-width is ample for 3/4" stock. If the stock is thicker, 1/4" will be better.

SPLINES. Splines (Figure 19-24), which are thin strips of material, are used to reinforce all types of miter joints as well as edge-to-edge joints.

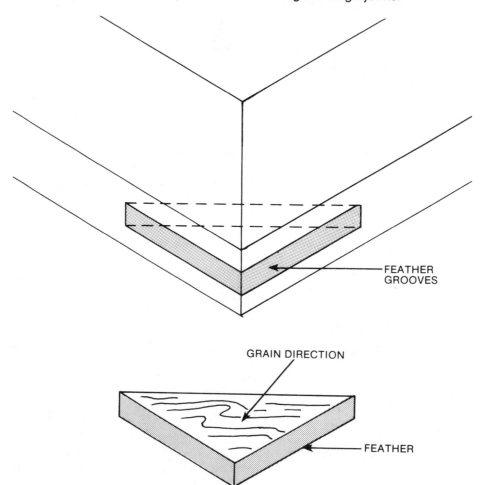

Figure 19-22: Feathers used to reinforce miter joints are cut from solid stock with the grain running as indicated.

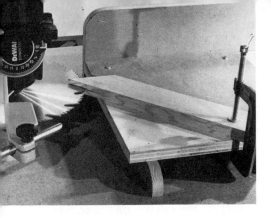

Figure 19-23: The grooves for the feathers are cut with the saw in horizontal position and the work supported by an auxiliary table.

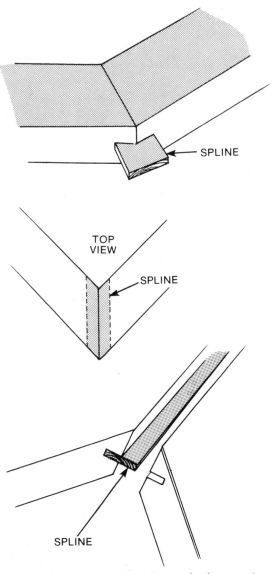

SPLINE

TOP
VIEW

SPLINE

SPLINE

Figure 19-24: Splines are used to reinforce miter joints and edge-to-edge joints. They are thin strips of material.

Splines are strongest when the grain direction runs across the short dimension, as shown in Figure 19-25. Short splines can be cut from solid stock by first making cuts with the saw blade in horizontal position and then separating the splines by making a routine crosscut. One eighth-inch thick splines are all right for 3/4" stock. Use 1/4"-thick splines on heavier stock. In the latter case, plywood or hardboard can be used as spline material. Always cut splines longer than necessary so they can be trimmed and sanded flush after assembly.

To cut spline-grooves in a cross-miter, tilt the blade so it is perpendicular to the miter cut (Figure 19-26). Use a stop block so the cut will be the same in all pieces. Work in rip position to form spline grooves in stock that has been beveled. Form spline grooves in simple miters by supporting the work on the auxiliary table and using the saw blade in horizontal position.

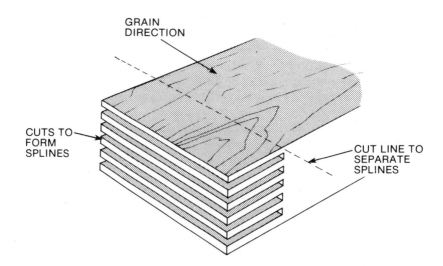

Figure 19-25: To form short splines, first cut with the saw blade in horizontal position, then separate the splines by making a crosscut.

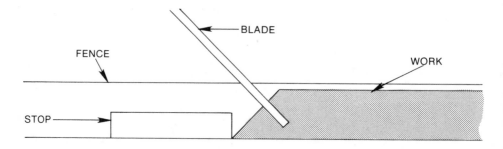

Figure 19-26: To cut spline-grooves in a cross-miter, the blade should be tilted so it is perpendicular to the miter cut. A stop block is used so the cut will be identical in all pieces.

THE SHIPLAP JOINT. The shiplap joint is formed when boards that have been edge-rabbeted are joined so the cuts overlap, as shown in Figure 19-27. Since the rabbet cuts are of similar size, the surfaces of the pieces will be even after assembly.

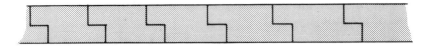

Figure 19-27: The shiplap joint consists of boards that have been edge-rabbeted to join with the cuts overlapping.

The rabbets can be cut by following a two-pass procedure. The saw blade, in horizontal position, is used with the auxiliary table (Figure 19-28). Set the blade height for the width of the rabbet; its projection for the rabbet's depth. Make passes with the stock placed on its edge. The second pass is made with the stock inverted and with the opposite surface against the fence.

Adjust the saw blade so its projection will equal the width of the rabbet and so its height above the table will be level with the bottom of the kerfs (Figure 19-29). Make passes with the stock flat on the table. Don't forget to invert the stock before making the second cut. This kind of work can also be done with a dadoing tool, in which case the full rabbet will be produced in a single pass.

Figure 19-28: The rabbets for a shiplap joint are formed by following a two-pass procedure.

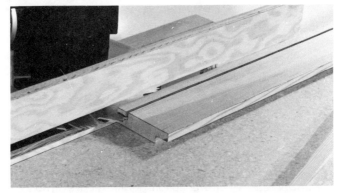

Figure 19-29: The saw blade should be adjusted so that its projection equals the width of the rabbet and its height above the table is level with the kerf bottoms.

THE CROSS LAP JOINT. The cross lap joint makes a strong connection when, for example, project components like table or chair stretchers must cross each other (Figure 19-30). It will be easier to work accurately if you clamp the pieces together so they can be cut simultaneously. The work can be done by making repeat passes with a saw blade or by using a dadoing tool. The depth of the cut should equal one-half the stock's width. The width of the cut should equal the thickness of the stock.

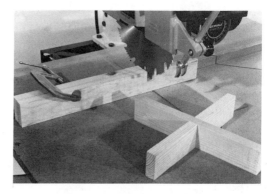

Figure 19-30: The cross lap joint is often used for table or chair stretchers when a strong connection between project components is required.

SOME TYPICAL ASSEMBLIES

Drawers. Nomenclature of a typical furniture drawer is shown in Figure 19-31. The bottom, which is cut a bit smaller than necessary, is let into grooves in the drawer's front and sides. It is not usually glued in place. This is done so the wood can "breathe"; that is, expand or contract without distortion.

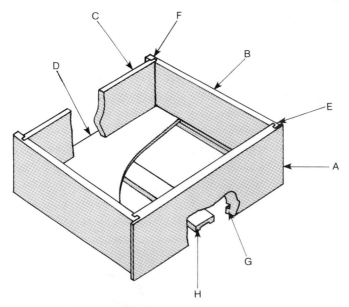

Figure 19-31: Nomenclature of typical furniture drawer: (A) Drawer front; (B) drawer sides; (C) drawer back; (D) drawer bottom (let into grooves in front and sides); (E) dado and rabbet joint (other joints may be used); (F) back can be let into sides with simple dado or dado-rabbet; (G) groove; and (H) centered drawer guide (ready-made commercial hardware also available).

Framed Panels. Framed panels are often used to construct doors and to form sides for furniture projects. The frame can be assembled with dowel-reinforced butt joints, as shown in Figure 19-32A. The panel (B) can be solid, tongue-and-groove lumber. It's better not to use glue in the center panel-joints so the boards can expand or contract without causing damage.

Framed panels can be fancier if you work along the lines shown in Figure 19-33. Cut the rails to shape on the saber saw. The grooves in the curved edges can be formed by working with the router or the shaper head. The panel (C) is plywood.

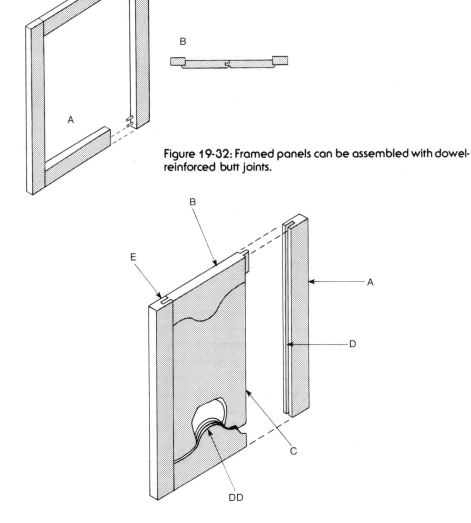

Figure 19-32: Framed panels can be assembled with dowel-reinforced butt joints.

Figure 19-33: The parts of a framed panel: (A) Stiles; (B) shaped rail; (C) inset panel—cut top and bottom to match curves; (D) groove; (D-D) grooves in curved rails can be done by routing or shaping; and (E) ends of rails are shaped to form tenons that fit grooves in stiles.

Figure 19-34 shows various ways to insert a panel in a frame. All the ideas can be used for doors and for sides of cabinets. Make a choice in relation to the overall design of the project.

Leg and Rail Assembly. The connection between rails or stretchers and legs is critical and must be done very carefully for the project to be long lived. Always use two dowels in each joint to resist twisting stresses (Figure 19-35). Mortise and tenon joints are also a good choice for this type of assembly. Fit corner blocks as carefully as you do other components.

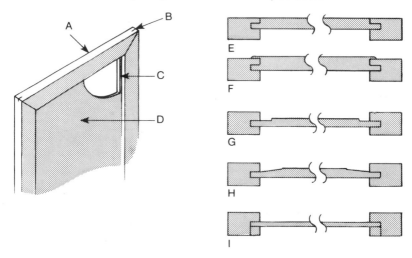

Figure 19-34: Parts of a framed panel and various methods of panel insertion: (A) Frame with mitered joints; (B) reinforcement (spline shown); (C) groove; (D) panel; (E) flush panel has a groove in the frame and a rabbet in the panel—this design is often used for the sides of case goods as well as doors; (F) elevated panel uses grooves in both the frame and the panel; (G) panel raised on one side but with square shoulders; (H) panel raised on one side but with beveled shoulders; and (I) rabbeted frame for a thin panel or glass insert—wood stops are used to secure the panel.

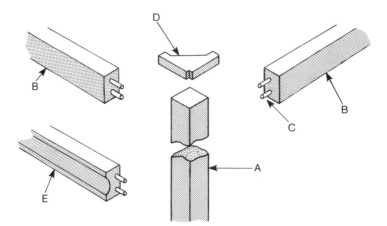

Figure 19-35: Always use two dowels for each joint in a leg and rail assembly. The assembly includes: (A) Leg; (B) rails; (C) minimum of two dowels each place; (D) well fitted corner block; and (E) stretcher (also doweled).

Bookcase Assembly. This kind of construction requires more time than assemblies that are simply nailed or screwed together, but the result is a good-looking and durable project (Figure 19-36). A back adds to the appearance of the project and provides strength to resist lateral stresses. This "engineering" can be used on many projects. The project can be closed in by adding front facing and then hanging doors.

Typical Base Cabinet. Box, or all-panel, construction is often used on kitchen cabinets and similar projects. The back is often omitted because cabinets of this type are usually placed against a wall, but including it is better craftsmanship. Doors are hung on the front framing (or facing), which is made of solid lumber (Figure 19-37). Note that either dadoes or butt joints are used throughout the assembly.

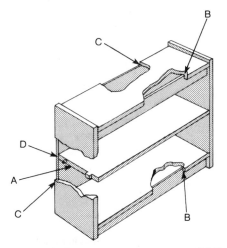

Figure 19-36: The bookcase assembly includes: (A) Dowel or tenon into sides (all shelves); (B) dado; (C) back inset in rabbets (sides and top shelf); (D) butt (bottom and middle shelf).

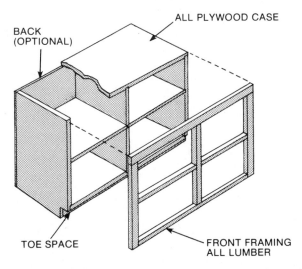

Figure 19-37: A typical base cabinet assembly. Doors are hung on the front framing.

Hiding Plywood Edges. Plywood edges are often covered with ready-made strips of veneer, but often, one of the methods shown in Figure 19-38 will be more suitable. On one hand, a heavy edge provides more protection than does veneer. Specially made strips can add a decorative detail, make the plywood look heavier, and provide a lip when, for example, a plywood slab is used as a desk or table top.

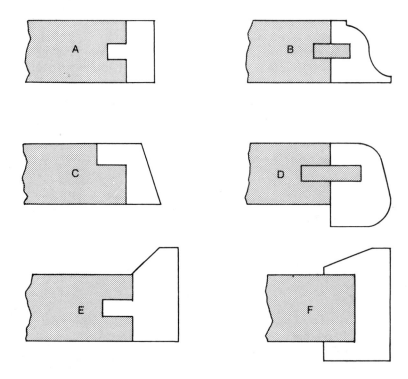

Figure 19-38: Methods for hiding plywood edges: (A) Wood strip with integral tongue—groove in plywood; (B) molding attached with spline; (C) rabbet cuts in both plywood and edging; (D) bulked edge attached with spline; (E) wood strip shaped to provide a lip has integral tongue—groove in plywood; and (F) strip is grooved for full thickness of plywood—adds bulk to edge and also provides a lip.

Index